Armed Conflicts in South Asia 2009

Armed Conflicts in South Asia 2009

Continuing Violence, Failing Peace Processes

Editors
D. Suba Chandran
P.R. Chari

LONDON AND NEW YORK

First published 2010 by Routledge

2 Park Square, Milton Park, Abingdon, Oxfordshire OX14 4RN
711 Third Avenue, New York, NY 10017

Routledge is an imprint of the Taylor & Francis Group, an informa business

First issued in paperback 2018

Transferred to Digital Printing 2010

Copyright © 2010 Institute of Peace and Conflict Studies

Typeset by
Star Compugraphics Private Limited
D–156, Second Floor
Sector 7
Noida 201 301

All rights reserved. No part of this book may be reprinted or reproduced or utilised in any form or by any electronic, mechanical, or other means, now known or hereafter invented, including photocopying and recording, or in any information storage or retrieval system, without permission in writing from the publishers.

Notice:
Product or corporate names may be trademarks or registered trademarks, and are used only for identification and explanation without intent to infringe.

British Library Cataloguing-in-Publication Data
A catalogue record of this book is available from the British Library

ISBN: 978-0-415-56444-1 (hbk)
ISBN: 978-1-138-38038-7 (pbk)

Contents

List of Tables and Figure	vii
List of Abbreviations	ix
Preface	xv

1. Armed Conflicts and Peace Processes in South Asia: An Overview   1
   P.R. Chari

2. Afghanistan: Tipping Point   19
   Shanthie Mariet D'Souza

3. Sectarian Violence in Pakistan   42
   Raghav Sharma

4. FATA and NWFP: Spreading Anarchy   62
   D. Suba Chandran

5. J&K: From Militancy to Jihad?   83
   Kavita Suri and D. Suba Chandran

6. Left-Wing Extremism in India: The Rule of the Maoists   103
   Devyani Srivastava

7. North-East: Minimal Gains of Counter-Insurgency Operations   125
   Bibhu Prasad Routray

8. Bangladesh: The Clampdown   150
   Sandeep Bhardwaj

9. Nepal: Out with the Old, In with the New   168
   Oliver Housden

10. Sri Lanka: Unprecedented Violence, Unclear Future   191
    N. Manoharan

11. Failed and Failing States and Armed Conflict
    in South Asia   211
    Sonali Huria

Notes on Contributors   230
Index   235

List of Tables and Figure

Tables

3.1	Year 2008	47
3.2	Year 2009	50
3.3	Reasons Given by Students for Joining a Madrasa	55
4.1	Suicide Terrorism in Pakistan, 2001–08	75
5.1	Party Performance in 2008 State Legislative Assembly Elections	97
6.1	State-Wise Details of Maoist Violence and Activity, 2008	109
6.2	Scheme for Modernisation of State Police Forces — Central Funds Released/Utilisation Position as on 30 June 2005 for Chhattisgarh, Jharkhand and Orissa	119
7.1	Security Situation in the North-Eastern States	133
7.2	Security Situation in Assam	134
7.3	Security Situation in Manipur	136
7.4	Security Situation in Tripura	138
7.5	Security Situation in Nagaland	140

Figure

6.1	Casualties of Police Personnel	113

List of Abbreviations

ACBAR	: Agency Coordinating Body for Afghan Relief
AF-PAK	: Afghanistan–Pakistan
AHAB	: Ahle Hadith Andolan Bangladesh
AI	: Ansarul Islam
AISC	: Army Integration Special Committee
AL	: Awami League
ANA	: Afghan National Army
ANAAC	: Afghan National Army Air Corps
ANP	: Afghan National Police
ANP	: Awami National Party
ANSF	: Afghan National Security Forces
ARTF	: Afghanistan Reconstruction Trust Fund
APHC	: All Parties Hurriyat Conference
ATMM	: Akhil Tarai Mukti Morcha
ATPLO	: All Tripura People's Liberation Organisation
ATTF	: All Tripura Tiger Force
BDI	: Backward Districts Initiative
BDR	: Bangladesh Rifles
BLT	: Bodo Liberation Tigers
BNCT	: Borok National Council of Tripura
BNP	: Bangladesh Nationalist Party
BSF	: Border Security Force
BTC	: Bodo Territorial Council
BVF	: Bodo Volunteer Force
BW	: Black Widow
CA	: Constituent Assembly
CBI	: Central Bureau of Investigation
CBREP	: Chure Bhawar Rastriya Ekta Party
CC	: Constitution Committee
CFA	: Ceasefire Agreement
CIA	: Central Intelligence Agency
CMEV	: Centre for Monitoring Election Violence
COBRA	: Combat Battalion for Resolute Action
CoIn	: Counter Insurgency
CPA	: Comprehensive Plan Agreement
CPI (M)	: Communist Party of India (Marxist)

CPI (Maoist)	: Communist Party of India (Maoist)
CPI (ML)	: Communist Party of India (Marxist–Leninist)
CPN-M	: Communist Party of Nepal (Maoist)
CPN-UML	: Communist Party of Nepal (Unified Marxist Leninist)
CPMF	: Central Paramilitary Forces
CRPF	: Central Reserve Police Force
DAN	: Democratic Alliance
DGFI	: Directorate General of Forces Intelligence
DHD	: Dima Halim Daogah
DoD	: US Department of Defence
EGoM	: Empowered Group of Ministers
EPDP	: Eelam People's Democratic Party
EPRLF	: Eelam People's Revolutionary Liberation Front
EROS	: Eelam Revolutionary Organisation of Students
FSI	: Failed States Index
GHI	: Global Hunger Index
GMF	: Gono Mukti Fouz
GNI	: Gross National Income
GoI	: Government of India
GoSL	: Government of Sri Lanka
GWOT	: Global War on Terror
HuJI	: Harkat-ul-Jihad-al-Islami
HuM	: Harkat-ul-Mujahideen
IAEA	: International Atomic Energy Agency
IB	: Intelligence Bureau
ICG	: International Crisis Group
ICRC	: International Committee of the Red Cross
IED	: Improvised Explosive Device
IPKF	: Indian Peace Keeping Force
ISAF	: International Security Assistance Force
ISF-IM	: Islamic Security Force - Indian Mujahideen
ISI	: Inter Services Intelligence
ISO	: Imamia Students Organization
J&K	: Jammu and Kashmir
JeM	: Jaish-e-Muhammad
JKLF	: Jammu and Kashmir Liberation Front
JMG	: Joint Monitoring Group
JMJB	: Jagrata Muslim Janata Bangladesh

JOC	: Joint Operations Command
JTMM-G	: Janatantrik Tarai Mukti Morcha-Goit
JTMM-JS	: Janatantrik Tarai Mukti Morcha-Jawala Singh
JTMM-R	: Janatantrik Tarai Mukti Morcha-Rajan
KCP	: Kangleipak Communist Party
KCP-MF	: KCP-Military Faction
KLA	: Kuki Liberation Army
KLNLF	: Karbi Longri North Cachar Hills Liberation Front
KNA	: Kuki National Army
KNF-Prithvi	: Kuki National Front (Prithvi)
KRA	: Kuki Revolutionary Army
KYKL	: Kanglei Yawol Kanna Lup
LeJ	: Lashkar-e-Jhangvi
LeT	: Lashkar-e-Toiba
LI	: Lashkar-e-Islami
LICUS	: Low-Income Countries Under Stress
LoC	: Line of Control
LTTE	: Liberation Tigers of Tamil Eelam
MCC	: Maoist Communist Centre
MHA	: Ministry of Home Affairs
MJF	: Madhesi Janadhikar Forum
MJF-YF	: Madhesi Janadhikar Forum-Youth Forum
MMA	: Majlis-e-Amal
MNF	: Minzo National Front
MoU	: Memorandum of Understanding
MULTA	: Muslim United Liberation Tigers of Assam
NA	: Nepali Army
NATO	: North Atlantic Treaty Organization
NC	: National Conference
NDA	: National Defence Army
NDFB	: National Democratic Front of Bodoland
NHRC	: National Human Rights Commission
NLFT	: National Liberation Front of Tripura
NNC	: Naga National Council
NREGA	: National Rural Employment Guarantee Act
NSA	: Non-State Actor
NSCN	: National Socialist Council of Nagaland
NSCN-IM	: National Socialist Council of Nagaland (Isak-Muivah)

NSCN-K	:	National Socialist Council of Nagaland (Khaplang)
NSCN-U	:	National Socialist Council of Nagaland (Unification)
NSP	:	National Sadbhavana Party
OCHA	:	Office for the Coordination of Humanitarian Affairs
OEF	:	Operation Enduring Freedom
OHCHR	:	Office of the High Commissioner of Human Rights
PBCP	:	Purba Banglar Communist Party
PDP	:	Peoples Democratic Party
PLA	:	People's Liberation Army
PLOTE	:	People's Liberation Organisation of Tamil Eelam
PMGSY	:	Pradhan Mantri Gram Sadak Yojana
PMO	:	Prime Minister's Office
PoK	:	Pakistan-occupied Kashmir
PPP	:	Pakistan People's Party
PREPAK	:	People's Revolutionary Party of Kangleipak
PRT	:	Provincial Reconstruction Team
PULF	:	People's United Liberation Front
PWG	:	People's War Group
RAW	:	Research and Analysis Wing
RBA	:	Royal Bhutan Army
RR	:	Rashtriya Rifles
RSVY	:	Rashtriya Sam Vikas Yojana
SASB	:	Shri Amarnath Shrine Board
SJMM	:	Samyukta Janatantrik Mukti Morcha
SLAF	:	Sri Lankan Air Force
SLFP	:	Sri Lanka Freedom Party
SLMC	:	Sri Lanka Muslim Congress
SLN	:	Sri Lankan Navy
SMP	:	Sipah-e-Mohammad Pakistan
SOG	:	Special Operations Group
SoO	:	Suspension of Operations agreement
SPA	:	Seven Party Alliance
SPO	:	Special Police Officer
SSP	:	Sipah-i-Sabah Pakistan
STF	:	Special Task Force
TELO	:	Tamil Eelam Liberation Organisation

TJP	:	Tehreek-i-Jafariya Pakistan
TMMT	:	Tarai Madhesi Mukti Tigers
TMVP	:	Tamil Makkal Viduthali Puligal
TNA	:	Tamil National Alliance
TNV	:	Tripura National Volunteers
TRC	:	Truth and Reconciliation Commission
TTP	:	Tekrik-i-Taliban Pakistan
TULF	:	Tamil United Liberation Front
UCPN-M	:	United Communist Party of Nepal-Maoist
ULFA	:	United Liberation Front of Asom
UNDP	:	United Nations Development Programme
UNLF	:	United National Liberation Front
UNP	:	United National Party
UPDS	:	United People's Democratic Solidarity
UPFA	:	United People's Freedom Alliance
UPA	:	United Progressive Alliance
WMD	:	Weapons of Mass Destruction
YCL	:	Youth Communist League
YF	:	Youth Force

Preface

The Institute of Peace and Conflict Studies (IPCS), since 2006, has been closely monitoring armed conflicts in South Asia — in particular the conflicts in Pakistan, J&K, India's North-East, Sri Lanka and Nepal, besides the Naxalite violence in India. The focus of this study, in the last three years, has been to comprehend these conflicts on an annual basis, in terms of the main issues and trends, and the efforts being made towards conflict management and their effectiveness.

The Institute hopes to convert this study into a long-term programme on armed conflicts in South Asia that would ultimately result in evolving a conflict database for this region. This will greaty benefit both policy-makers as well as the research community. Given the nature and intensity of conflicts in South Asia, it is essential to study them closely, identify early warning signals and provide alternative approaches to the actors involved in these conflicts. It is also imperative that there be regular policy recommendations to the state and to society from an independent think tank/research organisation. The project on Armed Conflicts in South Asia aims to fill this important space.

The focus of this volume, for the year 2009, is on armed conflicts in Afghanistan, FATA, J&K, India's North-East, Sri Lanka and Nepal, and sectarian and Naxalite violence in Pakistan and India, respectively. This volume also has a chapter focusing exclusively on the linkages between armed conflicts and the concept of failing/failed states in South Asia. Does state failure lead to armed conflicts or vice versa? It is hoped that the next edition will include few more thematic essays.

The Institute is extremely grateful to the Konrad Adenauer Stiftung (KSA), whose support has made it possible to undertake this study. The Institute is also grateful to Routledge, New Delhi, who agreed to publish these essays as an annual.

D. Suba Chandran
P.R. Chari

1

Armed Conflicts and Peace Processes in South Asia: An Overview

P.R. Chari

THE YEAR IN RETROSPECT

The year 2008 will be remembered whenever the history of these times is written as the year when a 'financial tsunami' struck the world. American ascendancy over the world's financial systems has ensured that no part of the globe could be insulated from its effects, including South Asia, one of the poorest regions, second only to sub-Saharan Africa. This manmade disaster is traceable to the greed of individuals and financial institutions, as well as to the profligacy of the United States, the world's most powerful country, adjudged on the basis of economic, military and technological parameters. It is fashionable to compare this 'financial tsunami' with the Great Depression of the 1930s; and while how long it will endure is a matter of intense speculation, it is painfully evident that the poor are hurting the most in both the national and international economy. Growing unemployment and food insecurity are prescriptions for social unrest, which will seriously affect peace and stability in poor countries.

At the physical level there was Cyclone Nargis, the year's most devastating natural disaster, which had its origins in the Bay of Bengal, veered off the coast of Bangladesh and finally struck Myanmar's Irrawady Delta on 10 May. Estimates of deaths reached 146,000; estimates of those made homeless were placed at the hundreds of thousands, and guesstimates of the monetary loss suffered are $10 billion. The paranoia of Myanmar's military junta made them reluctant to accept international relief, thereby adding to the sufferings of its people. It also drew attention to 'the historical connection between rice shortages and popular unrest (most notably in 1988)'; 'the cycle of explosive protest and regime crackdown is likely to continue'.[1]

2008 will be remembered also as the year when the likelihood of inter-state conflict receded further into the background, which was inevitable after nuclear weapons entered the equation between India and Pakistan — the two most persistent antagonists in South Asia who have fought several wars in their brief history as independent nations. In 2008, the most dangerous moments were end November, when the Mumbai terrorist attacks, resulting in 173 deaths and an estimated 300 being injured, raised India–Pakistan tensions to a new pitch. These attacks were traced back to Pakistan through cellphone intercepts of conversations between the terrorists and their handlers, and the perpetrators were identified as belonging to the extreme jihadist organisation, Lashkar-e-Toiba (LeT) — a creation of the Services Intelligence (ISI), functioning from within the Pakistan army. Beliefs that the LeT is no longer under ISI's control but has become an autonomous entity, were greeted with incredulity in India; other beliefs that rogue elements in the ISI had planned this outrage were dismissed outright as being fanciful. The military options available to India in retaliation against the Mumbai attacks, such as undertaking a surgical strike against Pakistan or launching a conventional attack on Pakistan but with limited objectives, and so on, were avidly discussed. But these options were rejected by the political leadership in New Delhi as impractical, largely due to the nuclear deterrence option available to Pakistan after its nuclear tests in May 1998. The limitations of the military option were, in fact, demonstrated earlier during the Kargil conflict (1999) and the border confrontation crisis (2001–02).[2] This left only the diplomatic option available to India, which has been assiduously pursued in tandem with the United States. Apart from India and Pakistan, Afghanistan and Pakistan are the only two other South Asian countries that could be embroiled in an inter-state conflict.

---

[1] Donal M. Seekins, 'Myanmar in 2009: Hardship Compounded', *Asian Survey*, 44(1), January/February 2009, p. 172.

[2] A distinction can be made between strategic stability (non-existent) and crisis stability (obtaining) in India–Pakistan crises, leading to the 'stability–instability' paradox. See P.R.Chari, Pervaiz Iqbal Cheema and Stephen P. Cohen, *Four Crises and a Peace Process: American Engagement in South Asia* (Washington, DC: Brookings Institution Press, 2007), pp. 196–201.

2008 would also be remembered in South Asia as the year which saw terrorist attacks acquiring greater virulence and becoming more spectacular. The Mumbai outrage attracted global attention because of the iconic nature of some of the targets attacked, although other terrorist strikes in the region have been equally catastrophic. For example, the suicide bombing of the Marriot Hotel in Islamabad led to 54 persons being killed and extensive damage to a popular haunt for local citizens. Afghanistan witnessed a suicide attack on the Serena Hotel in Kabul in January 2008, an attempt to assassinate President Karzai in April, and the deadly suicide attack on the Indian Embassy in Kabul in July that led to 54 deaths and over 100 people being injured. American intelligence linked the Embassy attack to the ubiquitous ISI, bringing India–Pakistan relations to a new low, which reached its nadir after the Mumbai attacks in November. A technical distinction is possible between suicide attacks where the attacker kills himself/ herself while seeking to destroy the target, and a suicidal attack in which the attacker has a chance, however infinitesimal, of escaping. The attack on the Indian embassy in Kabul and the Marriot Hotel in Islamabad were suicide attacks, but the Mumbai outrage provides a good example of suicidal attacks. The distinction is fine, but worth noting, since the level of professionalism required from the suicide bomber is much lower than that needed of a suicidal attacker.

2008 also witnessed a resurgence in armed conflicts and violence in South Asia amidst these escalating terrorist attacks. The spate of attacks on the International Security Assistance Force (ISAF) and Operation Enduring Freedom (OEF) forces in Afghanistan took a deadly toll of lives, estimated around 300 in 2008. Added to that were the casualties due to insurgency-related violence all over the country, estimated at 5,400, which also included the deaths of civilians in Afghanistan due to air strikes and drone attacks.[3] There is an increasing awareness now that the problem of militancy in Afghanistan lies in Pakistan, but having said that, no military solution to the Afghan imbroglio is possible without addressing the allied problems of civil governance, economic development, poppy cultivation and so on, which are inextricably linked to militancy in that country. Indeed, the question becomes relevant: how should one quantify success from an ISAF

---

[3] Adam B. Ellick and Abdul Waheed Wafa, '19 Killed in Attack in Afghanistan', *New York Times*, 13 November 2008. Casualty estimates vary, incidentally, from source to source.

and OEF perspective? Should it be equated with neutralising the Al Qaeda? Or does it require 'fixing' the Taliban menace in Pakistan? Does it require bringing about normalcy in India–Pakistan relations? These dilemmas facing the United States and NATO countries will become more acute in 2009.

In Sri Lanka, the campaign undertaken by the Sri Lankan armed forces against the Liberation Tigers of Tamil Eelam (LTTE), which was spearheading the Tamil ethnic struggle against Colombo, intensified during 2008. Difficulty in getting new recruits and military–financial support from overseas Tamils, and the steady loss of its major leaders due to defection or elimination by the security forces precipitated the LTTE's retreat over the last two years. It first lost control over the eastern provinces, then steadily lost ground in the Jaffna peninsula, finally getting sequestered within a sliver of territory in Mulaithivu district. Ultimately, even this last bastion fell. Prabhakaran and other LTTE leaders were killed, along with their cadres. Regrettably, a large number of Tamil civilians also fell victim to the crossfire between the LTTE and the Sri Lankan armed forces, with large numbers being displaced and incarcerated in camps in order to screen out the LTTE cadres seeking to escape. A massive humanitarian crisis is feared. There is some talk also that the LTTE will revive its fortunes with the passage of time, but this seems improbable, considering the manner in which it revealed its unprincipled character by using defenseless civilians as a human shield during its last stand. However, Tamil aspirations, that had led to this three-decade long armed struggle, can no longer be ignored again by Colombo.

Nepal has arrived at an uneasy truce between its warring parties after the Maoists, to the surprise of many observers and participants, came to power in April following national elections to the Constituent Assembly. The People's Liberation Army (PLA) has been sequestered in designated locations under a UN-mandated ceasefire. But violence in Nepal has continued between the Youth Communist League (YCL) of the Maoists and the youth wings of the other political parties, all of them functioning basically as storm troopers. Following the political crisis occasioned by the sacking and reinstatement of the Commander-in-Chief of the army, the resignation of the Prime Minister, and the subsequent election of a new Prime Minister who was clearly dependent on the goodwill of the Maoists, the future of the democratic process and the ceasefire in Nepal appears to be in jeopardy, with the likelihood of violence resuming being very high.

Insurgent violence in Kashmir has reduced markedly, but increased manifold in the Naxalite-affected states in central and eastern India. There is much concern about the growing strength and depredations of these Left Extremists, but little evidence of a co-ordinated plan involving both the union and State governments to deal purposefully with this menace. The insurgencies excoriating India's north-eastern states are in flux, but there is little to suggest that the state has the political will to deal with the basic issues of governance involved in countering these threats to security. Cross-border terrorist attacks on India, however, have not revealed any pattern, apart from the fact that large cities in the country being targeted.

Political violence has been distinguishing Pakistan since 9/11, starting with sectarian attacks on the minority Shia community that have taken place in different parts of the country. Exhibiting a classic 'blowback' symptoms, Pakistan is now suffering the consequences of the state-tolerated and state-sponsored violence perpetrated by the Taliban and other jihadist outfits like the LeT and the Jaish-e-Muhammad. In the past they were encouraged by Pakistan's military to mount attacks on India and Afghanistan. The new dimension that has been added is that, starting in mid-2007, after President Musharraf was forced to order an attack on the Red Mosque in Islamabad — some 200 persons therein lost their lives in consequence — the state and the Pakistan army has come under militant attack. Military establishments in Punjab and the North West Frontier Province (NWFP) have repeatedly been targeted. Classic examples would be the attacks in Lahore on the Sri Lankan cricket team, its police academy and, most brazenly, on the ISI headquarters, which are expressly designed to lower Pakistan's standing in the international community. With the Taliban gaining control over the Swat Valley, most parts of the Federally Administered Tribal Areas (FATA) region and Balochistan, Pakistan has been forced to take serious military steps to regain control; hopefully, this will be the initial step towards widening its operations and tackling the Al Qaeda/Taliban threat to Pakistan, Afghanistan and the wider Central Asian, Gulf and South Asian regions.

Turning to the political developments that had an impact on armed conflicts in the region, 2008 would be remembered as the year when, despite growing terrorist attacks, violence and disillusionment, general elections — comparatively free and fair — were held in the most problematical countries — Pakistan, Bangladesh, Nepal, Bhutan and the Maldives. Conventional wisdom tells us that holding successful elections celebrates the strength of democracy in that country, and portends greater peace and stability for the future. Is this true of South Asia, or do elections have a more limited relevance — insulating South Asian countries from the long-enduring and durable tensions and instabilities distinguishing the region? Democratic interludes, in truth, are fleeting interregnums in South Asia. Will 2008 be remembered then as the year when the vulnerability of the region to house weak and failing states added to its internal instability and armed conflicts? A related issue: how can South Asian countries, individually or collectively, deal with domestic and cross-border terrorism — the most urgent threat to their national security? Finally, what can be surmised about the viability of the peace processes in the region? These questions serve as a curtain raiser for the articles presented in this volume, addressing country-specific situations and issues of significance for all of South Asia.

DEMOCRACY'S FALTERING FOOTPRINT?

Democracy took long strides in South Asia during 2008, manifested by general elections being held all over the region with momentous results for the domestic polity. A tour d'horizon can be undertaken to review these events, significant for regional democracy. Whether they prove durable is, however, another matter.

Pakistan, has witnessed alternating periods of civilian and military rule over the past six decades of its tortured history. In 2008, its military-turned-civilian President, Pervaiz Musharraf, was forced out of office by a civil society movement protesting against his arbitrary removal of the Chief Justice of the Supreme Court in end-2007. It was led by the lawyer community in Lahore, but enjoyed widespread support in the country's intelligentsia and general public. This assertion of people's power resulted in general elections being held that led to the restoration of parliamentary democracy in the country. However, the coalition forged by its two major, though fractious, political parties — the People's Political Party and the Pakistan Muslim League (Nawaz) — proved an uneasy marriage of convenience, which fell apart under the imperative of providing governance to the State. Compromises and an uneasy truce saved the government from collapse. But descent into chaos with the growing Talibanisation of the country and/or a return of the military to power, remains distinctly possible. These developments illustrate the shallow roots put down by democracy in Pakistan. Several elections have been held, and many civilian governments have come to power in Pakistan since 1947. The essence of Pakistani polity, however, has not changed. The army remains the Praetorian Guard, the real power in the background, while the political parties bicker in the foreground, unable to reconcile the personal ambitions and feudal instincts of their warring leaders; hence a return of military rule over time seems almost inevitable. Civil society and people's awakening is a new factor now. How this will motivate the political leadership into strengthening democracy remains to be seen.

Elections in Bangladesh during 2008, on the other hand, have provided a dramatic re-assertion of the democratic process in South Asia. The Bangladesh Army, its Praetorian Guard, undertook the Herculean task of cleaning up Dhaka's Augean stables. It wound up Khalida Zia's corrupt Bangladesh Nationalist Party (BNP) government, addressed the corruption pervading its administration, held free and fair elections and then, most atypically, returned to the barracks. Prime Minister Sheikh Hasina came to power thereafter, enjoying the support of 280 out of the total 300 members in the legislature. All is not well, however, in Bangladesh, as revealed by the recent revolt of the Bangladesh Rifles. It should be recalled that the revolt of the Bangladesh Rifles and the East Pakistan Rifles in March 1971 had triggered the movement that eventually led to the creation of Bangladesh. The Hasina government reached a compromise solution, envisaging the exoneration and continuance in service of the mutineers, but this contradicts the basic traditions of the armed forces.

After suffering under an insensitive monarchy for generations, which had brutally suppressed the urge of the people for liberty and equal opportunity, Nepal held general elections in April 2008, which, most unexpectedly, brought its Maoists to power. The violence and intimidation that marked these elections have left scars, reflected also in the law and order problems that are still continuing in Nepal in the form of clashes between the youth wings of the Maoist and other political parties. This violence has exacerbated the existing Madhesi agitation in the Terai region. The major challenge before the Nepali government is to frame the country's first Constitution, requiring the willing support of all the parties, which is currently nonexistent. Serious doubts are also being cast on the ability of the Nepal government to usher peace into the war-torn country in the absence of enabling institutions. In fact, the situation deteriorated further with the confrontation between the Commander-in-Chief and the Prime Minister, reflecting the latent tensions between the Nepal Army and the People's Liberation Army. A new non-Marxist political dispensation has come to power in Kathmandu, but the major problem of integrating the PLA with the Nepal army remains unresolved. No efforts have been made to promote harmony between the various political and ethnosocial groupings in Nepal, or to prosecute those responsible for committing atrocities on the people during the armed struggle, which involved both the army and the Maoist cadres. It is premature therefore to believe that the democratic impulse, strengthened by the electoral process, will ensure that parliamentary democracy survives in Nepal. Instead, a Maoist autocracy, could emerge.

Bhutan, in sharp contrast, has seen the installation of Prince Jigme Khesar Namgyel Wangchuck, reputed for his modern and liberal outlook on the throne of the Dragon Kingdom. Earlier, Bhutans' enlightened and respected ruler, Jigme Singye Wangchuck, had voluntarily renounced his absolute powers, and held elections to a bi-cameral parliament on the pattern obtaining in India. He had no doubt concluded, in light of the happenings taking place in Nepal that only a constitutional monarchy could survive in the twenty-first century, and imbibed the true meaning of the people's revolution in Nepal. Next only to India, it can be surmised that democracy will not only survive but endure in Bhutan.

The Maldives had suffered the depredations of a corrupt coterie-based rule under President Gayoom for some three decades. The opposition had been suppressed and scattered; indeed, it largely operated from Sri Lanka and India. Again, as in the case of the other South Asian countries, relatively free and fair elections were held in 2008, resulting in the coming into power of parties and individuals who are opposed to Gayoom. With a new Constitution being adopted by the Maldives, its tryst with democracy has just begun.

Elections in Sri Lanka are not due for a while. The last elections brought the Rajapakse government to power in 2006 with a strong commitment to pursuing a military solution to resolve the ethnic conflict in Sri Lanka. The destruction of the LTTE was its avowed objective, which it set out to achieve with single-minded determination, without being deflected by either adverse international opinion or criticism of its ruthless military campaign. Following their victory over the LTTE it is but natural that the security forces will gain weight in the Sri Lankan decision-making processes. But wisdom dictates that a dialogue eventually be required to seek a political solution and ensure a settlement of the Tamil question in Sri Lanka. India cannot avoid getting involved in the Sri Lankan situation due to New Delhi's domestic compulsions (read securing the support of political parties in Tamil Nadu). But it cannot press its preferred solution of greater devolution of powers to the Tamil areas too vigorously, despite its commitment to the sovereignty and integrity of Sri Lanka, bearing in mind the domestic compulsions of the Sinhala-dominated government in Colombo.

Still on the subject of democracy, it is apparent that the Karzai government in Afghanistan, widely believed to be ineffective, is not on its way out, thanks to some dexterous political manoeuvring by Karzai and the forging of expedient alliances with his rivals. What kind of a government will be stitched together after the new elections are held in the summer of 2009 and how effective it will prove in dealing with Afghanistan's horrendous problems remains to be seen.

For that matter the elections in India (May 2009) have yielded results that have confounded the pollsters, analysts and political parties. The United Progressive Alliance (UPA) coalition has returned to power with a more dominant Congress party, its coalition partners lacking the numbers to be able to seriously embarrass it. But the unbridled competition among them for 'lucrative' ministries shows that nothing has changed despite the spectacular electoral success of the Congress party. Hopefully, the new UPA Government will be able to pursue its unfinished socio-economic programmes and national security agenda with celerity. But the caveat must be sounded that historical records reveals the contrary. In 1972, 1980 and 1984 also the Congress party had won the elections with huge majorities, but frittered away its support due to a combination of disabling factors — inaction, bad decisions and malfeasance.

The foregoing discussion makes it clear that the countries of South Asia are at different stages in the trajectories of democratic growth. Democracy remains fragile in Afghanistan and Pakistan, but is well entrenched in India and Sri Lanka, while it remains at different stages of evolution in Bhutan, Bangladesh and the Maldives. One must conclude this section with the ironical observation that equating the holding of elections with the establishing of democratic credentials is a useful typology to estimate the Third-World character of nation-states. How long will it take South Asia to transcend such humiliating characterisations?

FAILING STATES AND ARMED CONFLICTS IN SOUTH ASIA

In last year's volume it was noticed that, apart from India and the Maldives, the other South Asian countries had been included in the top 60 (most vulnerable) countries listed by the Failed States Index (FSI).[4] Drawn up by the Fund for Peace, Washington, DC, this listing is published each year in the journal *Foreign Policy*. The ranking of the South Asian countries in 2008 in their order of vulnerability, namely their weakness and susceptibility to failure, are: Afghanistan 7 (8); Pakistan 9 (12); Bangladesh 12 (16); Nepal 23 (21); Sri Lanka 20 (25); and Bhutan 50 (47). Figures in parentheses show their rankings in 2007. Clearly, the situation in all the South Asian countries listed, except Nepal and Bhutan, has worsened. Furthermore, Afghanistan, Pakistan and Bangladesh are designated as 'critical', while Nepal and Bhutan are included among the states 'in danger'. The Maldives is ranked 67 and India 98 in the current listing. It should be clarified that these ratings do not indicate when violence will erupt or when these states might collapse. Rather, they are a measure of their vulnerability to violence, armed conflicts and collapse.[5]

It is possible, however, for states to draw back from the brink, and the classic example of this is India — considered to be verging on failure in the 1950s and 1960s due to food scarcity and famine, economic mismanagement, population growth, high inflation, precarious foreign exchange situation and so on. Dire predictions were made about its imminent failure, which bears similarities with current predictions that it will become the world's third-largest economy in another decade. The institutional capacity of states is of the essence to ensure the viability of states and checking their vulnerability to failure. Five core institutions are germane here — the military, police, civil services, justice system and political leadership. The health of these institutions is a fair indication of the condition of the state.

---

[4] The parameters on the basis of which this Index is prepared and listing is done include extensive corruption and criminal behaviour; inability to collect taxes or otherwise draw on citizen support; large-scale involuntary dislocation of the population; sharp economic decline; group-based inequality; institutional persecution or discrimination; severe demographic pressure; brain drain and environmental decay. See FSI 2008, *http://www.foreignpolicy.com* (accessed on 8 April 2009).

[5] *Ibid*. This section is derived from an analysis of the FSI and its various characteristics.

In last year's volume it was also noted that:

> So many failed states being located in South Asia has serious implications for the region's security and the propensity for armed conflicts within the territory of states. The geo-strategic reality must be appreciated that India is ringed by a circumference of tensions and instabilities that react with tensions and instabilities subsisting in India.[6]

This situation, too, has worsened over 2008, raising grave implications for the stability of South Asia and India's stake in the peace, stability and development of its neighbours. Their weakness heightens their unease with India but, paradoxically enough, also increases their dependence on India. Fears of being overwhelmed by India are intermingled with hopes of being rescued by it. This is apparent from the postures towards India adopted by Sri Lanka, Nepal and Bangladesh, whenever they are confronted with an internal crisis.

The vulnerability of weak states derives from their lack of resilience in being able to confront adverse internal and external political developments, the influence of international organisations, inflationary pressures on the economy and the ill effects of natural and manmade disasters. Indeed, 'fragile states' are distinguished by

> the coexistence of weak central governments with opposing militias, drug lords, tribal affiliations or other 'centrifugal forces' on the nation's territory. It can include endemic civil violence over natural resources and commodities such as oil, and chronic religious and ethnic strife.[7]

These definitions have tremendous significance for South Asia. But, how does the fragility, weakness and propensity to failure of these states affect regional security? Clearly such a domestic situation heightens their susceptibility to internal violence. Afghanistan provides the classic example of this phenomenon, the writ of the central government does not run much beyond Kabul, while the rest of the country is controlled by warlords. A similar situation has developed in Pakistan, with the state's control over the FATA region, Swat Valley

---

[6] D. Suba Chandran and P.R. Chari, *Armed Conflicts in South Asia 2008: Growing Violence* (New Delhi: Routledge, 2008), p.18.
[7] Michael Kraig, 'Weak Nations, Big Threats', Star Tribune (Minneapolis edition), 9 April 2009.

and NWFP being shared with the Taliban and assorted jihadist groups. The area under Islamabad's control in Balochistan and, for that matter, Sindh and Punjab could also shrink in the coming years.

There is another important aspect related to these internal security threats: the tribulations of the populations in these weak and failing states. Human rights abuses are commonly associated with despotic, totalitarian regimes, but a recent study of 140 nations[8] suggests that weak states are also responsible for jeopardising the personal security rights of their citizens, manifested by the phenomena of state terror, extrajudicial killings and political imprisonment. The empirical data reveals that weak and failing states are more susceptible to become totalitarian rather than democratic polities.

Apart from the threats to internal security associated with the loss of control over its own territories for the failing states of South Asia, these areas are propitious for becoming the breeding grounds for terrorism, organised crime, the proliferation of weapons of mass destruction, and drugs and human trafficking. Again, Afghanistan and Pakistan are the obvious examples. The Mumbai attacks were traced back to terrorists trained and equipped in Pakistan, highlighting the danger that such lawless elements present to its neighbours, which includes India, but also Iran and the Central Asian countries. Nepal too could become the breeding ground for terrorist activities in the future. Anti-social elements in Nepal endanger its internal security, but a major threat arises from them extending their operations into Bihar and eastern Uttar Pradesh that are recognised weak spots in India. Such examples could be extended to include specific security threats. The flow of drugs from Afghanistan, for instance, threatens the security of Pakistan and India. Terrorists from Pakistan and Bangladesh have launched terrorist attacks on India. Now, terrorists located in Afghanistan and Pakistan, like the Taliban, have been indicted for a series of devastating suicide and suicidal attacks in both countries. Human trafficking from Nepal is a continuing problem, and the dangers of nuclear weapons, technology and materials spilling out of Pakistan is a constant source of concern. State weakness and its vulnerability to collapse have serious implications, therefore, for the security of South Asia and the world.

---

[8] N. Englehart, 'State Capacity, State Failure, and Human Rights', *Journal of Peace Research*, 46 (2), 2009, pp. 163–80.

CROSS-BORDER AND DOMESTIC TERRORISM

It is plain to see that the national security challenges confronting South Asia have radically altered in the post-Cold War and post-9/11 era. But the defence and armed forces establishments are loathe to accepting these new realities for institutional reasons. All bureaucracies are averse to reform and military bureaucracies are notoriously slow to change. It is widely recognised, for instance, that national security cannot be equated with military and state security. The non-military and human aspects of security have become as significant as military security, on which huge budgetary outlays and the attention of national leaderships is being lavished. South Asia is no exception to these anomalies.

Over the years internal security threats have greatly multiplied in South Asia. Issues like terrorism, insurgency, migration, climate change, education and public health have acquired greater salience for internal security, demanding more attention from their political executives and national security elites. These concerned elites are unwilling, however, to recognise this new range of security threats, since old habits of thinking are difficult to discard, and an unfamiliar approach to national security launches them into unexplored territory. Their fixation, therefore, with preparing for traditional conflicts continues, and there is a reluctance in conceding that irregular warfare will be the future pattern of conflict. Apropos, the American experience in Iraq and Afghanistan reveals that there is a discrete cost of entry by regular war strategy. But the recurring cost of irregular war to continue the US presence in these countries and extricate itself thereafter from these imbroglios has been far greater, and has been responsible, partly at least, for the present financial crisis facing the United States.

A new pattern of 'hybrid warfare'[9] has emerged therefore, wherein non-state actors confront the dominance of the State's armed forces 'asymmetrically, using cover, concealment, dispersion and blending with civilian populations'.[10] The unwillingness of national security establishments to think innovatively through these problems reflects

---

[9] Frank G. Hoffman, author of *Conflict in the 21st Century: The Rise of Hybrid Wars* (Arlington, VA: Potomac Institute for Policy Studies, 2007), explains this concept and its ramifications.

[10] Greg Grant, 'The Man Behind Irregular Warfare', *DoD Buzz,* 7 April 2009.

in the weapons procurement decisions of defence establishments across South Asia, but especially in India and Pakistan. Big-ticket items like tanks and artillery for the army, large surface vessels and submarines for the navy and long-range and air-superiority aircraft for the air force crowd the agenda. These weapons systems are irrelevant for countering insurgency and terrorism, and they may never be used in major conventional conflicts that are increasingly becoming unlikely. Still, these weapons systems continue to be procured, much to the delight of arms manufacturing companies, despite the foreknowledge that they will be relegated, like nuclear weapons, to serve only the alleged ends of deterrence.

On the other hand, the paucity of appropriate weapons and equipment to meet the real threats to national security from militancy and insurgency, cross-border and domestic terrorism is painfully apparent. The counter-terrorism operations conducted to repel the Mumbai attacks highlighted the lack of training and specialised equipment needed to deal with these new-style assaults. The police and armed forces, thrown into action unprepared, lost many lives due to the lack of night-vision glasses, thermal imagers, or even an approach to media management. In fact, the Mumbai attacks (November 2008), the multiple attacks in Kabul (December 2008) and the attacks on the Sri Lankan cricketers and the police academy in Lahore (March 2009) fall into the genre of urban guerrilla attacks, launched by highly motivated and trained commandos. Jihadi terrorism in South Asia is an urban phenomenon, very different from rural insurgency, which is also afflicting the region.

A counter-terrorism force with appropriate skills, organisation, training, equipment and motivation is required to deal with urban guerrilla attacks, as distinct from the forces needed for counter-insurgency operations in rural areas. Whether these urban counter-terrorism forces should be located within the armed forces or be kept as paramilitary forces or should an entirely new special force be raised can be debated, but they are there to undertake urban guerrilla operations, including intelligence gathering, interrogating captured terrorists, reducing collateral damage during conflict, and rescuing hostages. An intriguing question arises here: can this role be devolved on private establishments to ensure their own security. Maintaining a monopoly over the use of force by the state, approved in orthodox political theory, may not be feasible in future, since multiple targets are vulnerable to attack in urban settings, and the state cannot protect them at all times.

Proceeding further, the Mumbai attack, later Kabul, and the two attacks in Lahore in March 2009 revealed a new pattern of multiple and simultaneous terrorist attacks. Engaging several targets with a few groups of suicidal attackers creates immense problems for counter-terrorist forces trained to deal with a single crisis at one time. These forces, moreover, cannot be located everywhere; hence more units are required to be positioned around the country. Further, using overwhelming force increases the possibilities of collateral damage, breeding new recruits for terrorist organisations, imbued with the desire for revenge; hence, the need for small, highly trained and skilled units. Elite troops could be located around the country to function as a rapid reaction force, and serve as back-up forces, but greater use of the local police and paramilitary units is indicated. Local administrations in particular should be charged with forming counter-terrorism teams for their jurisdictions, while the central and State governments should ensure proper co-ordination between local and central/state forces to avoid delays in crisis situations.

The inadequacy of the armed forces, as currently structured, to neutralise contemporary threats to national security can be further dramatised by reviewing their maritime capabilities. Traditional navies are not trained to deal with pirates in the Straits of Malacca or the waters around Somalia, or denying the sea to terrorists, as it occurred in Mumbai. The United States is now inducting 'Littoral Combat Ships to deal with this deficiency...These fast, maneuverable ships have low drafts and are thus suited for many kinds of unorthodox missions close to shore.'[11] These innovations have obvious relevance for South Asia, and refurbishing maritime forces to meet these new security threats should be seriously considered.

A word about the use of air power for counter-insurgency operations, which has a siren lure for armed forces and defence organisations around the world. The mistakes of Laos, Cambodia and Vietnam are being repeated by the United States in Pakistan with the co-operation of Islamabad, but also by Pakistan. Basically, neither country has the stomach for committing troops to ground action, which means acceptance of higher casualties. But American and Pakistani air attacks, despite better intelligence being available, inevitably lead to 'collateral damage' and civilian deaths, which then become focal

---

[11] Robert D. Kaplan, 'Anarchy on Land Means Piracy at Sea', *New York Times*, 12 April 2009.

points for the creation of more militants, imbued with revenge motivations. The entire effort thus becomes counter-productive, since heightened air attacks and civilian casualties ensures that more terrorists are spawned, followed by suicide attacks being launched against American and Pakistani ground forces and installations.

Tactics must suit the terrain and local circumstances, but also encourage the local people to solve their own problems. Above all, command headquarters should concern itself with policy and logistics, leaving tactics to be worked out at the local level. The implications for counter-insurgency operations are clear: keep the footprint small. Those inducted, ideally, should be Special Forces personnel trained for such operations, who are also familiar with the region's language and local culture. These lessons of relevance to counter-insurgency and counter-terrorism operations in South Asia are well known, but are generally forgotten.

WHAT ABOUT THE PEACE PROCESSES?

The most significant interstate peace process in South Asia is that between India and Pakistan, initiated after an agreement was reached between Prime Minister Vajpayee and President Musharraf on the sidelines of the January 2004 SAARC Summit in Islamabad. Currently this peace process lies frozen after the terrorist attacks on the Indian embassy in Kabul (July 2008) and Mumbai (November 2008). Governments obviously cannot ignore public sentiments and while Indian public opinion is greatly incensed by these attacks, Pakistani public opinion remains in denial about its official agencies being complicit in nurturing, equipping, training and launching terror attacks into India. The terror attacks now being mounted in Pakistan by the Taliban and LeT, and the retreat of the Pakistani state from its own territories, is explained away by urging that they are only expressions of resentment felt against the American influence over Pakistan's leadership. Whether the 'composite dialogue' with India and other negotiations will be resumed soon, while the ruling clique in Islamabad remains embroiled in ensuring its own survival in power, cannot be predicted. But, the conclusions of the Indian elections and the return of the Congress-led UPA coalition to power, is a hopeful sign. It would be realistic, however, to appreciate that, even if the peace process should resume, it will take a long time for trust to be established, unless some spectacular breakthrough is achieved in the dialogue. That said, the internal peace processes in South Asia are also worth reviewing. We can start with India.

It is apparent that no dialogue proceeds between New Delhi and the separatists in the Kashmir Valley who are obstinately in denial. But their illogic of allying with Pakistan is becoming starker as the latter struggles to deal with insurgency and terrorism in its own territory, and serious doubts are being cast on the viability of the Pakistani state. Would the Kashmiris want to share a Taliban-dominated future by sharing the vision of the separatists to join Pakistan?

The issue of greater relevance for the moment though is that no dialogue proceeds between New Delhi and the Naxalites. The sporadic ceasefires that some of the State governments have reached with these Left extremists have proved ephemeral and impermanent. Perhaps a sense of triumphalism has imbued these outfits after the spectacular success achieved by the Maoists in Nepal, who were able to leverage their success in opposing the government.

India's peripatetic dialogues with the militant groups in its northeastern states have a fitful character. Apart from Mizoram and Tripura, these groups continue to operate and splinter, with new outfits being formed periodically, making a dialogue problematic. The presence of a multiplicity of militant and extremist groups also makes it difficult for New Delhi to negotiate a viable peace process with them. In truth, however, ceasefire agreements with them have become irrelevant since criminal violence and extortion continue unhampered during these ceasefires, making little difference to the lives of the citizens.

What is the state of peace processes within Afghanistan and Pakistan? The dominant theme now is the AF-PAK strategy devised by the Obama administration that has identified its goal 'to disrupt, dismantle and defeat' the Al Qaeda in Pakistan and Afghanistan.[12] For this purpose a 'standing, trilateral dialogue' among the United States, Afghanistan and Pakistan is also envisaged to 'enhance intelligence sharing and military cooperation along the border, while addressing issues of common concern like trade, energy, and economic development'. Since this strategy is linked with the provision of liberal grants and aid to both countries that are in danger of economic collapse, it

---

[12] 'Remarks by the President on a New Strategy for Afghanistan and Pakistan', the White House, Office of the Press Secretary, 27 March 2009, http://www.whitehouse.gov/the_press_office/Remarks-by-the-President-on-a-New-Strategy-for-Afghanistan-and-Pakistan/ (accessed on 28 May 2009).

is being hoped that financial incentives will persuade them to address the militant threat to their internal stability with greater seriousness, which also threatens the wider South Asian region.

In Sri Lanka, the LTTE has been eliminated from its last pocket of resistance in the Jaffna peninsula. There was little logic to the fond hopes in India (Tamil Nadu State has a symbiotic relationship with Sri Lanka), that the Rajapakse government would offer a ceasefire, and not insist on the total surrender of the LTTE leadership, leaving them the one other choice of biting their cyanide pills. As it happened, the LTTE leadership, including Prabhakaran, preferred to die fighting the Sri Lankan armed forces rather than to surrender. The Sinhala government cannot be denied a sense of triumph in their hour of victory. But they would be making an egregious error by ignoring the festering Tamil demands for greater autonomy and a larger proportion of the development cake. The role of the million-strong Tamil diaspora that had played an important role in supporting the LTTE struggle is of especial interest. Will it reconcile itself to the LTTE having lost their conflict for a separate Eelam? Will they desist from trying to establish new Tamil rebel groups in Sri Lanka? The international community, especially India, cannot step away from ensuring the establishment of enduring peace in Sri Lanka, while preserving the sovereignty and integrity of the country.

A similar situation obtains in Nepal. The ceasefire achieved after arduous negotiations lies in danger of unravelling, with the President having reinstated the dismissed Commander-in-Chief, leading to Prime Minister Prachanda's resignation and the Maoists threatening to leave the government. The new government sworn in, headed by Madhav Nepal and comprising political parties opposed to the Maoists, is brittle, and considerable political dexterity will be needed to put together a working relationship between the parties in power, the Maoists, the Nepal Army, the PLA and the President to save the ceasefire from collapse.

In Sri Lanka and Nepal, but more generally in all the other countries of South Asia, warring political parties have yet to appreciate the need for dialogue and compromise that is needed to restore peace and stability in their countries, and permit the onerous tasks of national reconstruction to proceed without hindrance. That said, it is realistic to appreciate that the ongoing peace processes in South Asia remain fragile and are easily vulnerable to disruption.

2

Afghanistan: Tipping Point

Shanthie Mariet D'Souza

A BRIEF HISTORY

The international military intervention in Afghanistan after the 9/11 attacks on the US homeland has exacerbated the conflict in that country. The early beginnings of the conflict and consequent instability in Afghanistan can be traced to the period preceding the Soviet intervention (1973–79). In the largest covert operation since the Vietnam War, the United States' Central Intelligence Agency (CIA)[1] started supporting the Afghan resistance parties based in Pakistan. Following the Soviet intervention in Afghanistan, Pakistan emerged as the 'frontline state' in directing the anti-Soviet jihad. The objective of the Americans seemed to be transforming Afghanistan into a 'Soviet–Vietnam' and bleeding the Soviet Union 'white'.

Having achieved this objective and the Soviet withdrawal from Afghanistan, the US policy-makers lost interest in the country. Afghanistan continued to be wracked by internecine conflict between the various mujahideen factions. In the ensuing chaos, the Taliban began their victory march with active support from Pakistan. The strictly puritanical Taliban regime was led by Mullah Omar, and comprised a ragtag motley group of former Pushtun military commanders, madrasa teachers and a large rank and file from the Islamist religious

---

[1] President Jimmy Carter decided that the US had a 'moral obligation' to help the resistance movement. In July 1979, six months before the Soviet invasion, President Carter signed a Presidential finding on covert action that began as a modest programme of medical aid to the rebels. The entire covert aid programme was channelled by the CIA through the Inter Services Intelligence (ISI), the Pakistani intelligence agency, to maintain deniability. See John H. Cooley, *Unholy Wars: Afghanistan, America and International Terrorism* (London: Pluto Press, 2000), p. 129. For CIA funding see Brigadier Mohammad Yousaf and Major Mark Adkin, *The Bear Trap: Afghanistan's Untold Story* (Lahore: Jang Publishers, 1992), p. 120.

schools in Pakistan. Their repressive rule was marked by large-scale human rights violations and the oppression of women.

The US remained indifferent to the rise of the Taliban due to Pakistan's reassurances that the regime would serve as a stabilising force to restore peace and order, which would help the US oil companies to exploit the rich energy resources in neighbouring Central Asia. However, these hopes were quickly belied when the Taliban became extremist and provided sanctuary to the Al Qaeda in 1996, following Osama bin Laden's flight from Sudan. The Al Qaeda and the Taliban have shared a symbiotic relationship since then, with the former financing and the latter providing a fighting force. When Osama bin Laden was indicted for the 1998 US embassy bombings in Africa, the Taliban refused to extradite him, a stance maintained by it till the 11 September 2001 (9/11) attack on the US. The Taliban, dictated by their tribal code of Pushtunwali, vowed to protect and provide hospitality to their Al Qaeda guests.

In the aftermath of the 9/11 attacks on American homeland, the US-led Operation Enduring Freedom (OEF) was primarily targeted at decimating the Taliban–Al Qaeda terrorist infrastructure in Afghanistan and depriving the Al Qaeda of its territorial base for carrying out future attacks. The military operations that commenced on 7 October 2001, along with the forces of the Northern Alliance and local warlords, resulted in a quick ouster of the Taliban from Kabul. The Taliban withdrawal from Kandahar on 9 December 2001 marked the end of the Taliban regime in Afghanistan. On 1 May 2003, US Secretary of Defense Donald Rumsfeld, declared an end to 'major combat operations'. The announcement of early victory and diverting of resources and troops (CIA specialists and elite Special Forces) to Iraq in early 2003 at a critical juncture in the war in Afghanistan adversely affected the counter terrorism operations. The Bush administration's policy of providing support to the warlords to maintain a light security foot print in Afghanistan led to a deteriorating security situation, besides promoting a 'culture of impunity'.

The insurgency, which had its early beginnings in 2002–03, continues to wrack the country after eight years of military action. In 2008, violence surged by 40 per cent over 2007 and is said to be precariously at the tipping point.[2] Fractured political processes, inadequate

---

[2] Allan Orr, 'Recasting Afghan Strategy', *Small Wars & Insurgencies*, 20(1), March 2009, pp. 87–117.

reconstruction, rising instability and an alienated populace provided a support base to the Taliban-led insurgency.[3] The year 2009 is being viewed as a 'crucial year' for the international forces to contain, if not arrest the tide of Taliban insurgency. Following the unveiling of the new AF-PAK strategy by the Obama administration and the upcoming presidential elections in Afghanistan in August 2009, the troop surge policy of the US is primarily directed at containing the conflict in the southern and eastern parts of the country.

THE PRINCIPAL ACTORS

The conflict in Afghanistan involves several internal and external actors with conflicting interests and competing agendas. Some ethnic, tribal, clan and community groups existed in this environment before the conflict, and were engaged in creative competition. However, the present conflict and involvement of new actors have accentuated the existing socio-ethnic cleavages and divisive tendencies. In Afghanistan, the ethno-tribal power competition, and the Pushtun domination of the political space, has always been an important factor in maintaining equilibrium in the political system.

The present conflict in Afghanistan includes a huge array of new actors — intervening counter-insurgent states (the United States-led OEF) and its coalition partners (NATO International Security Assistance Force [ISAF], foreign terrorists with transnational linkages (Al Qaeda and its affiliates), international institutions, non-governmental organizations (NGOs) media, and others. In the case of the Taliban insurgency, the Taliban–Al Qaeda symbiotic relationship provides Al Qaeda with a local partner (the Taliban), which has developed further linkages with various non-state armed groups in Afghanistan and Pakistan. This area has emerged as an 'arc of regional conflict formation',[4] linking conflicts from Chechnya to Kashmir.

---

[3] The Taliban-led insurgency includes a loose alliance of Taliban guerrillas, followers of the Afghan warlord Gulbuddin Hekmatyar's radical group Hizb-i-Islami, Al Qaeda recruits, foreign terrorists, narcotic traffickers, bandits and tribal fighters in the Pakistan–Afghanistan border areas. This inference was derived from interviews and discussions with the local people in various provinces in Afghanistan — Herat, Kabul, Balkh, Parvan, Baglan, Samangan, Kapisa, and Nangarhar, during a field visit to Afghanistan in May–June 2007.

[4] Barnett R. Rubin and Andrea Armstrong, 'Regional Issues in the Reconstruction of Afghanistan', *World Policy Journal*, 20(1), Spring 2003, pp. 31–41.

Despite a massive international commitment to rebuilding Afghanistan not much has been done towards institution building, improving governance and establishing the rule of law. The nascent democratic government led by President Hamid Karzai is seen as weak, corrupt and ineffective by the international community as well as the local populace. The 'rentier state' depends on external aid for its functioning and providing security to the population. The writ of the Karzai government is restricted to the capital and he is popularly known as the 'mayor of Kabul'. The fight against the Taliban is being led by the US, NATO and indigenous Afghan national security forces (ANSF), which includes the Afghan National Army (ANA) and Afghan National Police (ANP).

Afghan National Army

The ANA has been primarily employed to augment the Coalition's Coin operations. In 2007, the ANA led 45 per cent of all operations. By the spring and summer of 2008, its role had expanded and the ANA reportedly led 62 per cent of operations.[5] In March 2009, the Pentagon estimated that the Afghan army has nearly 83,000 troops, although only 52,000 were engaged in combat alongside international or US forces.

Structurally, the ANA is divided into five ground manoeuver corps consisting of two to four brigades. Each brigade comprises infantry kandaks (Afghan battalions), combat support kandaks, and combat service support kandaks. Of the 160 units 95 have 82,781 personnel (out of the total projected strength of 134,000 by December 2011) distributed over five ground manoeuver corps and one air corps.[6] Once the ANA is expanded, it will have five corps headquarters, a division

---

[5] C.J. Radin, 'Afghan National Army: February 2009 Update', *The Long War Journal*, 24 February 2009, http://www.longwarjournal.org/archives/2009/02/afghan_national_army_1.php (accessed on 26 February 2009); Greg Bruno, 'Afghanistan's National Security Forces Backgrounder', The Council on Foreign Relations, 16 April 2009, http://www.cfr.org/publication/19122/afghanistans_national_security_forces.html?breadcrumb=%2Fpublication%2Fby_type%2Fbackgrounder (accessed on 21 April 2009).

[6] The five ANA corps serve as regional commands that include the 201st Corps based in Kabul, 203rd Corps in Gardez, 205th Corps in Kandahar, 207th Corps in Herat, and the 209th Corps in Mazar-e-Sharif. These regional commands provide a permanent ANA presence in every region of Afghanistan. For further details, see 'Fact Sheet Afghan National Army, Combined Security Transition Command Afghanistan', *CSTC-A Public Affairs*, 15 March 2009, http://www.cstc-a.com/mission/Afghan%20Army%20Fact%20Sheet.pdf (accessed on 20 March 2009).

headquarters, 21 brigades, and 114 battalions. The current budget allocation of the ANA is $2.75 billion per year. However, the Government of Afghanistan is not capable of funding this force.[7]

Since August 2008, the ANA has assumed lead responsibility for security in Kabul and is extending its reach into some of the provinces. It is more of a success story than the ANP, however, its ability to operate independently has been delayed and curtailed due to limitations of funding, recruitment, training and equipment.

Afghan National Police

The ANP comprises the Afghan Uniformed Police responsible for general law enforcement and public safety; the Border Police patrolling the country's borders and conducting counter-smuggling operations; the Civil Order Police dealing with disturbances in urban areas; the Counter Narcotics Police fighting drug trafficking; the Criminal Investigation Police investigating crimes; and the Counter Terrorism Police for counter-insurgency operations.[8]

As of November 2008, there were 76,000 police officers and there is a plan to recruit 6,000 more. Military strategists estimate the proper ratio of police to people in peacetime to be around 1 per 400 citizens, while stability operations call for much high ratios.[9] Afghanistan, with an estimated population of 33 million, will have a ratio of 1 to 402 people once these forces are fully staffed.

The core component of any effective Coin force is a well-trained police force responsible for security and intelligence collection at the community level. Like the ANA, the ANP too is facing problems of funding, training, recruitment, equipment and desertions. The development of Afghanistan's police force 'has been hindered by lack of institutional reform, widespread corruption, insufficient US military trainers and advisors, and a lack of unity of effort within the

---

[7] The expansion of the ANA's strength to 134,000 will require American or allied funds to pay for trainers, equipment, food, and housing for the Afghan forces. This is will cost an additional $20 billion, over and above the existing budget. See C.J. Radin, 'Afghan National Army: February 2009 Update', *The Long War Journal*, 24 February 2009, http://www.longwarjournal.org/archives/2009/02/afghan_national_army_1.php (accessed on 26 February 2009).

[8] For details, see 'Fact Sheet Afghan National Police', Combined Security Transition Command-Afghanistan (CSTC-A), Public Affairs, 15 March 2009, http://www.cstc-a.com/mission/Fact%20Sheet%20Afghan%20National%20Police.pdf (accessed on 21 March 2009).

[9] Jarett Broemmel, Terry Clark and Shannon Nielsen, 'The Surge can Succeed', *Military Review*, July–August 2007, pp. 110–12.

international community'.[10] The ANP remains under-trained, under-manned, has minimal control in the Afghan urban centres and only a ghost presence in rural Afghan villages, where they are most needed. Wherever they are present, they inspire fear, not security.[11]

Afghan National Army Air Corps (ANAAC)

The Afghan air corps remains in its infancy. As of late 2008 the Afghan air corps operated and maintained seven medium-sized cargo planes and 13 helicopters, though future plans envisage equipping the Afghan commando battalions with helicopter detachments for rapid-response missions. Pentagon trainers say the ANAAC will eventually include 'reconnaissance and light attack air-to-ground fixed-wing aircraft', but implementation is years away. A 2009 summary of international activities in Afghanistan by NATO reported that the ANAAC seeks to employ 7,000 personnel and 126 aircrafts by 2016.

Armed Groups

The Taliban-led insurgency includes a symbiotic relationship between Taliban guerrillas, followers of Gulbuddin Hekmatyar's radical Hizb-i-Islami, the Haqqani network, Al Qaeda and its affiliates, religious clerics, narcotic traffickers, anti-government armed groups, unemployed and alienated men in Afghanistan and tribal fighters in Pakistani tribal areas.[12] While most of these groups may not share

[10] Greg Bruno, 'Afghanistan's National Security Forces Backgrounder', The Council on Foreign Relations, 16 April 2009, http://www.cfr.org/publication/19122/afghanistans_national_security_forces.html?breadcrumb=%2Fpublication%2Fby_type%2Fbackgrounder (accessed on 20 April 2009).

[11] International Crisis Group,'Policing in Afghanistan: Still Searching for a Strategy', Asia Briefing No. 85, 18 December 2008, http://www.crisisgroup.org/library/documents/asia/south_asia/b85_policing_in_afghanistan___still_searching_for_a_strategy.pdf (accessed on 10 January 2009).

[12] This inference was derived from interviews, briefings and discussions with local people, government officials, academics, media persons, and aid workers in various Afghan provinces in May–June 2007. For further details on the insurgency, see Seth Jones, *Counterinsurgency in Afghanistan*, RAND Counterinsurgency Study, Vol. 4 (Arlington: Rand Corporation, 2008); Antonio Giustozzi, *Koran, Kalashnikov and Laptop: The Neo-Taliban Insurgency in Afghanistan* (New York: Columbia University Press, 2008); Ahmed Rashid, *Descent into Chaos: How the War against Islamic Extremism is being Lost in Pakistan, Afghanistan and Central Asia* (London: Penguin, 2008), pp. 240–61; Ron Synovitz, 'Afghan Insurgency Diversifies as Taliban Forges Alliances with Other Factions', Radio Free Europe / Radio Liberty (RFE/RL), 29 August 2008, http://www.rferl.org/Content/Insurgency_Diversifies_As_Taliban_Forges_Alliances_With_Other_Factions/1194808.html (accessed on 1 September 2008).

the political goals of the Taliban, they do share a common agenda in preventing or limiting the writ of Afghan state authority.

Taliban

The Taliban primarily consists of rural Pashtuns from the Ghilzai confederation. Following their resettlement under Durrani rule in the early twentieth century, Pushtun communities can also be found in the centre and the north of the country.[13] Though Taliban emerged as a social and religious movement, it has a strong ethno-tribal base.

Several Taliban leaders are reported to be living in Balochistan, around Quetta,[14] from where they are able to direct anti-Afghan activities. The Taliban has a wide support base in the Pakistan–Afghanistan border areas, which has serious ramifications for the security of Pakistan and Afghanistan. These areas have historically remained ungoverned and are predominantly inhabited by Pushtun tribes with strong ethno-tribal affiliations to the Taliban.

There is no accurate estimate of the number of Taliban fighters, though their strength seems to be increasing with recruits becoming available from madrasas in Pakistan. There has been a marked improvement in the sophistication of the weapons available with the Taliban and the attacks carried out by them. Their influence has been dominant in the southern and eastern provinces of the country and is spreading to its relatively stable north.

Al Qaeda

The Taliban–Al Qaeda relationship has further strengthened in post-9/11 Afghanistan. Al Qaeda, reportedly, has forged alliances with the Pakistani terrorist groups like the Jaish-e-Muhammad (JeM, proscribed in 2002 and presently operating under the banner of Jamaat-ul-Furqan),[15] Harkat-ul-Jihad-al-Islami (HuJI) and Harkat-ul-Mujahideen

---

[13] Thomas H. Johnson and M. Chris Mason, 'Understanding the Taliban and Insurgency in Afghanistan', *Orbis*, 51(1), Winter 2007, pp. 7–8.

[14] Declan Walsh, 'Balochistan feeds Taliban's growing power', *San Francisco Chronicle*, Chronicle Foreign Service, 31 May 2006, http://www.sfgate.com/cgibin/article.cgi?file=/c/a/2006/05/31/MNGT1J4ULI1.DTL (accessed on 21 June 2006).

[15] In Pakistan, the JeM operated at least four major military training camps located in Balakot, Muzzaffarabad, Hajeera, and Mansehra. For further details, see Evan F. Kohlmann, 'The Jihadists of Pakistan', The NEFA Foundation Occasional Report, August 2006, http://www.nefafoundation.org/miscellaneous/pakistanjihad0806.pdf (accessed on 8 September 2007).

(HuM) that are responsible for anti-Western attacks in Pakistan and terrorism in Jammu and Kashmir. These groups, along with Al Qaeda, have created a 'lethal concoction' with overlapping linkages, membership and ideologies.

Warlords and Private Militias

The Afghan warlords were regarded as staunch allies of the Western powers during the initial phase of OEF. Rather than marginalising the warlords and dismantling their militias, the US has relied upon the warlords (particularly from the Northern Alliance) for intelligence and co-operation in efforts to capture the Taliban and Al Qaeda remnants.[16] With the objective of maintaining a light security footprint due to preoccupation with planning for the war in Iraq, security for the Afghan population was the responsibility of regional warlords until a new ANA could be recruited, trained and deployed.[17] This promoted a 'culture of impunity',[18] and has created a problem in the security sector reform for the Afghan government and the international community.

Other Anti-Government Forces and Non-State Actors

The spread of insecurity and instability beyond the south and east to other areas, including the relatively stable north, is primarily due to the coalescence of the Taliban insurgency with the anti-government forces, warlords, militias, narcotic traffickers and criminal networks in a self sustaining 'conflict eco-system'. The present-day highly fluid and complex nature of the threat environment has been aptly described

---

[16] Richard Rupp, 'High Hopes and Limited Prospects, Washington's Security and Nation-Building Aims in Afghanistan', *Cambridge Review of International Affairs*, 19 (2), June 2006, p. 291.

[17] See James Dobbins, 'Preparing for Nation-Building', *Survival*, 48 (3), Autumn, 2006. Also see James Dobbins, 'Ending Afghanistan's Civil War', testimony presented before the House Armed Services Committee on 30 January 2007, http://armedservices.house.gov/pdfs/FC%20hearing_013007/Dobbins%20Testimony.pdf (accessed on 27 April 2007).

[18] International Crisis Group, 'Countering Afghanistan's Insurgency: No Quick Fixes', Asia Report No. 123, 2 November 2006, http://www.crisisgroup.org/home/index.cfm?l=1&id=4485 (accessed on 24 January 2007).

as a 'complex adaptive system'.[19] More importantly, since early 2002, US analysts point to the sharp increase in the number of non-state armed groups that are active in Afghanistan, including the migration of some groups that have been active in other fronts. For example, Laskhar-e-Toiba (LeT), which has historically focused its activities on Kashmir and India, is now active in provinces like Kunar and Nuristan.[20]

International Forces

United States — OEF

In post-9/11 Afghanistan, the US is heading a coalition of countries as part of the OEF. However, compared to Iraq, the US presence in Afghanistan is inadequate, although there are indications of change under the new US administration. The limited US forces[21] remain focused on offensive 'clear and sweep' operations and aerial bombings, resulting in collateral damage and mounting civilian deaths that further antagonise the population. In the new 'AFPAK' strategy, President

---

[19] The term refers to systems that are diverse (made up of multiple interconnected elements) and adaptive (possessing the capacity to change and learn from experience). For further details, see C. Christine Fair and Seth G. Jones, 'Securing Afghanistan: Getting on Track', United States Institute of Peace, Working Paper, 23 January 2009, http://library.usip.org/articles/1012068.1022/1.PDF (accessed on 10 February 2009).

[20] This increasingly complex system has important parallels with the Iraqi insurgency. See C. Christine Fair and Seth G. Jones, n. 19, *infra*.

[21] According to estimates provided by the US Department of Defense (DoD), there are approximately 19,000 US service members in Afghanistan. DoD figures show that there were about 139,000 troops in Iraq and 19,000 in Afghanistan as of 1 October 2006. For further details see Amy Belasco, 'The Cost of Iraq, Afghanistan and Other Global War on Terror Operations Since 9/11', Congressional Research Service Report RL33110, updated 16 July 2007, p.13. In addition to troops involved in combat operations, about 5,000 US troops are involved in training and advising the Afghan security forces and another 2,000 are involved in logistical operations and providing manpower for 12 Provincial Reconstruction Teams (PRTs). Between 23,000 and 24,000 American service members are in Afghanistan, the highest troop presence the United States has had in the history of the nation. Jim Garamone, 'Afghan Forces Battling Taliban in Afghanistan', American Forces Press Service, 16 January 2007, http://www.globalsecurity.org/military/library/news/2007/01/mil-070116-afps01.htm (accessed on 7 March 2007).

Obama has committed 17,000 new troops for combat and other activities to Afghanistan, as well as another 4,000 to train Afghan troops.[22]

Nato-ISAF

ISAF commenced its mission in Afghanistan on 20 December 2001 as a UN-mandated European organisation but later evolved into a NATO-led mission in 2003.[23] Initially, the ISAF mission, led by the US, was limited to Kabul. Subsequently, in August 2003, NATO took command of ISAF over Afghanistan's territory to assist 'the Afghan Government in exercising and extending its authority and influence across the country, paving the way for reconstruction and effective governance'.[24] The UN expanded NATO's role by Resolution No. 1776 on 17 September 2007, calling upon the alliance 'to disarm militias, reform the justice system, train a national police force and army, provide security for elections, and combat the narcotics industry'. Over the years, the number of ISAF troops has grown from the initial 5,000 to around 56,420 (as on February 2009), with troops from 41 countries, including all 26 NATO members.

Regional Powers

Pakistan

Given its geo-strategic position, Pakistan remains a 'crucial partner' for addressing Taliban insurgency. It continues its quest to regain 'strategic depth' in Afghanistan and use it as a 'strategic asset and a bargaining chip', to accrue unlimited American aid. Its external intelligence agency, the Inter Services Intelligence (ISI), is actively involved in supporting, funding and training the Taliban forces in its territory.[25] The US policy of interspersing drone attacks in Pakistan

---

[22] Stephen Biddle, 'Obama's Afghanistan–Pakistan Strategy: "A Reasonable First Step"', The Council on Foreign Relations, 30 March 2009, http://www.cfr.org/publication/18982/ (accessed on 12 April 2009).

[23] For further details see Paul Gallis, 'NATO in Afghanistan: A Test of the Transatlantic Alliance', Congressional Research Service Report RL33627, updated 16 July 2007, p. 3.

[24] 'NATO's role in Afghanistan', http://www.nato.int/issues/afghanistan/index.html (accessed on 12 July 2009).

[25] James Risen and David Rohde, 'A Hostile Land Foils the Quest for Bin Laden', *New York Times*, 13 December 2004. Also see Christopher Heffelfinger (ed.), *Unmasking Terror: A Global Review of Terrorist Activities* (Washington, DC: Jamestown Foundation, 2005).

with cajoling the military regime to co-operate with them in capturing the Taliban–Al Qaeda leadership has yielded few results.

Iran

Another external actor contributing to instability in Afghanistan is Iran. US officials have accused Iran of shipping advanced weaponry to militants for destabilising the Karzai government, a charge which Iran has denied. The reported discovery of Iranian arms and accounts of gunmen in pickup trucks crossing over into Afghanistan's western Farah province suggests that Tehran could be raising the ante for Washington in Afghanistan. During the Bush presidency, Iran's involvement in Afghan affairs was viewed as a 'point of pressure' for the US. However, frequent attacks on NATO supply lines in Pakistani territory is compelling the Obama administration to engage Iran in a diplomatic relationship.

CONFLICT IN 2008

Afghanistan in 2008 appeared to be teetering on the brink of failure and chaos. 2008 was the deadliest year since 2001 in being witness to record-breaking violence, exceeding 2007 levels by mid-year itself. Insurgency inspired incidents rose almost 50 per cent, from 12.4 attacks per day in 2007 to 18.4 in 2008.[26] The impact of this violence and the propaganda war launched by the Taliban has been significant for the Afghan population, most of whom are not supporters of the Taliban. This regime of intimidation and violence, combined with the ineffectiveness of international community's Coin campaign to provide security, and the sluggish progress in rebuilding the country, has impacted on the Afghan government's legitimacy among its people. Optimism among the Afghans, after the toppling of the Taliban regime, is fast giving way to despondency. Afghan villagers

---

[26] Roggio and Radin, 'Afghanistan: Mapping the Rising Violence', *The Long War Journal*, 5 August 2008, http://www.longwarjournal.org/archives/2008/08/afghanistan_mapping.php (accessed on 15 August 2008).

in the south and the east are beginning to hedge their bets and are withholding support from international and government forces. In practice, numerous Afghans now openly co-operate with and/or support the Taliban and Al Qaeda, be it out of fear, apathy or genuine support.[27]

In light of the increased violence levels, recent public opinion polls indicate that the percentage of Afghans viewing their security environment positively has dropped from 72 per cent in 2005 to 55 per cent. This becomes lower in high-conflict provinces with a corresponding decline in the capacity of the international forces to provide security.[28] These daunting statistics has generated active public discourse in the US that focuses on past failures in Afghanistan by the Soviets and the British, making the country a 'graveyard of empires'.[29]

Insecurity in Afghanistan due to the Taliban-led insurgency has spread to parts of north, north-west and central Afghanistan, like Badghis, Ghor, Farah and Kunduz, including provinces close to and bordering Kabul, like Ghazni, Logar and Wardak. The Taliban had announced their strategic objective of encircling Kabul in 2008, and resorted to high-profile attacks — Hotel Serena (January), President Karzai (April) and the Indian Embassy (July). The Taliban leadership enlisted the support of local militia factions and anti-government forces in its bid for geographical expansion. Given that they could not make much progress outside their traditional strongholds in south and east Afghanistan, they resorted to forming loose alliances and are transforming their jihad movement into a national struggle.

---

[27] Allan Orr, 'Recasting Afghan Strategy', *Small Wars & Insurgencies*, 20(1), March 2009, pp. 87–117.

[28] Only one-third of the Afghans acknowledge that US or NATO forces have a strong presence in their areas, down from 57 per cent just two years ago. Similarly, 42 per cent, down from 67 per cent in 2005, see the Western forces as capable of providing security. In the conflict ravaged south-west (Helmand, Kandahar, Nimroz, Uruzgan, and Zabul provinces), only 26 per cent feel secure from crime and violence; in Helmand alone, just 14 per cent feel safe. See Gary Langer, 'Frustration with War, Problems in Daily Life Send Afghans' Support for U.S. Efforts Tumbling', ABC News/BBC/ARD National Survey of Afghanistan, 9 February 2009, http://abcnews.go.com/PollingUnit/story?id=6787686&page=1 (accessed on 18 February 2009).

[29] Milton Bearden, 'Afghanistan, Graveyard of Empires', *Foreign Affairs*, November/December 2001, http://www.foreignaffairs.org/20011101facomment5771/milton-bearden/afghanistan-graveyard-of-empires.html (accessed on 21 March 2000).

With the Afghan government controlling only around 30 per cent of the country,[30] the rest is open for the Taliban and their affiliates to expand their control.

Nature of International Intervention

The pessimistic assessments by the US officials of the current security situation in Afghanistan indicate that the US strategy in Afghanistan is desperately off-course and needs to change. In the absence of adequate troops and the inability to secure the countryside, the international forces have relied on clear and sweep operations and aerial strikes. The resulting 'collateral damage' has acted as a force multiplier for the Taliban insurgency. Rather than marginalising the warlords and dismantling their militias, the US, in numerous cases, have relied upon the warlords for co-operation in their efforts to nab the remnants of the Taliban and Al Qaeda leadership. This undermined the Afghan government's legitimacy, thereby undoing efforts to strengthen the Afghan national security forces or building the political institutions of that country. More importantly, the US bid to increase 'military to military cooperation' and counter-terrorism co-operation with Pakistan has not yielded any tangible results to address the issue of sanctuary in that country.

Serious flaws in the international community's Coin campaign and differing threat perceptions, coupled with the varied strategies adopted to address them, have contributed to the deteriorating security situation and instability. The absence of a unified Coin strategy, lack of co-ordination in aid distribution and minimal measures to strengthen the role of the Afghan government remain the problems afflicting the international effort. The divergent perceptions of reconstruction prevalent among aid agencies, differing operational approaches of the American and NATO militaries, the unwillingness of external agencies to co-ordinate their efforts with the Afghan government, are

---

[30] US National Intelligence Director Michael McConnell, in a bleak assessment before the Senate Armed Services Committee of the security situation in Afghanistan, pointed out that the Taliban controls 10–11 per cent of the country, while the government controls 30–31 per cent. J. Michael McConnell, Annual Threat Assessment of the Director of National Intelligence for the Senate Select Committee on Intelligence, 5 February 2008, 'NATO chief disputes US intelligence assessment on Afghanistan', *The International Herald Tribune*, 29 February 2008, http://www.iht.com/articles/ap/2008/02/29/america/NA-GEN-US-NATO.php (accessed on 1 March 2008).

undermining the international CoIn efforts towards long-term stabilisation of the country.[31]

With international aid coming from some 80 different countries and aid groups, each with its own national agenda, less than one-third of the aid received has been delivered through the Afghan government's national budget, thus contradicting and undermining a basic requisite for the Afghan government to develop governance capacity and gain credibility among it's people. Important development initiatives like the National Solidarity Programme are suffering funding shortfalls.[32] Moreover, only a fraction of the aid promised by the international community has actually been delivered to the country. According to a June 2008 report by the Agency Coordinating Body for Afghan Relief (ACBAR), donors pledged $25 billion in aid from 2002 to 2008, of which only $15 billion has actually been spent. The US, providing a third of all developmental aid to Afghanistan, dispersed only $5 billion of its promised $10.4 billion. The report further indicates that some 40 per cent of that $15 billion ended up in consultants' salaries and company profits.[33]

Major Trends in 2008–09

Rising Violence and Increased Civilian Casualties

The Taliban-led insurgency has shown no signs of abatement with a significant rise of violence level in parts of the south, south-east and south-west, leading to an overall increase in casualties from 2007. In 2008, violence continued to escalate with a reported 30 per cent

---

[31] Shanthie Mariet D'Souza, '"Unity of Effort": The Missing Link in the Afghan Counter-Insurgency Campaign', *Strategic Analysis*, 32(5), September–October 2008.

[32] The National Solidarity Programme, which takes a community-managed approach to rural infrastructure and reconstruction, thereby limiting corruption and empowering citizen participation, will face a $160 million shortfall in its second phase. US contributions to the Afghanistan Reconstruction Trust Fund (ARTF) fell from $74 million in 2006 to $50 million in 2007. Caroline Wadhams, Colin Cookman and Ben Dear, 'Afghanistan Needs More Than Money: Greater US Leadership is Needed to Fix Development Problems', Center for American Progress, 11 June 2008, http://www.americanprogress.org/issues/2008/06/afghanistan_needs.html (accessed on 22 June 2008).

[33] 'Vast sums of aid are lost in the corporate profits of contractors and subcontractors, which can be as high as 50 per cent on a single contract', the report said. Caroline Wadhams, Colin Cookman and Ben Dear, 'Afghanistan Needs More Than Money', n. 32, *infra*.

increase nation-wide and an estimated 40 per cent rise in attacks over 2007 in the US-led eastern sector.[34] There has been a marked rise in both civilian and military casualties, as well as among the insurgents. Attacks against Afghan civilians and the international community using improvised explosive devices (IEDs) caused the greatest loss of life, while insurgents increasingly targeted isolated and vulnerable ANP facilities, resulting in a significant rise in police fatalities. Furthermore, instability in Pakistan allowed insurgents to use safe havens there to mount attacks from across the porous border into Afghanistan.[35]

In 2008, a total of 2,118 civilians were killed, compared to 1,523 in 2007. The 2008 figure is, in fact, the highest since the Taliban government was ousted in November 2001.[36] The mounting civilian casualties were primarily a result of the over-reliance on aerial bombings by the international forces, in the absence of adequate troops on the ground and the lack of 'human intelligence'. Such casualties have had a disastrous effect on popular perceptions by eroding support for the Afghan government and causing serious resentment towards the international forces.

Asymmetric Warfare

The Taliban and its affiliates have not been able to fight 'set-piece battles' with the coalition forces. This is the rationale behind the Taliban's strategy of avoiding aggregation and resorting to asymmetric warfare. Instead of gathering in company-sized units to take on foreign troops, Taliban forces are also increasingly resorting to use of IEDs, suicide bombings and roadside bombings. Statistics compiled by ISAF reveal that explosives attacks rose by 33 per cent in 2008 over the previous year and there was a 25 per cent increase in direct-fire incidents in 2007. Suicide attacks have been accompanied by attacks on students and schools, assassinations of officials, and the targeting of policemen in a deliberate attempt to impede the establishment of legitimate government institutions and undermine popular confidence in the authority and capability of the Government of Afghanistan.

[34] Vincent Morelli and Paul Belkin, 'NATO in Afghanistan: A Test of the Trans-Atlantic Alliance', Congressional Research Service Report RL33627, 23 January 2009.
[35] NATO, 'Afghanistan Report 2009', p. 6, http://www.nato.int/cps/en/natolive/index.htm (accessed on 21 June 2009).
[36] According to the United Nations' data, in the first eight months of 2008, 1,445 civilians were killed in Afghanistan, representing a rise of 39 per cent over the same period of 2007. Also see Dexter Filkins, 'Afghan Civilian Deaths Rose 40 Per Cent in 2008', *International Herald Tribune*, 18 February 2009.

Increased Linkages of Non-State Actors

A complex web of international networks of armed groups, linked by opium trafficking, ethnic ties and Islamic fundamentalism, connects Afghanistan with Kashmir, Chechnya, Tajikistan, Kyrgyzstan, Uzbekistan, Pakistan, Iran and Central Asia in an arc of 'regional conflict formation'.[37] Their trans-national nature is intertwined and interconnected also by the exchange of illegal goods (weapons, drugs and human trafficking), which provides fighters and funds for the Taliban–Al Qaeda insurgency in Afghanistan.

Following Al Qaeda's 2001–02 expulsion from Afghanistan and the relocation of some of its core elements in Pakistani cities, many Al Qaeda activists are known to have joined forces with indigenous Pakistani Sunni militant groups, including LeT, JeM, SSP, and Lashkar-e-Jhangvi (LeJ). Links between Al Qaeda and these Pakistani Islamic militant groups are informal and extensive, with existing Pakistani religious extremists facilitating Al Qaeda activities in that country. Hence, despite the absence of any physical infrastructure of the Al Qaeda in Pakistan, the acts of terror are carried out by Pakistani terrorist groups by a system of 'sub-contracting'.[38]

Sources of Funding

Narco-trafficking continues to remain a major source of funding for Taliban insurgency. The opium trade in Afghanistan, which supplies more than 90 per cent of the world's opium, is worth about $3.1 billion, and contributes about a third to Afghanistan's total economy. The huge array of Taliban affiliated groups and warlords, narcotics traffickers and organised criminals involved in the drug trade have formed cross border networks, enabling an easy flow of drugs from Afghanistan into Central Asia, Iran, Pakistan, China and India. The Taliban insurgents make an estimated $100–200 million each year by taxing opium poppy production and trafficking. Thus, a fall in opium production is critical for shrinking the war chest of the insurgents. Despite the fact that opium cultivation fell by 19 per cent in 2008, significant differences exist in the Allies' approach to countering opium

---

[37] See Barnett R. Rubin and Andrea Armstrong, 'Regional Issues in the Reconstruction of Afghanistan'.

[38] C. Christine Fair, 'Militant Recruitment in Pakistan', *Studies in Conflict and Terrorism*, May 2004.

production in Afghanistan. While US policy insists on using forceful means for complete eradication like aerial spraying, the NATO allies are reluctant to do so mainly for reasons of losing the battle for heart and minds. Forceful poppy crop eradication campaigns without providing alternative livelihood programmes have created economic hardships for the people, thereby increasing their discontent with the government and foreign forces and expanding the support base for the Taliban, particularly in the south and the east.

CONFLICT MANAGEMENT

The central focus of the international community is to contain the conflict in the Afghanistan–Pakistan tribal areas, which is spilling over into Pakistan and leading to greater instability and violence in that country.

Arming the Tribal Militia

The recent 'peak' in violence in Afghanistan has led senior US commanders and military planners to explore a 'ground-up' tribal reconciliation programme and the feasibility of recruiting Afghan tribesmen to fight the Taliban–Al Qaeda combine. Taking a page out of the so-called 'Sunni Awakening' in Iraq, which set the Sunni tribesmen first against the militants in Anbar province and then elsewhere, there are views about replicating this model for the country's multiple tribal militias.

Perhaps the most closely watched, though least understood, element of Afghanistan's security forces is the Afghan Public Protection Force, an experimental militia programme, modelled on a similar programme in Iraq. These units are being recruited and vetted by regional leaders, who assume responsibility for their performance and discipline. However, critics warn that arming local tribes could awaken deep-rooted tribal blood feuds and do more harm than good. The Afghan tribal structure is different and less hierarchical than in Iraq, and has been radically transformed through decades of war and conflict. Both in Afghanistan and Pakistan, the Taliban have further weakened the tribal structures by systematic targeting and elimination of moderate tribal leaders, like those who support the counter-narcotics campaign. Moreover, the Taliban are equally adept at tribal co-option by providing them protection against poppy eradication.

Even if successful in halting the progress of the Taliban, it is hard to see how this tribal option could stop the division of the country into small fiefdoms. Without a serious Disarmament Demobilisation Reintegration (DDR) and Disarmament of Illegal Armed Groups (DIAG) programme, the reliance on tribal militias could be counter-productive and promote a 'culture of impunity'. According to former Afghan Interior Minister, Ali Jalali, 'manipulating the tribal would be a tactical gain, but also an immense strategic loss'. It would do little to help the state-building project in Afghanistan.

Talks/Negotiations with the Taliban

Discussions on the possibility of talks with the Taliban gathered momentum in 2008. During an October interview with TIME magazine, US President Obama, who was then a Democratic party nominee, maintained that opportunities to negotiate with the Taliban should be 'explored'. Not surprisingly, this policy has gained ground in the plans of action of the new administration. United States Central Command (CENTCOM) chief, General David Petraeus, has said that one element of the Coin strategy in Iraq that might be applicable in Afghanistan is reaching out to the 'reconcilable' elements among the insurgents, who have gained ground in the past year. Similarly, Defense Secretary Robert M. Gates has favoured some form of reconciliation in Afghanistan. These ideas of negotiations with reconcilable elements of the Taliban is also supported by the Afghan government, Saudi Arabia, the UN and by Western diplomats. The Afghan government is in fact pursuing such talks under the auspices of Saudi Arabia.[39]

There are reports of differences between the British and American approach in Afghanistan.[40] The US approves Karzai's moves to include

[39] However, spokesmen for Taliban leader Mullah Omar have denied any participation, and it is unclear if the Taliban interlocutors who were present in Riyadh have the power to speak for any of the major elements of the insurgency. See Caroline Wadhams, Colin Cookman and Jenny Shin, 'A "Downward Spiral" in Afghanistan', Center for American Progress, Washington DC, 9 October 2008, http://www.americanprogress.org/issues/2008/10/downward_spiral.html (accessed on 20 October 2008); Shanthie Mariet D'Souza, 'Talking to the Taliban: Will it Ensure "Peace" in Afghanistan?', *Strategic Analysis*, March–April 2009.

[40] Disagreement has reportedly surfaced over the US military's desire to spray poppy fields from the air with herbicide and to continue its bombing strikes on Afghan villages, which Britain complains undermines its strategy of 'winning hearts and minds'. See 'Britain Tells US: We're Winning Afghan Battles But Not the War', 7 September 2007, http://www.timesonline.co.uk/tol/news/politics/article2402986.ece (accessed on 12 September 2007).

moderate elements within the Taliban in the future peace process. On 10 September 2007, President Hamid Karzai offered to negotiate with the Taliban. On 11 September a Taliban spokesman responded saying, 'For the sake of national interests... we are fully ready for talks with the government.' He added that the Taliban had a 'limited' number of conditions, but did not explain further.[41] This response is being viewed with scepticism as the Taliban has a history of rebuffing earlier offers for negotiations.

The prospect for peace talks, however, is a highly controversial subject for those nations that have committed troops to NATO's Afghan mission and for those aiding the reconstruction efforts.[42] As a result, the international community considers the very idea of negotiations as weakening the military effort. Nonetheless, despite the lack of consensus on addressing the long term challenges in Afghanistan, there is a growing recognition that the insurgency in southern and eastern Afghanistan will not be defeated on the battlefield alone. Strategic negotiations with the Taliban need to be distinguished from a reconciliation process for those who lay down their weapons. Moreover, with the top Taliban leadership linking the process of negotiation with the total withdrawal of international forces from Afghanistan and the imposition of the shariah, the prospect for talks tread the realm of the non-negotiable.

President Karzai's Attempts at Political Reconciliation

The Karzai government has made numerous gestures towards political reconciliation and negotiations with the Taliban. While steering clear of the NATO classification of 'tier-based Taliban', the Afghan government's approach of inclusion is based on the tribal milieu of Afghan society. The objective is to exploit the differences between the tribes and communities supporting the Taliban and drive a wedge between

---

[41] Syed Saleem Shahzad, 'Al-Qaeda Fights Back at Afghan Peace Bid', *Asia Times*, 13 September 2007, http://www.atimes.com/atimes/South_Asia/II13Df01.html (accessed on 20 September 2007).

[42] Although officials from the UK, US, Canada, Denmark, and Italy have expressed some optimism in talking to the so-called 'moderate' elements of the Taliban, a growing number of countries like Iran, Russia and India are opposed to such talks. Increasingly, NATO countries like Canada are giving diplomacy priority, given the perceived failure of defence and development. See Gar Pardy, 'Held Hostage by Afghanistan', *Ottawa Citizen*, 8 September 2007.

the Afghan and Pakistani Taliban. Processes like the Loya Jirga and the elections were directed at 'inclusion' — bringing all the excluded actors back into the political process. President Karzai's efforts at reconciliation have been variously interpreted as signs of weakness, desperation, political manoeuvring and hope. Observers speculate that Karzai might be interested in securing a peace agreement with the Taliban to bolster his flagging support base before Afghanistan's upcoming presidential elections.[43]

Troop Surge

True to his campaign pledge of diverting troops from Iraq to Afghanistan, President Obama approved the sending of 17,000 troops adding to the existing 38,000 stationed in Afghanistan, signalling his first significant move to change the course of the conflict in that country. The reinforcements include about 8,000 marines, who would be deployed in Afghanistan by late spring, and a 4,000-strong army brigade that would arrive in the summer of 2009. These units will be joined by 5,000 army 'enablers' 'at a later date' to provide logistical support. President Obama's written statement explained, 'This increase is necessary to stabilize a deteriorating situation in Afghanistan, which has not received the strategic attention, direction and resources it urgently requires'.[44] Most of these new forces are expected to be deployed in southern Afghanistan, where a shortage of US and NATO forces to hold ground has crippled the Coin and counter-narcotics efforts.

The previous US administration had taken a decision in the winter of 2008 to send an additional 3,000 troops to Afghanistan in response to the escalation in Taliban activity that had lasted through the last winter. These troops, from the 10th Mountain Division that has repeatedly been deployed in Afghanistan since the start of the

---

[43] Richard Weitz, 'Afghanistan: Nato Allies Experiencing "Battle Fatigue"', *EurasiaNet Commentary*, 19 May 2008, http://www.eurasianet.org/departments/insight/articles/eav051908a.shtml (accessed on 21 May 2008).

[44] Mark Thompson, 'Obama's Yes-We-Can War: More Troops to Afghanistan', *Time* (Washington edition), 18 February 2009, http://www.time.com/time/nation/article/0,8599,1880253,00.html (accessed on 24 February 2009).

war in October 2001, are now based in Logar and Wardak provinces, south of Kabul, and will be followed by a larger number — possibly as many as 30,000 — that are likely to be sent to Afghanistan during the remainder of 2009.

As explained by senior US commander in Afghanistan General David McKiernan, this additional troop deployment, 'allows us to…change the dynamics of the security situation, predominantly in southern Afghanistan, where we are at best stalemated'. While this mini troop surge, is seen as quintessential to stabilise South Afghanistan, this initial deployment of extra forces could be the beginning of a larger US troop surge in Afghanistan. The new US forces will have a dual mission — double the size of the Afghan Army to 134,000 by the end of 2011 and provide security to Afghan communities, which are increasingly falling under Taliban control. The additional forces are expected to end the over-reliance on air strikes, which have been responsible for the bulk of civilian casualties and have increased tensions between the US and Afghan President Hamid Karzai.

CONCLUSIONS

Afghanistan today stands at a critical juncture in its struggle to quell the rising insurgency, and 2009 is a crucial year for this purpose. Reconstruction efforts have been hampered by insurgency and the problem is deepening despite the high casualties inflicted by the international forces. The security situation in Afghanistan will remain unstable and deteriorate further since the Taliban have increased their area of operation and stepped up their use of guerilla tactics. Mere emphasis on economic reconstruction without adequate security measures and the lack of Afghan state institutions will only assist the insurgents. Abducting people and holding them to ransom is likely to continue, and the Taliban is likely to resort to more such tactics and use them as bargaining tools. The overall impact of such developments on international participation in the reconstruction process could be disastrous.

The international Coin effort in Afghanistan is, in fact, floundering. While it has focused narrowly on an instant quick-fix, the larger goal of institution building and restoring the Afghan state's capacity to deal with its internal problems has been missed. The international community, particularly the US, has reneged on the commitment made during the 2006 London Conference on the 'Afghan Compact' which identified 'three critical and interdependent areas or pillars of activity' over five years: security; governance; rule of law and human rights; and social and economic development. It is important to have a unified political–diplomatic, socio–economic, psychological–moral, and security–stability effort against those who wish to depose the government. The plethora of international actors in the aid and reconstruction arena has only added to the chaos and the dissipation of energy and resources. International efforts must be unified by the UN, with a co-ordinator directing nation-building efforts in Afghanistan.

The raging Taliban-led insurgency may not be able to topple the Karzai government for as long as it is supported by the international forces. However, popular discontent with the slow pace of reconstruction and lack of security could tilt peoples' support towards the insurgents. After all, in Afghanistan no one has ever claimed national power by fighting decisive battles, rather by winning people's support in times of chaos, anarchy and insecurity. The Taliban took advantage of such a scenario in the past and they will exploit every available opportunity to exploit the present situation, particularly as Afghanistan prepares itself for the presidential elections in August this year.

While the insurgency in Afghanistan has an external–internal interface, with common borders, ethnicities and cultures creating transnational networks of criminal groups sustaining the insurgency, a regional approach that is based on co-ordinating responses would help to disrupt these networks. The inability of the participants at the 2001 Bonn Conference to involve and elicit the support of the regional powers to play a useful role reveals their inability to comprehend the complexity of regional power dynamics. Afghanistan's neighbours, in alliance with the provincial leaders, could tilt the power balance among the ethnic groups if the Karzai government fails to extend its authority, or should the international community wash its hands off Afghanistan. More importantly, the way the international community engages with Afghanistan's problematic neighbours, Iran and Pakistan, would go a long way towards the emergence of a peaceful and stable Afghanistan.

According to available indications, the initiatives of the new US administration do not mark a break from the past, but are a continuation of its earlier policies and risks pushing Afghanistan further into the abyss. While this may reflect the lack of options available with the US administration, it remains to be seen whether it will exploit the available opportunities to shift from the 'minimalist approach' of the past to a comprehensive policy that includes building a stable and legitimate Afghan government capable of providing security, development, governance and basic services to its people. Unfortunately, time is neither on the side of the Afghans nor the US forces, who are looking for an exit strategy. However, before this occurs, a civilian surge must take place in Afghanistan. Local institutions for security and governance must be established, but the local people must have the capacity to protect and sustain them. Mere troop surges without a tangible difference in the lives of Afghans would be tantamount to nothing but foreign occupation for the local Afghans.

The festering problem of 'sanctuary' in Pakistan also needs to be addressed. This calls for a new US approach towards that country. Its degeneration necessitates critical intervention, not merely by transferring large amounts of military assistance without accountability, but by making the leaders of Pakistan work towards recovering the state from chaos. Neither a degenerated Pakistan nor a Pakistan in its current *avatar* is in the interests of the international community in general and for Afghanistan in particular. In ensuring that Afghanistan becomes a permanently neutral country, there is a need for another conference on the lines of Bonn that includes all the regional and great powers, ensuring their commitment to non-interference in Afghanistan.

The war in Afghanistan has reached a 'pivotal moment' or 'tipping point'. A huge array of international actors and their attention is geared towards changing the tide of this war in Afghanistan. The year 2009 will be crucial to assess whether President Obama's promise of a 'change' in the situation is realised. Whether conflict-ravaged Afghanistan continues its downward spiral or moves towards becoming a 'stable country' will be a test case for the new US administration.

3

Sectarian Violence in Pakistan

Raghav Sharma

A BRIEF HISTORY

The seeds of an exclusivist Islamic identity were sown in the early years of Pakistan's birth, with the launching of a sustained campaign in which Shias and Sunnis had closed ranks to declare Ahmadis 'non-Muslims'. However, it was Zia-ul-Haq's ascendance to power in 1977, coupled with developments at the domestic and international level, that ruptured the Shia–Sunni consensus characterising Pakistan's sectarian landscape. Zia's drive to Islamise Pakistan's identity on distinctly Sunni lines led to introduction of the Sunni Hanafi–Deobandi system of jurisprudence, evident from the promulgation of the Hudood ordinances in February 1979, followed by the Zakat ordinance in 1980.[1] Both these measures caused widespread resentment amongst the Shias and acquired political overtones with the Shiite scholar Mufti Jaffar Hussein founding the Tehreek-e-Nifaz-e-Fiq-e-Jafariya (TNJF or 'movement for the implementation of Shiite jurisprudence') on 12–13 April 1979.[2]

On the international stage, the year 1979–80 witnessed the Shi'i Islamic revolution in Iran, followed by the Soviet invasion of Afghanistan, which whipped up resistance in the form of a puritanical jihad supported with US and Saudi money, with Pakistan being its launch pad. The 1980s onwards saw a mushrooming of Deobandi *Deeni Madrasahs* (religious seminaries), which in addition to generous foreign funding also got state support from the *zakat* funds.[3] By 1984,

---

[1] Ashok K. Behuria, 'Shia–Sunni Relations in Pakistan: The Widening Divide', *Strategic Analysis*, 28(1), January–March 2004, p. 159.
[2] *Ibid.*, p. 160.
[3] Mehtab Ali Shah, 'Sectarianism—A Threat to Human Security: A Case Study of Pakistan', *The Round Table, Commonwealth Journal of International Affairs*, 94(382), October 2005, p. 617.

for instance, 9.4 per cent of the *zakat* funds went to support some 2,273 madrasas that catered to 111,050 students,[4] who, along with semi-educated unemployed youth, became the foot soldiers for extremist sectarian outfits. Iran too supported a galaxy of Shia groups and set up Shia madrasas. Pakistan thus emerged as the central turf for playing out the regional and ideological struggle between Riyadh and Tehran.

Zia actively encouraged the growth of Sunni sectarian groups like the Sipah-i-Sabah Pakistan (SSP), founded by Maulana Haqq Nawaz Jhangvi in 1985 in Jhang,[5] to serve as a counterweight to growing Shia political activism, fears of which were greatly accentuated by the Iranian revolution. By 1986 the sectarian fires had spread to the frontier regions, as Zia settled and armed large number of Sunni Afghan refugees in the Parachinar region of the NWFP leading to a violent confrontation with the Shia Turi tribe in the region.[6] Thus the state emerged as the key player in Pakistan's sectarian cauldron.

Sectarian strife reached its zenith following the Soviet withdrawal from Afghanistan in 1989, as men armed to the teeth and taught to kill and die in the name of an exclusively defined Islam, channelled their energies to either waging a jihad in Kashmir or pursuing a rabid sectarian agenda within Pakistan. Thus, by the early 1990s, targeted political assassinations of leaders from rival sects and attacks on religious processions or places of worship became common, which provoked violent cycles of revenge killings. However, sectarian violence after 9/11 shifted from targeting religious processions and leaders to attacking symbols of the Pakistani state, often involving the use of suicide and car bombings.

The insincerity of successive governments of various political complexions in Islamabad to rein in sectarian organisations has allowed them to gain in strength, with sectarian violence reaching yet another peak in 2008. The problem has been further exacerbated by

---

[4] S.V.R. Nasr, 'The Rise of Sunni Militancy in Pakistan: The Changing Role of Islamism and Ulema in Politics', *Modern Asian Studies*, 34, 2000, pp. 142–45.

[5] Jhang is a middle-sized city in the Punjab province that emerged as one of the nerve centres of sectarian conflict in its early stages. The economic setting of the region, characterised by the dominance of the Shia landed aristocracy, provided the ideal setting for pursuing a sectarian agenda. Interestingly, the Taliban skilfully played on the sectarian and the class faultlines in Swat to consolidate their hold. It plans to replicate this tactic elsewhere.

[6] Shah, 'Sectarianism — A Threat to Human Security', p. 618.

many Sunni Deobandi groups forging alliances with jihadi groups like the Tehrik-i-Taliban Pakistan (TTP) who share a similar worldview.

THE PRINCIPAL ACTORS

Apart from the state, whose role as a key actor is fleshed out in this chapter, there are numerous sectarian groups, some of whom have enjoyed tacit support from the state. The section below briefly sketches out the contours of six actors who have played a critical role in fuelling sectarian strife in Pakistan.

Sipah-i-Sabah Pakistan (SSP) and Lashkar-e-Jhangvi (LeJ)

Founded with the blessings of the Zia regime, the SSP's proclaimed objectives are to fight the corrupting cultural influence of Shi'ism at all levels,[7] having Pakistan declared a Sunni Muslim state and the Shias as infidels. The SSP enjoys substantial support not just on its home turf in Punjab but also in the Lower Kurram Valley and the neighbouring Orakzai agency. While the financial support for SSP comes through private donations from Saudi Arabia, Pakistan and *zakat* donations, its social base comprises the emerging class of traders, shopkeepers and transport operators who are demanding a greater political voice, thus challenging the established order.[8] To meet its objectives it has taken recourse to violence, though of late there has been an attempt to embed the movement in the mainstream political discourse. This change of strategy created a schism in the ranks of the SSP and led to the formation of the LeJ in 1996, though some interpret it as a clever tactic by the SSP to dodge a potential ban — in light of mounting sectarian violence — by separating its extremist core and urging it to carry on with its programme of *tafkir* (purging the community of Shias).[9] Essentially, the, SSP and LeJ are two sides of the same coin and have forged linkages with jihadi groups like the Taliban, Al Qaeda,

---

[7] Behuria, 'Shia-Sunni Relations in Pakistan', p. 162.
[8] South Asia Terrorism Portal, http://www.satp.org/satporgtp/countries/pakistan/terroristoutfits/ssp.htm (accessed on 31 March 2009).
[9] Azmat Abbas, 'Sectarianism in Pakistan: The Players and the Game', *South Asia Partnership-Pakistan,* February 2002, pp. 14–17.

Harkat-ul-Ansar, Jaish-e-Muhammad (JeM) and Lashkar-e-Toiba (LeT) that share a similar worldview. Following the closure of training camps like Saroi and Kahled bin Waled in Afghanistan in the aftermath of the US-led intervention in 2001, the LeJ established an elaborate training facility for its cadres in Muridke (near Lahore) where the jihadi group LeT is also headquartered.[10] The LeJ, which is currently led by Muhammad Ajmal, is amongst the most violent sectarian organisations that not only targets Shias in Pakistan but also Iranian interests in Pakistan. Police reports indicate that the LeJ operates under a loose organisational structure comprising sub-units of five to eight members, each which operates independently.[11] Its current active cadre strength is estimated to be about 300. Official patronage to LeJ leaders like Riaz Basra by the political elite, like former Punjab Chief Minister Mian Manzoor Ahmad Watoo, has helped these groups to flourish.[12]

Sipah-i-Mohammed Pakistan and Tehreek-i-Jafariya Pakistan (TJP)

The roots of TJP, formed in 1992 by Allama Arif Husseini, can be traced to the TNJF, discussed earlier. TJP has a considerable social base in Jhang. Its proclaimed objectives centre around the protection of the social, political and religious rights of Shiites and the propagation of Shia ideas.[13] The organisation's youth wing, known as the Imamia Students Organisation (ISO) made the movement a potent force; however, differences over the present TJP Chief Allama Sajid Ali Naqvi's policies estranged the ISO. The TJP's image was severely undermined as Allama Naqvi refused to lend support to Mehram Ali, a Shia political activist, who was hanged after his conviction in the bombing of a Lahore sessions court which killed 19 policemen and three leaders from the rival SSP.[14]

Allama Naqvi's attempts into steer the TJP into becoming a political as opposed to a religious organisation and hence refraining from violence,

---

[10] Abbas, 'Sectarianism in Pakistan', p. 17.
[11] South Asia Terrorism Portal, http://www.satporgtp/countries/pakistan/terroristoutfits/lej.htm (accessed on 1 April 2009).
[12] Abbas, 'Sectarianism in Pakistan', p. 14.
[13] South Asia Terrorism Portal, http://www.satp.orgtp/countries/pakistan/terroristoutfits/tjp.htm (accessed on 1 April 2009).
[14] Abbas, 'Sectarianism in Pakistan', pp. 8–9.

created a schism in the TJP ranks in 1993, leading to the formation of the Sipah-e-Mohammad Pakistan (SMP) under Ghulam Raza Naqvi. The SMP was formed to physically counter Sunni militancy; it has a cadre base of 30,000 followers, drawn largely from Punjab. Apart from being supported by Iran, the SMP attracts funding from Shias living in Kuwait, the United Arab Emirates, besides individual and public donations from within Pakistan. Headquartered at Thokar Niaz Beg, a Shia-dominated Lahore suburb, it initially enjoyed support from the influential people of the area like Major (retd.) Ashraf Hussain Shah, which allowed the SMP to defy the law with impunity. The suburb was out of bounds for the police.[15] However, following factional clashes in 1996, which led to the arrest of some SMP leaders like Riaz Naqvi, its support base has dwindled and its pool of finance has shrunk, thus blunting its lethal edge. Nonetheless, police officials believe that the SMP continues to enjoy support in pockets of Baluchistan and the Northern Areas, apart from Punjab.

Sunni Tehreek (ST)

The birth of organisations like the ST highlights the intra-sectarian faultlines between the Deobandi Sunnis, backed by their Ahl-e-Hadith counterparts, and the Barelvis. The ST was founded in 1992 by Maulana Saleem Qadri, who was assassinated by the SSP in 2001. Commenting on the rise of intra-sectarian strife, eminent journalist Mehreen Zahra Malik opines that

> Barelvis found themselves hemmed in by the state funding of Deobandi groups, the exponential increase in Deobandi seminaries and the tussle in urban centres, especially Karachi, to capture mosques, a good source of revenue for various groups. The fight over mosques and other property brought a Barelvi backlash in the form of the ST, which aimed to protect Barelvi mosques and interests against the Deobandi onslaught.[16]

The Karachi business community, dominated by Gujarati-speaking Memons and Bohras, provides the ST with its financial sinews. On 28 February 2009, the ST plunged into the political fray with its chief Sarwat Ejaz Qadri announcing the formation of ST's political wing, the Pakistani Inqalabi Tehreek.

[15] *Ibid.*, p. 15.
[16] Mehreen Zara Malik, 'In Pakistan Sunni Against Sunni', *The Indian Express*, 24 May 2006.

Lashkar-i-Islami (LI)

This group's violent confrontation with its Barelvi counterpart, Ansarul Islam, has fuelled intra-sectarian strife, claiming several hundred lives since 2006 in the Khyber Agency of FATA where both of them hold competing Sharia courts.[17] In addition, the LI has clashed with the powerful *gaddi nashin*, who are descendants of Sufi saints. The group has also been involved in targeting the syncretic shrine culture, seen for instance in the bombing of the shrine of seventeenth-century Pashto poet Rehman Baba on 9 March 2008.[18] LI, which has links with the TTP, is particularly strong in the town of Bara, and its current chief, Manghal Bagh Afridi, claims to have an active armed strength of 10,000 men.[19]

THE CONFLICT IN 2008

Course of the Conflict

Sectarian violence continued to show a secular increase with the number of sectarian incidents jumping from 80 in 2007, resulting in 521 deaths and 757 people being injured[20] to 191 incidents in 2008 which claimed 1,336 lives and injured 1,662 (see Table 3.1).[21] The opening months of 2009 were not very different with the period January–March being marked by 65 incidents of sectarian violence, which claimed 111 lives and left 215 injured. The overall violence

Table 3.1: Year 2008

Attacks/clashes	Incidents	Killed	Injured
Inter-tribe sectarian clashes	191	1,336	1,662

Source: *Pakistan Security Report 2008*, p. 4.

---

[17] International Crisis Group, 'Pakistan: The Militant Jihadi Challenge', Asia Report No. 164, 13 March 2009, p. 13.
[18] Tom Hussain, 'Pakistani Taliban Target Sufi Shrines', *The National*, 9 March 2009.
[19] www.globalsecurity.org/Pak/lei.htm (accessed on 1 April 2009).
[20] Pakistan Institute of Peace Studies (PIPS), *Pakistan Security Report 2007* (Islamabad: PIPS, 2008), p. 24.
[21] PIPS, *Pakistan Security Report 2008* (Islamabad: PIPS, 2009), p. 4.

levels in Pakistan have shows a huge jump of 746 per cent since 2005.[22] This spiralling violence index has to be contextualised against the backdrop of steady collapse of state authority in Pakistan, and the consequential expansion of ungovernable spaces that provide an ideal environment for the sectarian jihadi groups to operate in.

The restoration of civilian authority, and the strategy to defeat extremism announced in September 2008, has failed to curtail the spread of violence. This is not surprising. Under President Musharraf no serious attempt was made to target sources of homegrown extremism, evident from Musharraf's retreat on curriculum reform and the madrasas registration law, apart from his reliance on religious groupings like the Majlis-e-Amal (MMA) in order to strengthen his rule in return for pursuing an Islamist agenda in the NWFP.[23] Thus, the fragile civilian government inherited a grave situation as it faced a robust network of extremist groups challenging the government's writ. Although on 20 September 2008 President Asif Ali Zardari announced a three-pronged strategy in Parliament to tackle extremism, his government could do little on the ground given its internal weaknesses and preoccupation with intense political squabbling, coupled with the precipitate degeneration of the state machinery available at its disposal. Ahmed Rashid notes that democratic governments have a poor record in reining in radical extremist groups for 'democracy has failed to take root largely because the army has never allowed it to take root, but also because politicians have never practiced democratic norms of behaviour and tried to build institutions, rather than personal power bases'.[24]

As in 2007, a large majority of the sectarian clashes in 2008 took place in the NWFP and other tribal pockets bordering Afghanistan. However, what is more worrying is the deepening nexus between Sunni Deobandi and transnational jihadi outfits which is blurring the gap between internal and external jihad. This dangerous intertwining of the two was underscored on three occasions when Pakistan's major cities were rocked by unprecedented terror strikes. First, Interior Minister Rehman Malik in a statement before the National Assembly

---

[22] South Asia Terrorism Portal, http://www.satp.org/Pak/sectkilling.htm%20figures.htm (accessed on 1 April 2009).

[23] International Crisis Group, 'Pakistan: The Militant Jihadi Challenge', p. 4.

[24] Ahmed Rashid, 'Militancy Will Not Run Out of Steam', *BBC*, 4 August 2008, http://news.bbc.co.uk/2/hi/south_asia/7530272.stm (accessed on 1 April 2009).

on 22 December 2008 said that the LeJ was behind the 20 September 2008 bombing of the Marriot Hotel in Islamabad, which killed 60 persons, including the Czech ambassador, two Indian diplomats, two US marines and several other foreign guests. Second, on 22 March 2009, security agencies named Matiur Rehman of the LeJ as having planned the daring attack on the Sri Lankan cricket team in Lahore on 3 March. Finally, Benazir Bhutto in an interview following a deadly attack on her during welcome procession in Karachi on 18 October 2007, named 'Abdul Rehman Sindhi, an Al Qaeda-linked Lashkar-e Jhangvi (LeJ) militant from the Dadu District of Sindh' as being the mastermind behind the attack.[25]

2008 opened on a bloody note with the Shiite holy month of Ramadan being marked by a suicide attack by the LeJ on the Imambargah in Peshawar on 17 January 2008 that killed 12 persons. Sectarian violence throughout the month of March in NWFP claimed 40 lives. On 21 June 2008 an intra-sectarian clash between Lashkar-i-Islami (LI) and Ansarul Islam (AI) in the Tera area of the Khyber agency led to 31 deaths and 50 people being injured. On 23 June 2008, 17 security officials escorting a food convoy to the town of Parachinar were abducted by pro-Taliban militants in the Sunni-dominated area of Pir Qayyum. They beheaded eight securitymen from the Shia Turi tribe, sparking tensions in the Kurram agency which has seen intense sectarian fighting since the resumption of violence in August 2008. The abduction and beheading of Shia truck drivers by the Taliban militia at Shasho Village — where the Taliban are believed to be running a training camp — is on the rise. Similarly, in South Waziristan of the 19 paramilitary troops captured by the Taliban, they beheaded only one soldier, a Shia, reflecting the strong sectarian sentiments prevailing in the Taliban ranks.[26]

On 19 August 2008 a suicide bomber targeting Shias killed 30 and injured 40 at a hospital in Dera Ismail Khan. The TTP claimed responsibility for the attack,[27] which again underscores the powerful linkages between the Taliban and Sunni Deobandi groups. Horror revisited the area in November when a bomb ripped through a Shia funeral procession leaving 10 dead and 40 wounded. Ramadan eve saw a surge in this kind of sectarian violence. On 30 August tensions

[25] Kanchan Lakshman, 'Sectarian Implosion', *South Asia Intelligence Review, Weekly Assessments and Briefings*, 7(38), 30 March 2009.
[26] Rahimullah Yusufzai, 'Much Ado About Nothing', *Newsline*, September 2007.
[27] '30 Killed in DI Khan Suicide Attack', *Daily Times*, 20 August 2008.

flared up and in the ensuing clashes between the Shia Turi and Sunni Bangash tribes in the Kurram agency (which shares a border with Afghanistan on three sides and is of immense strategic significance for the Taliban) more than 95 people lost their lives and over 200 were injured.[28] The intensity and scale of sectarian violence is noteworthy for it indicates the meticulous planning and organisation involved, indicating a sense of purpose and strategy behind the violence, making it difficult to classify sectarian clashes in Pakistan as instances of simple rioting. Moreover, the violence in Kurram emphasises the state's role as an actor in the sectarian quagmire. Parachinar houses an army garrison, and Shia tribal council leaders like Hajji Gulab Hussain have levelled serious allegations, stating that 'the lower ranking soldiers are ready for action...but the army is supporting the Taliban...the army did nothing'.[29]

The month of Muharram witnessed sectarian skirmishes spreading to settled parts of NWFP like Hangu, Kohat, Bannu and even the provincial capital of Peshawar. What is noteworthy is that over the course of these clashes the Shia Turi tribes from Kurram openly supported their counterparts in other provinces, thus reflecting the increasing polarisation and showing that sectarianism in Pakistan cannot be ignored by the state as a local or inter-tribal issue.

On 6 October 2008, in a daring attack, a LeJ suicide bomber attacked the Shia Pakistan Muslim League (Nawaz) parliamentarian Rashid Anwar Niwani's residence in Bhakkar district of Punjab, close to NWFP, killing 25 and injuring 60, including Niwani.[30] On 5 December 2008, a car bomb went off in a Shia mosque in Peshawar targeting the local Shia community hailing from Parachinar that resulted in over 34 fatalities while injuring more than 120. In the neighbouring Orakzai agency sectarian skirmishes were centred primarily on the control of Mir Anwar Shah's shrine at Kalaya. Efforts to settle the shrines ownership dispute with the Sunnis in Kalaya by convening a jirga in December were sought to be thwarted as a car bomb attack on the jirga venue killed six people.[31] Thus, the sectarian groups clearly have a vested interest in ensuring that the conflict continues.

---

[28] www.globalsecurity.org/G:/Pak/AUG%202008.htm (accessed on 4 April 2009).
[29] Abdul Majeed, 'Power Rising, Taliban Besiege Pakistani Shiite's', *New York Times*, 26 July 2008.
[30] International Crisis Group, 'Pakistan: The Militant Jihadi Challenge', p. 6.
[31] Mariam Abou Zahab, 'Sectarianism in Pakistan's Kurram Tribal Agency', *Terrorism Monitor*, 7(6), March 2009, http://www.jamestown.org/programs/gta/single/?tx_ttnews[tt_news]=34730&tx_ttnews[backPid]=26&cHash=ac2e288618 (accessed on 4 April 2009).

The year 2009 began on an equally grotesque note, with January — the Shia month of Ramadan — alone accounting for more than 50 per cent of the casualties that have taken place in the first quarter of 2009. On 10 January sectarian clashes erupted in Hangu as local Shias protested against the imposition of curfew during the Shia festival of *Ashura*, resulting in the death of 30 persons and injuring 50. Significantly, three prominent local commanders, Maulvi Nadeem, Momin and Ihsanullah, were among the six militants killed in sectarian clashes in Saidan Banda and Pass Kellay area of Hangu.[32] On 14 January, the LeJ in targeted killings assassinated four policemen in a shootout in Quetta; significantly, three of the four slain policemen belonged to the Hazara Shia community. Close on its heels, on 26 January 2009, the Shia leader Hussain Ali Yousufi of the Hazara Democratic Party was assassinated in Quetta by LeJ militants; his killing provoked widespread unrest in Quetta.[33] Both incidents once again brought to the fore the vulnerability of Hazara Shias, who have been marginalised and targeted in the past by the Taliban, who carried out a systematic massacre of the community with the active participation of LeJ cadres. Hence it is not surprising to find the community turning to outside players like Iran for more than just spiritual guidance. On 5 February a suicide bomber blew himself up outside a Shia mosque in Dera Ghazi Khan killing 32 and injuring 48, and on 20 February a Shia funeral procession in Dera Ismail Khan was bombed, killing 32 and injuring 145 people.[34]

Table 3.2: Year 2009

Month	Incidents	Killed	Injured
January	54	53	64
February	7	43	147
March	6	15	4
April	3	27	146
Total	70	138	361

Source: South Asia Terrorism Portal, http://satp.org/satporgtp/countries/pakistan/database/sect-killing.htm (accessed on 4 April 2009).

---

[32] South Asia Terrorism Portal, www.satp.org/Pak/lej.htm (accessed on 4 April 2009).
[33] South Asia Terrorism Portal, www.satp.org/Pak/Pakistan%20Timeline%202009.htm (accessed on 4 April 2009).
[34] Kanchan Lakshman, 'Sectarian Implosion'.

In what appeared to be a cycle of revenge killings, Shia extremists struck by using a remote-controlled bomb, targeting the SSP leader Khalifa Abdul Qayyum, who escaped unhurt. However, the attack left six persons dead and injured 26, followed closely in February by a grenade attack on a Sunni mosque that killed one and injured 18. The same month witnessed the bombing of another Shia funeral procession that claimed more than 30 lives.[35]

In the first major sectarian strike in Punjab in 2009, a suicide bomber targeted the main Imambargah in Chakwal where over 1,200 Shia Muslims had gathered for the religious ceremony of a *majlis*. The attack led to 26 fatalities and injuries to over 40.[36] Incidentally, Chakwal, which is rife with sectarian divisions, constitutes an important recruiting centre for the army in Punjab.

Major Trends

What stands out in this string of attacks is that banned Sunni outfits like the LeJ and SSP have been extremely active and are striking at regular intervals, reflecting their better finances and organisational structures that have improved because of linkages with the Taliban and Al Qaeda. In contrast, their Shia counterparts, namely the TJP and SMP, although have not been disbanded yet, no longer exhibit the same degree of lethality. Sectarian violence is no longer confined to its original nerve centre in Punjab or to its traditional urban turfs like Karachi, but has spread to the countryside. It has acquired particularly alarming proportions in the frontier regions of Pakistan from where it is spreading towards settled areas that had previously not experienced any significant sectarian friction. Moreover, the magnitude and intensity of violence suggests that it is increasingly becoming organised and lethal with the use of rocket launchers, mortars and grenades, which are easily available in Pakistan's flourishing arms bazaars. The Pakistan Ministry of Interior estimates that the number of illegal weapons in the country at an astounding 18 million, which is in addition to the 2 million legally acquired.[37]

---

[35] International Crisis Group, 'Pakistan: The Militant Jihadi Challenge', pp. 16–17.

[36] 'Bloodbath in Chakwal Leaves 26 Dead, 40 Injured', *Dawn*, 6 April 2009.

[37] International Crisis Group,'The State of Sectarianism in Pakistan', Asia Report No. 95, April 2005, p. 27.

Further, an increasingly large proportion of attacks seem to be relying on the use of car and suicide bombers to carry out their mission, with 2008 witnessing 59 incidents of suicide bombings. These tactics stand out as they were not used in Pakistan and Afghanistan prior to 9/11. Commenting on the use of this grotesque new technique an analyst in the Special Investigation Group opined that 'from the 26 suicide attacks where we recovered a head, we made a startling discovery… The vast majority [of suicide bombers] came from just one tribe, the Mehsuds of central Waziristan, all boys aged 16 to 20…Qari Hussain, also known as Ustad-e-Fidaeen (teacher of suicide cadres), a Mehsud tribesman in his early 30s, is identified as the "commander" who manages Baitullah Mehsud-led Taliban suicide bombing training centres and is directly responsible for indoctrinating the youth for suicide missions.'[38]

Intra-sectarian cleavages also appear to be sharpening and skirmishes are no longer limited to a tussle for control over mosques, but aim also to challenge the powerful syncretic shrine culture shared by the Shias, Sufis and Barelvi Sunnis. This has brought Sunni Deobandi groups into conflict with the *gaddi nashin*, who had hitherto not been involved in the conflict.

Factors Sustaining the Conflict

A number of factors have worked towards sustaining the sectarian conflict while giving it a new dimension. To begin with, the merging of the Taliban with Sunni sectarian groups has greatly accentuated the problem. The Taliban, with the help of Sunni Deobandi groups who share the same objectives, provide the Taliban with access to a vast network of madrasas across Pakistan. This is facilitating the Taliban's endeavour to entrench themselves in Pakistan's ungovernable frontier regions and enabling them to spread further north and challenge the government's writ with impunity. Extremist outfits are also attempting to drum up local support for their cause by playing up existing sectarian cleavages and throwing their weight behind the local Sunni population against the Shias. For the Sunni Deobandi groups linkages with better financed transnational jihadi groups have not only lent a more lethal edge to the latter but have also made it difficult to segregate the home-grown from foreign terrorists.

---

[38] South Asia Terrorism Portal, http://www.satp.org/satporgtp/countries/pakistan/index.htm (accessed on 5 April 2009).

The lack of political will to rein in sectarian tendencies has allowed these groups to gain in strength and to multiply. The state's ineptness, seen, for instance, in its retreat on key issues such as the madrasas bill in 2001 — which would have made their registration mandatory — and the proposed change in curriculum, apart from the ability of proscribed groups like the SSP to hold public rallies in cities like Karachi, like the one that took place on 1 March 2008, and openly give a call for jihad against the West, have boosted the confidence of the religious right. Commenting on the ability of officially proscribed groups to operate with impunity, Fredric Grare states that 'the objective of the ISI was to maintain violence at an acceptable level, not to eliminate groups.... the SSP was allowed to hold rallies under a new name after a series of negotiations with the ISI'.[39]

This problem becomes even more difficult to address due to the infiltration of the law and order machinery by sectarian elements, seen, for instance, in the conviction of police personnel who were subsequently discovered to be affiliated with the SSP in two sectarian attacks in March and May 2004.[40] The police's capacity to investigate and act in cases of sectarian violence is impaired due to corruption, political interference and the lack of proper equipment and training. Moreover, all the civilian wings of the law and order machinery, like the police and Intelligence Bureau, are at the mercy of the notorious ISI and its strategic interests[41] for access to information, thus further curtailing their ability to stem the rising tide of sectarian violence.[42] Further, the abysmal rate of conviction for sectarian crimes, the ability of elements associated with sectarian organisations to threaten with impunity judges hearing cases of sectarian violence have all contributed to bolstering the determination of radical extremist forces.

Apart from a general breakdown of the state machinery and the spread of Taliban to the ungovernable tracts of Pakistan, a number of

---

[39] Fredric Grare, 'Reforming the Intelligence Agencies in Pakistan's Transitional Democracy', Carnegie Endowment for International Peace, 2009, p. 28, www.carnegieendowment.org/files/pakistan_intelligence_transitional_democracy.pdf (accessed on 6 April 2009).

[40] International Crisis Group, 'Pakistan: The Militant Jihadi Challenge', p. 17.

[41] ISI's strategic interests in Kashmir and Afghanistan allowed for the mushrooming of elaborate training camps along the Afghanistan–Pakistan border, Punjab as well as Pakistan Occupied Kashmir (POK). They have provided militant groups an opportunity to acquire training in combat, and the use of sophisticated weaponry.

[42] International Crisis Group, 'Pakistan: The Militant Jihadi Challenge', p. 19.

other factors too have played a role in sustaining the cycle of sectarian violence. Most sectarian extremist groups, apart from being lavishly financed by foreign funds and private donations in Pakistan, also run 'protection and extortion rackets from both Shia and Sunni banks and businesses'.[43] These groups have emerged as a breeding ground for drug traffickers, smugglers and criminals. A recent report of the International Crisis Group commenting on this linkage, states:

> Karachi has witnessed a marked increase in crime since 2008, as radical Sunni groups increasingly turn their attention to raising funds and acquiring weapons for FATA-based Pakistani Taliban through robberies, kidnappings for ransom and snatching weapons from police, guards and even paramilitary Rangers Force. Money stolen in two major robberies was eventually traced to FATA's Waziristan agencies.[44]

The rapid expansion of print and electronic media in Pakistan, which has helped in reaching a wider audience and rapidly disseminating ideas, facilitates the stoking of these sectarian fires. The problem is particularly acute in FATA and NWFP as federal laws do not apply here and therefore the state does not have the legal power to curb what it considers illegal. The media boom, coupled with better transport services that allow for the increased mobility of sectarian activists, has helped sustain and enlarge the social base of sectarian conflict.[45]

Ahmed Rashid asserts that militancy of the type found in this region flourishes in the vacuum created by the lack of social, economic and political development. Growing poverty and lack of access to education and avenues of employment have played a major role in pushing people into the arms of extremists. Two successive surveys in 2002 and 2003 by the Islamabad Institute of Policy Studies underscore this proposition as they reveal that a majority of the madrasa students, who serve as foot soldiers for sectarian and jihadi groups, come from poor agrarian families in the countryside, with only 5.71 per cent of

---

[43] http://www.ag.gov.au/agd/WWW/nationalsecurity.nsf/Page/What_Governments_are_doing_Listing_of_Terrorism_Organisations_Lashkar_I_Jhangvi (accessed on 5 April 2009).
[44] International Crisis Group, 'Pakistan: The Militant Jihadi Challenge', p. 10.
[45] Moonis Ahmar, 'Sectarian Conflicts in Pakistan', *Pakistan Vision*, 9(1), July 2008, p. 7.

the students joining madrasas for religious reasons.[46] Moreover, these religious seminaries provide food and shelter to a large number of students free of charge, making it very hard for families with meagre resources to resist sending their children to them (see Table 3.3).[47] This link between poverty and the rising levels of extremist violence in Pakistan was officially acknowledged by Interior Minister Rehman Malik, who while commenting on the Chakwal suicide bombing of 5 April 2009, stated that 'the price of a suicide bomber ranges from Rs 5 lakh to Rs 15 lakh'.[48]

Table 3.3: Reasons Given by Students for Joining a Madrasa

Reason	Percentage
Economic	48.95
Social	40.63
Religious	5.71
Educational	3.12
Political	2.09

Source: Tariq Rehman, 'Madrassas: Religion, Poverty and the Potential for Political Violence in Pakistan'.

The breakdown of the traditional tribal system has also encouraged the rapid spread of sectarian violence — actively supported by the Taliban — to the frontier regions. A number of young people are attracted to the Taliban not out of sympathy for their cause, but out of frustration with the tribal system which cannot 'harness their potential to meet modern day needs and rampant illiteracy, chronic poverty and unemployment. Thus, pragmatism draws young people to the Taliban. They are building a new form of social capital, a network that offers the opportunities and prestige that the tribal system once did.'[49] With the collapse of traditional social structures and the state abdicating its responsibilities the possibility of credible alternatives emerging to fill this vacuum appears bleak. These problems are

---

[46] Tariq Rehman, 'Madrassas: Religion, Poverty and the Potential for Political Violence in Pakistan', *Islamabad Policy Research Institute (IPRI) Journal*, 5(1), Winter 2005, http://ipripak.org/journal/winter2005/madrassas.html (accessed on 9 April 2009).

[47] Abbas, 'Sectarianism in Pakistan', p. 28.

[48] 'Hire a Suicide Bomber for Just Rs 5 lakh', *The Times of India*, 7 April 2009.

[49] David Montero, 'Why the Taliban Appeal to Pakistani Youth', *Christian Science Monitor*, 16 June 2006.

likely to grow if concrete steps are not taken to arrest the slide of the Pakistani economy to bankruptcy and to integrate its tribal areas with mainstream Pakistani society.

However, though poverty and lack of access to education are important contributors to the swelling ranks of foot soldiers for extremist causes, it would be naïve to assume that this logic holds in all situations. The profile of many Lashkar recruits — like medical students in Australia and MBA graduates in Pakistan — strongly reinforces Oliver Roy's claim regarding the changing social profile of the 'holy warriors'.[50] The rapid Islamisation of school education in Pakistan has also contributed immensely to changing the social contours of Islamic extremist organisations through the crystallisation of identities, often conceived in opposition the 'other'.

CONFLICT MANAGEMENT

As Pakistan finds itself increasingly being pushed to the brink by rising levels of extremism and militancy, President Zardari in his speech to the Parliament on 20 September 2008 outlined his government's three-pronged strategy to deal with the rising tide of extremism. He envisaged making peace with those willing to renounce violence, dealing firmly with those who challenge the government's writ and promoting economic development in the tribal regions. He also spoke about setting up a Counter Terrorism Authority, with help from the 'Friends of Pakistan', and to raise 20,000 additional police forces for each province, who would receive special pay and equipment.[51] Zardari's policy pronouncement was greeted a few hours later by the deadly truck bombing of the Marriot Hotel in Islamabad. Intelligence reports stated that the attack was executed by LeJ militants in collaboration with jihadi groups.

Hopes for the successful execution of the government strategy have been bleak from the very outset given the multiplicity of authorities — each pursuing its own agenda — a lack of political will and the weak state of the civilian law enforcement agencies. This explains the government's lack of progress on following through its pledge of establishing a Madrasa Regulation Authority that would

---

[50] Raghav Sharma, 'Pakistan as a Nation State and Flag Bearer of Islam', VDM Verlag Publications, Saarbrücken, Germany, January 2009, p. 51.

[51] http://www.app.com.pk/en_/index.php?option=com_content&task=view&id=72005&Itemid=2 (accessed on 11 April 2009).

oversee the functioning of religious seminaries.[52] In fact, the government has failed even to use existing legal tools such as the Anti-terrorism Act promulgated in 1997 and amended twice in 2004, to bring the perpetrators of sectarian violence to book. The January 2004 amendment brought under its purview financing and supporting structures of banned organisations.[53] In October, another amendment specifically enhanced punishment for attacks on places of worship through the 'use of firearms and explosives by any device including bomb blasts in a mosque, imambargah...whether or not any hurt or damage is caused thereby'.[54]

Throughout 2008 the government continued with its piecemeal approach in dealing with the rising violence and anarchy resulting from a toxic mix of internal sectarian jihad and external jihad. The government's response has oscillated between striking with arms and striking tenuous peace deals with extremist groups that have collapsed at the slightest provocation. Moreover, deals with the Taliban, negotiated by Islamabad from a weak position, even if successful, will not be able to rein in other sectarian organisations. In all likelihood they will either detach themselves from their current marriage of convenience with the Taliban or, as Islamabad cedes more authority to the Taliban, these sectarian groups will be able to operate with greater ease.

Inspite of rising levels of sectarian strife in 2008 there has been no consequential crackdown against sectarian extremist groups. In fact, the government has been in a state of denial as a response to demands for government intervention raised, for instance, at a parliament sit-in demonstration in Islamabad by people from the Kurram in June 2008. Demands to prevent a sectarian flare-up in the region were met with the government denying the existence of any sectarian problem. It chose instead to blame the ubiquitous foreign hand for pitting tribes against each other.[55]

As a result Shias, who have largely been at the receiving end in the recent spate of violence, are losing faith in the state's ability and sincerity to protect them. Past ceasefire agreements between the

---

[52] International Crisis Group, 'Pakistan: The Militant Jihadi Challenge', p. 18.
[53] International Crisis Group, 'The State of Sectarianism in Pakistan', p. 26.
[54] Act No. II, *An Act to Further Amend the Anti-terrorism Act, 1997*
[55] Inamullah Khattak, 'Kurram Tribes Ready to Bury the Hatchet', *Dawn*, 26 September 2008.

Shia Turi and Sunni Bangash tribes have collapsed. After the recent sectarian clashes on 30 August 2008, Shias justifiably complain that 'making peace is not in the hands of the Sunni tribes anymore. They have come under the thumb of the Taliban...they have to pledge that they will not allow the Taliban into their villages, that they will not give any more opportunities for the Taliban to make their own strongholds here, or to launch attacks on the Turi. Only then there can be peace.'[56] The ability of the region's ancient tribal system, which was the most effective forum to resolve conflicts and even unite tribes of different sects in the face of a common enemy, has been therefore compromised.

After much delay and bloodshed a peace jirga was finally convened in Islamabad under the supervision of the Political Agent of Kurram. An agreement was reached, under which the roads under siege by the rival groups were reopened, power was restored and dozens of people abducted by rival clans were released in December 2008 after prolonged negotiations that had been initiated on 25 September 2008.[57] Although a tenuous ceasefire holds in Kurram as of now, past experiences have not been particularly encouraging, as ceasefires have broken down on the slightest provocation. Moreover, mutual suspicions continue to simmer below the surface, the leadership on both sides remains rigid, and strong vested interests prevent the graduation of a ceasefire to a peace process.

The extremist elements amongst the clerical elite who have larger political ambitions, criminal elements who find refuge in sectarian organisations, the galaxy of extremist groups that have loosely rallied under the umbrella of the Taliban, the ISI and the powerful guns lobby are some of the the most significant actors who have a stake in ensuring that the embers of sectarian strife continue to glow.

CONCLUSIONS

Levels of sectarian violence have shown a steady increase in 2008, particularly in the frontier areas bordering Afghanistan, but even more worrying has been the growing enmeshing of Sunni Deobandi

---

[56] Nirupama Subramanian, 'In Pakistan a Shia–Sunni War to Oust the Taliban', *The Hindu*, 3 September 2008.

[57] Mariam Abou Zahab, 'Sectarianism in Pakistan's Kurram Tribal Agency'.

sectarian and jihadi groups. Although officially proscribed in 2002, Sunni Deobandi extremist groups like the LeJ have struck regularly and their agenda has broadened to include striking at targets associated with the West and symbols of the Pakistani state. The state's inept response reflects both its unwillingness and incapacity to deal with the threat posed by the militant jihadi challenge, which has become sharper as traditional mechanisms of conflict management like the jirga have proved incapable of dealing with the conflict.

In continuance of the trend in 2007 and 2008, besides the opening months of 2009, it was the frontier regions, which bore the brunt of sectarian violence; over the last two years they have replaced Punjab as the primary site of sectarian strife. Violence has been most intense in the Kurram agency where sectarian clashes have claimed 400 lives and injured and displaced thousands of people since the renewed outbreak of hostilities in the region in August 2008. The failing government writ in FATA and NWFP, coupled with the expansion of the Taliban in these regions, has transformed the areas into a sanctuary for Sunni Deobandi groups, who are fanning the sectarian fires that have spread to the neighbouring Orakzai and Khyber agency and settled parts of NWFP like Hangu, Bannu, Kohat and Peshawar. There has also been a rise in car and suicide bombings for executing sectarian attacks in 2008, reflecting that these methods are increasingly gaining favour as an operational tactic.

As the Pakistani state retreats — most powerfully symbolised by the recent peace deal in Swat that leaves the Taliban in defacto control of the region — its ideological fallout does not augur well for the country's sectarian landscape. With the Taliban determined to consolidate its hold in the frontier agencies so as to secure the base and supply routes for their fight against the US in Afghanistan and make a decisive push into Pakistan, it is likely to play up the existing inter- and intra-sectarian cleavages to the hilt, and further exacerbate the conflict both in terms of its intensity and geographical scale. If the conflict does escalate further and Pakistan continues to display its inability to manage the conflict, it is likely that groups like the SMP, that are currently lying low, will be rekindled.[58] The conflict will also draw in outside players, notably Iran, in favour of the Shias. The virtual besieging of the Shias in Parachinar in 2008 attracted the

---

[58] Already there are visible signs to the effect. For a detailed report see 'Banned Outfits Re-emerging in Karachi', *Daily Times*, 13 July 2008.

attention of the Grand Ayatollah Ali al-Sistani, who has called upon Shias in Pakistan to do all they can to help their brethen.

Violence inspired by a radical religious ideology is likely to continue plaguing Pakistan in the foreseeable future. If the US and its allies were to withdraw from the region the sectarian jihadi combine will channelise its energies to challenge the Pakistani state more vigorously. For Pakistan to effectively reverse this trend it will have to address issues pertaining to the reform of its law and order machinery, to allow it to decisively crack down on extremist groups and their infrastructure. But, more significantly, Pakistan needs to seriously address questions pertaining to the very character of the Pakistani nation state, which would entail among other things reversing the Islamisation policies that have been pursued in the field of education and public life.

4

FATA and NWFP: Spreading Anarchy

D. Suba Chandran

In 2008, armed conflict in Pakistan's Federally Administered Tribal Area (FATA) continued and became more violent, expanding into some settled districts of the North West Frontier Province (NWFP) as well as some other parts of Pakistan. The most important development in 2008 was the expansion of armed conflict into Swat, a settled district and valley, nestled along with Dir, Malakand and Chitral in the north. Though the military only started fighting the Taliban in Swat in 2009, the damage had already been done by the incoherent policies pursued by the state and its military vis-à-vis the Taliban, both in the NWFP and the FATA.

A BRIEF HISTORY

The NWFP, situated between the Indus and the FATA in east and west respectively, consists of 24 districts. These districts are 'settled', and are governed by the rules and regulations of Pakistan in line with its Constitution, like the three other provinces — Punjab, Sind and Balochistan. The people in these settled districts elect their own government; after the 2008 elections the Awami National Party formed the government, along with the Pakistan People's Party (PPP). The FATA is a small region, comprising seven tribal agencies — Bajaur, Mohmand, Khyber, Khurram, Orakzai, North Waziristan, and South Waziristan. Except for Orakzai Agency, all the others share borders with Afghanistan in the west and the NWFP in the east.

The differences between the NWFP and the FATA relate to their administration and the state's writ. While the NWFP elects its own government, the FATA is directly administered by Islamabad. Historically, the writ of the state in FATA was never complete. As part of their larger strategy vis-à-vis Afghanistan and Russia, what came to be known as the Great Game, the British created the NWFP in 1901, along with five tribal agencies, which were subsequently increased to seven. After repeatedly failing to establish their writ over these tribal areas, the British formulated an administrative system, premised on the Frontier Crimes Regulation (1901), which vested all administrative, executive and judicial powers in government officials. Though the Durand Line (1893) distributed the numerous Pashtun tribes between Afghanistan and British India, it was never respected by the local population then and nor is it now, which is a major historical factor linked to the armed conflicts that one is witness to today. These agencies witnessed several armed conflicts between the local tribal population and the British Army in the late nineteenth and early twentieth centuries.

Of the 24 settled districts, there has been intense violence in Peshawar, Hangu, Bannu, Malakand and DI Khan — all districts bordering the FATA — and a full-scale armed conflict in Swat, which later spread to Buner and Dir. Of the seven agencies in FATA, today there is a sustained armed conflict in at least four — North and South Waziristan, Mohmand and Bajaur, while a sectarian armed conflict continues in Kurram.

In FATA, the armed conflict started in South Waziristan in 2002–03, and spread to North Waziristan in 2003–04. By 2005, both these Agencies were under complete control of the Taliban. Wazirs and Mehsuds, the two main tribes in these Agencies, were deeply embroiled in the armed conflict. During this phase, there was also a parallel conflict between the militants and their local supporters against the secular local tribal leadership, which was seen by the Taliban as being pro-government and anti-Taliban. The government, during this phase led by General Musharraf, adopted the dubious policy of appeasing the Taliban whenever they confronted the state, and only took limited action when under pressure from the US. During this phase, numerous pro-government elders were murdered, their relatives kidnapped and the secular jirgas attacked by suicide bombers. As a result, the Taliban succeeded in establishing their writ, now popularly recognised as the Talibanisation of the FATA.

In 2006, the armed conflict expanded to Bajaur Agency and later to Mohmand Agency. In 2007–08, as a result of increasing Taliban influence in the FATA, the sectarian conflict, lying dormant in the Kurram Agency, became violent. Also, during this period, the militants started expanding their presence in the settled districts so as to establish their writ more fully, as they have done in the FATA. Swat, for historical and governance-related reasons, became the first to fall victim to this expansion.

Swat has witnessed the maximum violence in recent years, and in 2008 was under the control of Maulana Fazlullah. The state succumbed to his threats, and passed the Nizam-e-Adl regulations in early 2009, popularly referred to as the imposition of Shariah in the Malakand region. Fortunately, the state realised its folly. Following intense pressure from civil society and the international community, especially the US, the state has deployed its military to fight the Taliban in Swat, and clear them out of the region. As of May 2009, the armed forces are engaged in fighting in Swat, Dir and Buner districts, which have witnessed violence, the retreat of the Taliban and a mass exodus leading to serious internal displacement of population. These issues are discussed in this chapter.

THE PRINCIPAL ACTORS

The State: Government of Pakistan

The Government of Pakistan is a principal actor in the armed conflict in the FATA and the NWFP. The strategies employed in these two tribal regions are distinctly different since the objectives are different. The main objective of the federal government in the FATA is to not alienate the local tribal Pashtun population, for that would have larger implications for Pakistan–Afghanistan relations and Pashtun nationalism. Any all-out military action, the federal government fears, would alienate the local population from Pakistan, leading to the emergence of anti-Pakistani and pro-Pashtun sentiments.

This could be a major reason for Pakistan's dilemma in waging an all-out war against local militants, Al Qaeda and Taliban in this region. While Pakistan is willing to target the Al Qaeda and foreign militants like the Uzbeks in the FATA, the federal government is extremely reluctant to pursue a confrontationist policy with the Taliban and its local supporters in this region. It is for this reason that the federal government has attempted to reach understandings with the tribal population in North and South Waziristan, Mohmand and Bajaur Agencies.

The provincial government in the NWFP led by the Awami National Party is keen to reach a political understanding and sign peace agreements with the Taliban groups. After coming to power in 2008, a major initiative was launched during April–June, which witnessed ceasefires and secret negotiations. The NWFP government released some of the arrested leaders and pressurised the federal government to go slow on the military approach. The secret negotiations produced mixed results: it completely failed with Baitullah Mehsud, while it seems to be working with Maulana Fazlullah. There was moderate success in North Waziristan, but complete failure in South Waziristan. Other negotiations were intermittent, for example, in the Mohmand, Bajaur and Kurram Agencies.

The Militants: Taliban/Al Qaeda/ Tehreek-i-Taliban Pakistan (TTP)

The militants who are fighting the state in the FATA and NWFP region are not part of a monolithic formation. Five separate groups can be identified, which include the Taliban, who are primarily Afghan Pashtuns; Al Qaeda, whose cadres are from all over the Middle East, including Chechens and Arabs; other foreign militants who are not a part of the Al Qaeda, but still fight along with the Taliban, like the Uzbeks; the local Taliban, primarily comprising the Pahstuns from the FATA and NWFP, fighting under the banner of the TTP; and sectarian militants, from this region and from Pakistan, primarily belonging to the Punjab.

The TTP in particular is also not monolithic; it should be viewed rather as a franchisee organisation.[1] Though Baituallah Mehsud is considered to be the leader of the TTP, there is no strict hierarchy in the TTP. Even the Wazirs, who inhabit South Wazirstan with the Mehsuds, do not concur completely with Baitullah. For example, Hafiz Gul Bahadur in North Waziristan and Maulvi Nazir in South Waziristan, though part of the TTP, say that they do not agree with Baitullah. Though these three have recently formed a coalition, in 2009, differences do exist between them.[2] Invariably, every Agency has its own local militant group, which owes allegiance to the TTP and is using its banner although they fight their own battles on their own terms. For example, Maulana Fazlullah has been a part of the Tehreek-e-Nafaz-e-Shariat-e-Mohammadi (TNSM), which was founded much before the TTP, and even before the Taliban were established in Afghanistan; but now considers himself a part of the TTP.

---

[1] See Hassan Abbas, 'A Profile of Tehrik-i-Taliban Pakistan', *CTC Sentinel*, 1(2), January 2008, pp. 1–4.
[2] 'Three Taliban Factions form Shura Ittehad-ul-Mujahiden', *News*, 23 February 2009.

The main objectives of these militant groups are to continue their operations in Afghanistan against the US-led forces, overthrow the Karzai government and re-establish Taliban control over Afghanistan, establish a pro-Taliban administration and/or society in the FATA and to confront the Pakistani state — politically and/or militarily — if it comes in the way of these three objectives. However, in 2008, the primary objectives of these groups have become internal — in terms of establishing their writ in their respective regions. Their attacks on Pakistan, though part of a sectional TTP drive to control the entire state, are more likely to be retaliations and warnings to Islamabad to stop interfering with their plans for the FATA and NWFP.

The US-led Forces in Afghanistan

The US-led security forces in Afghanistan, though not allowed formally to operate inside the FATA by Pakistan, could be considered the third principal actor in the armed conflicts in this region. The main objectives of the US-led forces include the following: to ensure that the FATA is not used as a sanctuary or base for military operations by the militants; to pressurise the Pakistani government not to support the militants politically or militarily; and to force the Pakistani security forces to launch military operations against militants in the FATA.

Towards achieving these ends, the US-led forces have used hot pursuit, cross-border firing and drones and missiles to attack targets inside the FATA. It is also believed that the US has built an excellent network of human and signal intelligence in the region, which it is using either to attack targets or sharing the information with the Pakistani security forces and pressurising them to act.

Despite the rhetoric in public, there appears to be a trust deficit between the US security forces and those in Pakistan. The latter does not completely believe in the intelligence inputs received from the US; there were many instances when they were proved wrong. Conversely, the US forces have reservations regarding the 'leaks' which warn of an impending attack or a search, hence the unilateral actions.

ARMED CONFLICT IN 2008

The armed conflict in the FATA during 2008 expanded to include all seven agencies, besides spreading to the settled districts of the NWFP. Swat, in particular, became a major battleground between the Taliban and the state. The fallout of the armed conflict in these two regions could also be tracked to numerous other terrorist attacks in Pakistan.

Armed Conflict in the FATA and NWFP: An Overview

January 2008 started with abductions and military action on the one hand, and an extension of the ceasefire by the Taliban on the other. South Waziristan remained very violent in January 2008; there were more encounters between the security forces and the Taliban as the latter attempted to evict the security forces from forts, especially in Ladha, Siplatoi and Sararogah. More than 200 militants were killed in January in South Waziristan.[3] However, in North Waziristan, the militants extended the ceasefire twice in January 2008, which they had declared earlier in December 2007.[4] It was widely believed that the militants and the government were negotiating a secret deal to reach an understanding in North and South Waziristan. There was also a missile attack, perhaps the first drone attack of the year, near Mir Ali, in which 15 people were killed.[5] The remaining part of the year followed the same pattern: abductions, limited military action and temporary ceasefires. Outside Waziristan, in Mohmand Agency, more than 20 militants and seven soldiers were killed in an ambush on a military convoy.[6] In Kurram Agency, the sectarian conflict, which had intensified in 2007, continued unabated in January 2008.[7]

Outside the FATA, the armed conflict in Swat has intensified; the military operations against the Taliban, which were launched in 2007, continued in January 2008. According to the government, more than 200 militants belonging to the Taliban have been killed since November 2007.[8] There were at least two major suicide attacks, one in Swat on a military base and another in an Imambargah in Peshawar.

---

[3] See 'Five Killed in S Waziristan Clashes', *The News*, 2 January 2008; '27 Militants Killed in S Waziristan', *News*, 3 January 2008; 'Another Waziristan Fort Falls to Militants', *Dawn*, 18 January 2008; '90 Militants Killed in S Waziristan Clashes', *The News*, 19 January 2009; 'Army Says Some Areas Cleared of Militants: Clashes in S. Waziristan', *Dawn*, 25 January 2008.
[4] See 'Militants Extend Ceasefire', *Dawn*, 2 January 2008.
[5] 'Missile Strike Kills 15 in North Waziristan', *The News*, 30 January 2008.
[6] '23 Taliban, 7 Soldiers Die in Fighting', *The News*, 15 January 2008.
[7] 'Eight More Killed in Kurram Agency', *Dawn*, 3 January 2008.
[8] 'Troops Capture 52 Militants in Swat', *Dawn*, 4 January 2008.

This has been a major feature in the growth of the Taliban phenomenon in the FATA, leading to the deepening of sectarian faultlines both in the FATA and in the NWFP. Besides, there were regular attacks and kidnappings in the districts of Bannu, Mardan, Buner, Lakki Marwat, Kohat and Hangu.

February 2008 was comparatively peaceful. Perhaps the election fever that had gripped Pakistan had a salutary influence on the levels of violence. There were no major military operations against the militants, although there were two suicide attacks in the FATA — the first in Mir Ali in North Waziristan and the second in Parachinar in the Kurram Agency; more than 40 people were killed in these two attacks.[9] Towards the end of the month, there was a major drone attack in South Waziristan.[10] Outside the FATA, Swat remained the focus of militant activities, including a deadly suicide attack towards the end of the month in Mingora, during the funeral of a police officer.[11]

March 2008 was dominated by Mohmand and Bajaur Agencies in terms of violence. There were repeated clashes between the security forces and the Taliban.[12] Khyber Agency witnessed what later became a major trend along the Peshawar–Torkham Highway — militant attacks on the supply route for carrying materials for the NATO troops fighting the Taliban in Afghanistan.[13] There were also major drone attacks in South Waziristan, in which more than 20 people were killed, followed by a suicide attack.[14] The sectarian violence between Shias and Sunnis in Khyber Agency, including one suicide attack, and between two Sunni organisations in Khyber Agency, further intensified.[15] Outside the FATA, most of the violence was centred around Swat. Hangu also witnessed some sectarian clashes, following the celebration of *Nauroz*, the Persian new year.[16]

---

[9] 'Six Pro-govt Elders Killed by Suicide Bomber', *Dawn,* 12 February 2008; '38 Killed in Parachinar Pre-poll Carnage', *Daily Times,* 17 February 2008.

[10] 'Six Foreigners Among 8 Killed in Waziristan: Locals Suspect Missile Strike From Across Border', *Dawn,* 29 February 2008.

[11] '40 Die as Bomber Hits DSP's Funeral', *The News,* 1 March 2008.

[12] 'Five "militants" killed in Mohmand Agency', *Daily Times,* 4 March 2008.

[13] '50 Injured in Torkham Oil Tanker Blaze', *Dawn,* 24 March 2008.

[14] 'US Plane Attacks Wana House with Precision Bombs: Foreign Militants among Nine Killed', *Dawn,* 17 March 2008; 'Suicide Car Bomb Kills Five Troops in Wana', *Daily Times,* 21 March 2008.

[15] '8 Killed in Clash Between Rival Groups near Bara', *Daily Times,* 4 March 2008.

[16] 'Mehsud Orders Taliban Not to Attack Pak Forces', *Daily Times,* 24 April 2008.

April–June 2008 was marked by sectarian violence, primarily in the Kurram and Khyber Agencies, but also by peace negotiations. In the Kurram Agency, more than 100 persons were killed in sectarian conflicts between Sunnis and Shias. The conflict later spread to Dera Ismail Khan in May 2008. In Khyber, the conflict within the two Sunni organisations continued; in May, for the first time, there was a suicide attack that was linked to the ongoing conflict between two Sunni organisations – Ansar-ul-Islam (AI) and Lashkar-e-Islam (LI).[17] The new government in the NWFP initiated a fresh political process aimed at restoring peace in the region. Sufi Mohammad, leader of the TNSM, was released in April, along with some other tribal leaders in North Waziristan. Baitullah Mehsud announced a ceasefire in the FATA and the NWFP in April, while the NWFP government reached some kind of an understanding with the Taliban in Swat.[18]

July 2008 witnessed the continuation of sectarian clashes in the Khyber Agency, while numerous minor incidents took place in Mohmand and Bajaur Agencies as part of the local Taliban effort to impose their writ. Typical Taliban diktats were issued emphasising women wearing the veil, Shariah courts and so on in these two Agencies.[19] Also, in Mohmand and South Waziristan, the divisions within the various Taliban groups came to the fore once again, and there were open armed conflicts between the various groups. In South Waziristan, the old divide between the Wazirs and the Uzbeks came into the open after the local Taliban leaders in a jirga decided to expel the foreigners.[20] In Mohmand, after the local TTP chapter fought with another group led by Shah Khalid, considered to be closer to the government, there was intense fighting that led to killings and abductions of members from the rival groups.[21]

---

[17] '17 Injured in Mosque Suicide Attack', *Dawn*, 2 May 2008; '15 Killed in Fighting between Militant Factions', *Dawn*, 23 June 2008; 'Fierce Gunbattle Erupts in Khyber Agency', *Dawn*, 22 June 2008.
[18] 'Government, Fazlullah Agree on Ceasefire in Swat', *Daily Times*, 10 May 2008. 'Swat Taliban "Renounce Militancy": Peace Pact Signed with Fazlullah's Men', *Dawn*, 22 May 2008.
[19] 'Taliban Order Mohmand Women to Veil', *Daily Times*, 4 July 2008; 'Taliban Set up Sharia Courts in Bajaur Agency', *Dawn*, 7 July 2008.
[20] 'Taliban, Tribal Elders Agree to Expel Uzbeks', *Dawn*, 8 July 2008.
[21] 'Mohmand Militant Group Surrenders to TTP', *Daily Times*, 19 July 2008.

Outside the FATA, July 2008 was an important month because it marked the beginnings of renewed violence in Swat after the dialogue process between the Taliban and the NWFP government broke down. By end July, the Taliban had renewed its violent activities; in the first three days itself more than 80 people were killed.[22] July also witnessed a military confrontation between the security forces and the Taliban in Kohat district; the Taliban attacked a local fort, took it over temporarily and even promised the paramilitary soldiers in the fort a safe passage! The paramilitary forces surrendered without fighting. The government had to plan a full-blown operation to remove the Taliban from their strongholds in the district.[23]

Since August 2008 the unprecedented violence in Swat has subsumed the entire tribal belt. After that, there were attacks and counter attacks everyday in Swat. While the government used heavy weapons and helicopter gunships against the militants, the latter continued to fight the state and also tried to impose their writ by enforcing their brand of Islam, specially separate codes of conduct for the men and women of the region. More importantly, Fazlullah, the leader of Swat Taliban, was particularly severe on girls' education; since then, more than 200 schools have been destroyed by his men.

Outside Swat, in August 2008, there was a major military operation in Bajaur. The state used fighter jets, helicopter gunships and heavy artillery against the Taliban forces in Bajaur.[24] The battle for Bajaur was the most significant operation that Pakistan's security forces were involved in during 2008. In terms of sectarian conflicts, while the violence between Sunni groups continued in Khyber, in Kurram it restarted after a brief lull. Bajaur witnessed the killing of Haji Namdar, leader of Tanzim Amr bil Maroof Wa Nehi Anil Munkir (Suppression of Vice and Promotion of Virtue), while the fighting in Kurram resulted in more than 150 people getting killed.[25]

---

[22] 'Fresh Operation in Swat; Five Troops, 25 Militants Killed', *Dawn*, 31 July 2008; '33 More Killed as Swat Operation Continues', *Daily Times*, 1 August 2008.

[23] 'Militants Storm Fort Near Hangu', *The News*, 16 July 2008; 'Taliban Renew Threat to Kill Hostages', *Dawn*, 20 July 2008; 'Normality Returns to Hangu', *Dawn*, 22 July 2008;

[24] 'Militants Forced to End Khar Siege', *Dawn*, 12 August 2008; 'Troops Pull Out of Lowi Sam', *Dawn*, 10 August 2008; 'Air Power Used to Rescue 180 Besieged Soldiers', *Dawn*, 10 August 2008; 'Three Civilians among 17 Killed in Bajaur', *News*, 21 August 2008.

[25] '35 Killed in Kurram Clashes', *Dawn*, 13 August 2008; '10 Killed in Kurram Agency Clashes', *Dawn*, 10 August 2008; 'Over 100 Killed in Kurram Agency in Last Week', *Daily Times*, 14 August 2008; 'Fresh Fighting Leaves 47 Dead in Kurram', *Daily Times*, 18 August 2008.

September–December 2008, witnessed the violence in Swat reaching its peak, military operations intensifying in Bajaur, while drone attacks by the US from across the Durand Line started increasing. There were almost 10 drone attacks in four months, which is twice the number that were carried out in the previous eight months. Almost all these drone attacks took place in North and South Waziristan.

Major Trends in 2008

My chapter in the 2008 volume of this annual publication on the armed conflict in the FATA 2008 identified three major trends: first, the spread of armed conflict into the other Agencies of the FATA outside North and South Waziristan and other parts of the NWFP; second, an armed conflict within the militant groups, especially between the local militants and the Uzbeks, and between the Taliban and the local population; and, third, increasing suicide attacks all over Pakistan. In 2008, some of these trends continued, but there were some new trends as well, which are discussed below.

Intensifying Taliban Expansion in the FATA and the NWFP

In last year's volume it was assessed that the armed conflict in North and Waziristan would have a domino effect on the other Agencies in the FATA as well as on some settled districts of the NWFP like Tank, Kohat, Peshawar and DI Khan.

Within FATA, the spread of the Taliban can be placed under three categories: those Agencies that are totally under the control of the Taliban, like North and South Waziristan; those Agencies, where the Taliban has a major presence but is witnessing intense fighting between the militants and the security forces, like Bajaur and Mohmand Agencies; and those Agencies, where the Taliban's presence in the other Agencies is exacerbating the sectarian conflicts between the Shias and Sunnis, or within the Sunnis, like the Kurram and Khyber Agencies.

As seen in the overview, there was not much military confrontation in North and South Waziristan during 2008. This is not because the militants do not exist, but because they are effectively controlling the situation. Major attacks in these two Agencies were led by the US through drone attacks from across the Durand Line. In fact, South and North Waziristan suffered the most drone attacks in 2008.

Khyber too witnessed violence in 2008, but is was not uniform either in terms of the perpetrators or in terms of their objectives. Most of the violence that took place was between two Sunni organisations, led by the AI and LI. In addition, there was violence led by the Taliban in Khyber, mostly in the form of attacks on NATO supply routes.

Exacerbating Sectarian Faultlines

The armed conflict being led by the Taliban is exacerbating the sectarian faultlines between the Shias and Sunnis, as well as the differences that exist amongst the various Sunni organisations. In 2008 Kurram was worst affected by the Shia–Sunni conflict. Kurram's geographic and ethnic profile makes it an ideal site for sectarian violence. Its boundaries lie mostly along the Durand Line, making it appear almost like a triangle projecting into Afghanistan. For administrative reasons Kurram is divided into three regions — Upper, Central and Lower Kurram. The main access into the Kurram, especially to its administrative headquarters Parachinar, is from Kohat, through Hangu. Turis are the main inhabitants of the region, especially upper and lower Kurram, and are perhaps the only Pashtun tribe that is wholly Shia. Bangash is the second biggest Pashtun tribe in Kurram, comprised of both Shias and Sunnis.

There have been sectarian conflicts between the Shias and Sunnis in Kurram earlier, for example, in 1983–87, 1996–98 and 2001. However, the present sectarian violence, which started in April 2007 and continues even now, is due to the growing influence of the local Taliban in the FATA. The high level of violence which started in April 2008 is the third phase of the recent sectarian conflict in Kurram; the first phase started in April 2007, subsided later but was renewed in November 2007 and continued till January 2008. Apart from a suicide attack in February 2008, which killed more than 45 persons, there were regular attacks on the movement of people, blockading of the only route that takes essential supplies into the Shia areas of Kurram, and the systematic targeting of hospitals, ambulances and the electricity network. More than 300 people were killed during April–June 2008.

Apart from the Shia–Sunni conflict in Kurram, the violence between the two Sunni organisations in Khyber also continued. This conflict is a parallel one, like the sectarian conflict in Kurram, having its own history but also being exacerbated by the overall Taliban growth. Khyber is perhaps the most important Agency for Pakistan and

Afghanistan for strategic reasons. The main road link between Pakistan and Afghanistan (the other road is from Quetta to Kandahar via Chaman) goes via Bara and Landikotal in the Khyber Agency, connecting Peshawar with Kabul. From the Greeks to the British, numerous armies, including those of the Persians, Mughals, Afghans and Sikhs, crossed what later came to be known as the Durand Line, mainly through the Khyber Pass.

The violence in 2008 between two Sunni groups led by Mufti Munir Shakir and Pir Saifullah was the result of an ongoing conflict that had begun in 2005. Surprisingly, neither Munir nor Saifullah belong to Khyber; Munir is from the Kurram Agency, while Saifullah is an Afghan. And even though the local population was upset with the two and with the violence, their efforts to expel them through various jirgas did not yield the desired results. The violence taking place today is an offshoot of this divide, but is being led by two armed groups — LI and AI.

LI is led by Mangal Bagh Afridi, who is a part of Mufti Munir's group. Mangal Bagh, after tasting power under Munir in terms of issuing fatwas and imposing fines, does not want to lose his control. LI has been attempting to impose its own code of Islam; there have been reports linking them to the stoning and killing of people committing adultery, and issuing fatwas on women who go to markets and public places without blood relatives, and those who do not offer regular prayers. Those who defied LI edicts were imprisoned and kept in illegal confinement. Journalists writing on the activities of LI have been threatened and illegally detained, and their papers have been banned. LI has also been running an illegal FM radio station, through which Mangal Bagh is issuing his edicts and fatwas.

In addition to all this, LI is also engaged in a violent conflict with AI, another group which has gained an element of support from the local population. Both groups have been attacking each other's supporters and properties. Capturing illegal weapons and FM stations, and demolishing houses and shopping complexes belonging to each other, have become a regular phenomenon in Khyber Agency. But this generally goes unnoticed as the reports coming in from other agencies are more sensational. LI has also been attacking the checkposts of the paramilitary forces, capturing and killing soldiers.

The Jihad Within

The last volume's chapter on armed conflict in the FATA highlighted the divides within the various militant groups that are fighting in the region.

There was an open confrontation between a section of Uzbek militants under the leadership of Tahir Yuldashev and the local militants being led by Maulvi Nazir. This conflict resulted in the killing of more than 200 militants in 2007, most of them Uzbeks. While Maulvi Nazir belongs to the Wazir tribe, a section within the Wazir and the Mehsud tribes are reported to be supporting the Uzbeks. Baitullah does not have any serious objections to the presence of the Uzbeks, therefore he was not in total agreement with Nazir. This Uzbek vs Nazir fight continued sporadically in 2008, primarily in South Waziristan. When the Uzbek militants attacked Maulvi Nazir and his supporters, the latter retaliated.[26] Later in 2008, Maulvi Nazir organised a jirga in July in Wana which included people from South Waziristan and some from the North Waziristan Taliban Shura. The Uzbeks were blamed for the attacks carried out on Nazir's supporters and on some pro-government tribal elders that took place earlier. It was decided then that the Uzbeks should be expelled from South Waziristan.

There were also reports about a divide between Maulvi Nazir and Baitullah Mehsud, as the former is considered to be close to the security forces.[27] Besides the dispute over the Uzbeks, Baitullah, Maulvi Nazir and Hafiz Gul Bahadur differed on various other issues. Like Nazir, Gul Bahadur is also a Wazir, and is a veteran who took part in the Afghan jihad. He has been pursuing peace deals with the government in North Waziristan during 2008, while Baituallah was busy organising attacks against the state all over Pakistan. When Baitullah wanted to open another front in North Waziristan, Gul Bahadur refused as he was negotiating a deal with the government. Though Gul Bahadur is considered the number two in the TTP network, he does not play a major role. There are even reports indicating that Nazir and Gul Bahadur formed a Muqami-Tehrik-e-Taliban in 2008 against Baitullah.

In Mohmand Agency there were violent clashes between two Taliban groups, led by Shah Khalid and and Omar Khalid. The latter is closer to the TTP and Baitullah, while the former was Ahle Hadith and against any attacks on the Pakistani security forces. There was a cold war between these two groups for a long time. Both have separate

---

[26] 'Two Uzbek Fighters Killed in Waziristan', *Dawn*, 14 January 2008; 'Wazir Tribesmen Wary of Uzbek Militants' Return to South Waziristan', *Daily Times*, 31 January 2008.

[27] 'Tension Grips Waziristan as Uzbeks Find New Sanctuary', *The News*, 21 May 2007.

training camps and their own areas of influence, with their own checkposts. Whenever there were fights between these two groups, the Afghan Taliban commanders used to mediate. In July 2008, there was a bloody battle, in which Shah Khalid and his men were killed by the TTP led by Omar Khalid. According to reports, Omar Khalid invited guest fighters from the TTP in other tribal agencies such as Bajaur, South Waziristan and Khyber, and organised a bloody coup using heavy weapons and ammunition, including mortars and rockets to wipe out the Shah Khalid group.[28]

Continuing Suicide Attacks

Like in the previous year, 2008 also witnessed numerous suicide attacks. In 2007 there were 60, while in 2008 there were 54 suicide attacks within Pakistan. Further analyses of suicide attacks in Pakistan will reveal that they were concentrated in the FATA and the NWFP, both in 2007 and 2008; these two regions witnessed thrice the number of suicide attacks during 2008, compared to the rest of Pakistan (see Table 4.1).

Table 4.1: Suicide Terrorism in Pakistan, 2001–08

Year	FATA and NWFP	Outside FATA and NWFP
2002	01	–
2003	02	–
2004	06	01
2005	04	–
2006	02	05
2007	44	16
2008	41	12

Source: Compiled by author based on open newspaper sources.

The following trends can be identified in suicide terrorism within Pakistan, especially in the FATA and NWFP regions. First, there is a direct correlation between the US-led action in Afghanistan and suicide terrorism in Pakistan. Until 9/11, there were no suicide attacks inside Pakistan — either in FATA or the NWFP or elsewhere. Available data clearly proves that suicide terrorism in Pakistan is a post-9/11 phenomenon. Second, in the FATA and the NWFP, suicide attacks

[28] '50 Killed as Two Militant Groups Clash in Mohmand', *The News,* 19 July 2008.

began only in 2004, after the armed conflict became entrenched in Waziristan. While there were no suicide attacks in 2005 in this region, there were five in 2006 and 11 during the first eight months of 2007. Third, most of the suicide attacks in FATA and the NWFP have been anti-state, with Pakistan's security forces being targeted. Till 2007, sectarian causes had motivated these suicide attacks. In FATA and the settled districts of NWFP, they have primarily been anti-state.

Three distinct strategies have been used by the Taliban in pursuing their suicide attacks. First, in those areas that are completely under their control, or which the Taliban want to bring under their total control, they have used suicide attacks primarily against the security forces. At times they have also used suicide attacks against tribal jirgas, which they believed were secular and pro-government. The objective of these attacks was to ensure that no other institution — state or tribal, formal or traditional — questions the Taliban's writ. Suicide attacks in Waziristan and Swat are a part of this strategy. Second, the Taliban has also used suicide attacks as a strategy in settled districts, mostly bordering the FATA, as part of their efforts to increase their areas of operation. Unlike in FATA, the border districts like Bannu, DI Khan, Kohat and even Peshawar, do not have a Taliban presence, as in the FATA. The mainstream institutions of the state continue to function in these border districts and the Taliban aims to destroy them by carrying out suicide attacks. As a part of this strategy, the Taliban has also targeted secular political parties, primarily the Awami National Party. Third, the Taliban has been mounting suicide attacks in other parts of Pakistan, mainly in Punjab and Islamabad, as a punishment and warning against the military operations being carried out by the state in FATA and Swat. Though the suicide attacks in Islamabad and Lahore are not a part of the Taliban's strategy to take over these two capitals — political and cultural — the objective is to warn the Pakistani state of consequences. In most cases the targets of these suicide attacks were either related to the security forces or were places where an international audience would be readily available.

CONFLICT MANAGEMENT

Conflict management in the FATA and the NWFP involves four key actors: the government of the NWFP led by the Awami National Party, the Government of Pakistan, the US-led international forces stationed in Afghanistan and the local tribal leadership of the region.

Secret Negotiations and Political Deals

Secret negotiations and political deals with sections of the Taliban have been the primary strategies of the state in dealing with the conflict. As mentioned above, the Taliban in Pakistan is not a monolith and includes different tribal affiliations with various leaders. For example, in North and South Waziristan, there are three major leaders — Gul Bahadur, Maulvi Nazir and Baitullah Mehsud. While the first two are Wazirs, whose fighters are based in North and South Waziristan, the last one is a Mehsud, whose base is in South Waziristan. While the state was engaged in a serious military operation against Baitullah Mehsud in the beginning of 2008 in South Waziristan, it was secretly negotiating a deal with Gul Bahadur in North Waziristan. The latter agreed to prolong the ceasefire in place, which had been established in 2007. In Mohmand Agency, the state was closer to Shah Khalid's group and was using him against the TTP.

After the elections, the new government in the NWFP, led by the Awami National Party initiated a different negotiation with the TTP and with Maulana Fazlullah. During mid-2008, the NWFP government released Sufi Mohammad, the leader of the TNSM as part of these negotiations. The provincial government was also in negotiation with Baitullah Mehsud, who announced a ceasefire in February 2008. In 2009, as part of the understanding with the Taliban in Swat, the Parliament even passed a resolution — Nizam-e-Adl, popularly referred to as the Shariah regulations.

However, the secret negotiations and political deals with the Taliban achieved very little success in 2008. The various factions of the Taliban, with whom the state had entered into negotiations, never fulfilled their commitments, leading to renewed violence.

The Internal Jirgas and Tribal Lashkars

Tribal jirgas have traditionally played a major role in resolving conflicts in the Pashtun community, especially in the FATA. Numerous jirgas were called after armed conflict broke out in this region, in the various sub-regions, and amongst the different tribes. Some of these jirgas are inter-tribal and some are intra-tribal, some were convened between the local tribes and the government, and some between the local population and the Taliban.

The involvement of the local tribes and the use of jirgas never had the same objectives. They were convened by different tribes for different reasons and supported by different parties. The use of tribal jirgas as a conflict management tool in 2008 could be divided into three categories: first, used for the Taliban, to obtain the release of tribal leaders or elders kidnapped by the Taliban, or in retaliation to the Taliban killing local leaders, for instance. These jirgas allowed the tribes to negotiate with the Taliban on the subject of limiting their sphere of influence or, alternately, accepting it, but, more importantly, these jirgas at times also raised a tribal *lashkar* (militia) to proceed against the Taliban. In 2008, the tribal jirgas used all these strategies to deal with the Taliban.[29]

The second category of local jirga involvement in conflict management took the form of brokering ceasefires between the Taliban and the government whenever serious military operations were launched. The local tribal leadership, caught in the crossfire between militants and the security forces, initiated such measures on its own to broker a ceasefire. At times, the government reached the tribal leadership through its Political Agent to assist them in this process or to pressure the Taliban to continue the ceasefire. Though the role of these jirgas in brokering ceasefires between the militants and the government could never be extended into negotiating a long-term truce, they did play a major role in providing temporary relief to the civilian population.

The third category of jirga involvement was offensive, in terms of organising themselves into militias, mainly under pressure from the government. The government actively helped such militias in 2008, for example, by supporting Shah Khalid in Mohmand and Maulvi Nazir in South Waziristan. Without active help from the state, Nazir's cadres would not have been able to evict the Uzbeks from South Waziristan.

The tribal jirgas were especially useful while trying to address the plight of the internally displaced people from the tribal agencies. To conclude, the jirgas remain a potential tool for conflict management, but are being exploited by the state and the Taliban to achieve their immediate interests. Unfortunately, unlike the role they played

---

[29] 'Tribesmen Raising Anti-Al Qaeda Lashkar: Official', *Dawn*, 10 January 2008.

historically, these tribal jirgas have today lost or are losing their importance, resulting from the growing differences in perception between the secular elders, who believe in Pashtun traditions, and the younger generation, which is being buoyed by the Taliban version of Islam.

Military Operations

The state was also engaged in anti-militant operations. There were at least three major operations in the FATA — in South Waziristan, Mohmand and Bajaur during 2008, and two in the NWFP — in Kohat and Swat. The state used heavy weapons, including fighter aircrafts, helicopter gunships and artillery. These were intense operations, spanning over a period of two to six weeks.Unfortunately, none of them operations were taken to their logical conclusion, due principally to three reasons. First, the reluctance of the state to fight militancy for political reasons. Many in Pakistan believes that this is not their war, therefore, why should they fight the Taliban. They reason that the problem in the FATA and the NWFP is primarily a fallout of the US-led War on Terror being conducted in Afghanistan. This section believes that once this War ends in Afganistan peace will return to these two regions. Second, there is also some reluctance in the security establishment, comprising the military and intelligence agencies. A section within the security establishment believes that the US presence in Afghanistan is unlikely to be long term; and that the Taliban is their trump card in Kabul in a post-US, post-Karzai Afghanistan. So, they ask: why should Pakistan fight against its future trump card in Afghanistan? Finally, there is great pressure from the NWFP — both the ANP and Muttahida Majlis-e-Amal (MMA) — on Islamabad, to ensure that military operations are kept to a minimum in the FATA.

The Awami National Party, which had formed the government in the NWFP provincial assembly in 2008, is apprehensive about the spreading violence and growing number of internally displaced persons (IDPs). As discussed above, the Taliban is using suicide bombings and hit-and-run attacks in the settled districts of the NWFP as their revenge strategy. Also, military operations in the FATA have resulted in a huge exodus of people from the tribal Agencies into the settled districts of the NWFP, creating a huge social and economic issue for the government in Peshawar. In particular, the districts of Bannu, DI Khan, Kohat, Peshawar, Mardan and Buner have borne the brunt of this displacement. On the other hand, religious parties are also against military operations, since their sympathy lies with the Taliban. They accuse Islamabad of being a stooge of Washington in carrying out military operations against their own people. Anti-American sentiments and the rhetoric of Pakistan's sovereignty have been powerful tools in their hands in opposing the military operations.

Drone Attacks

Besides the military operations by Pakistan's security forces, drone attacks by the US from across the Durand Line should also be seen as part of the conflict management process. Though these drone attacks against targets in the FATA started in 2004 itself, they increased tremendously in 2008. During 2004–07, there were less than 10 drone attacks in four years; in 2008, there were at least 15 such attacks. One can in fact see a clear pattern emerging; between January and August in 2008, there were only five drone attacks in the FATA, which doubled in the last four months of the year, and are continuing with increasing frequency in 2009.

It is obvious that the US considers the drone attacks to be an effective strategy to counter the Taliban in the FATA for the following reasons: drone attacks have resulted in neutralising key Taliban and Al Qaeda figures, who the US considers high-value targets in the FATA. From Nek Mohammad to Sheikh Ahmed Salim Swedan, the drones successfully targeted some key leaders of the Taliban and Al Qaeda. The year 2008 in particular was highly successful, for the drones were able to effectively neutralise Abu Laith al-Libi, Abu Sulayman Al-Jazairi, Khalid Habib, Abu Akash, Mohammad Hasan Khalil al-Hakim aka Abu Jihad al-Masri, Rashid Rauf and Abu Zubair al-Masri.[30] The drone attacks have also been very successful in neutralising foreign fighters in the FATA belonging to the Al Qaeda; many of whom were Arabs, Chechens and Uzbeks.[31]

---

[30] 'Drone Strikes Killed High Value Targets, US tells Pakistan', *Dawn*, 9 February 2009. Also 'Missile Strike Kills 15 in North Waziristan', *The News*, 30 January 2008; '12 Killed as Missile Hits House in S Waziristan', *The News*, 29 February 2008; '12 Killed in Drone Attack on Damadola', *Dawn*, 15 May 2008; 'Qaeda Weapons Expert Slain in Waziristan strike', *Daily Times*, 29 July 2008.

[31] See '7 Arabs Among Missile Victims', *Dawn*, 31 January 2008; 'Six Foreigners among 8 Killed in Waziristan', *Dawn*, 29 February 2008; 'Two Foreigners Killed in Missile Attack', *Dawn*, 17 October 2008.

Drone attacks from across the Durand Line are also a part of the trust factor, or the lack of it there of, between the American forces and Pakistan's own security forces. The US is sceptical about Pakistan's seriousness in fighting the Taliban and Al Qaeda. Besides, the US is convinced that the drone attacks are the best way to neutralise high-value targets, as this reduces the time required for eliminating these targets, as compared to conventional search-and-destroy operations. Finally, the drone attacks have been limited to the FATA and, so far, have not expanded into the settled districts in NWFP. Even within the FATA, the attacks have primarily focused on North and South Waziristan, Mohmand and Bajaur Agencies. Two-thirds of the drone attacks in 2008 took place in North and South Waziristan.

Though the government and the opposition in Pakistan have condemned the drone attacks as a violation of its sovereignty, it is unlikely that the US could have carried out these attacks by disregarding Islamabad's concerns. It appears that the state tacitly supports the drone attacks, but publicly condemns them, for purely political reasons.

CONCLUSIONS

Where is the armed conflict in FATA and NWFP heading? Are there signs of its decline and eventual cessation? What can Pakistan do to reduce the armed conflicts in these two regions?

As mentioned in last year's volume, the armed conflict in these regions is likely to continue and expand further. First, the state in Pakistan is not fully geared to fight the Taliban militarily. The Pakistani armed forces, moreover, is not keen to fight the Taliban, especially in the FATA, since a section of the military believes this is not in its interests. The full fledged military operations conducted in 2009 in Swat, Dir, Malakand and Buner should be seen as being NWFP-specific. It is unlikely that such military operations will be carried out in the FATA.

Second, a section within the local population in the NWFP and FATA supports the militants and is opposed to the state. The Awami National Party government in the NWFP, though it does not support the Taliban, but nor is not in favour of full-scale military operations against them for security and economic reasons. They fear that military operations in the FATA will only increase Taliban attacks in the settled districts of the NWFP, leading to massive internal population displacement. Precisely for these reasons, the they were even willing to sacrifice Swat and Malakand, despite both being part of the settled districts.

Third, anti-US feelings are likely to continue and increase further. The drone attacks in particular will further exacerbate anti-American sentiments in the region. It is unfortunate that the leadership in Pakistan — political, religious and military — are not focusing on certain facts relating to the drone attacks, especially the nationality of the targets and their supporters. While these attacks are highlighted in terms of Pakistan's sovereignty and the killing of innocent people, what is being deliberately ignored is that the targets include high value Al Qaeda targets, foreign fighters and their local supporters.

Fourth, Pakistan is likely to continue with its dual strategy for dealing with militancy and the Taliban in the NWFP and FATA. The country's political and military leadership seems to believe that an element of radicalisation of the FATA is acceptable, as long as it does not affect the rest of the NWFP and Pakistan. The state seems willing to further dilute its writ (or whatever remains of it) in the FATA, as long as the TTP does not look further east. The provincial government in the NWFP also pursued a similar strategy vis-à-vis Swat; as long as Maulana Fazlullah was willing to be a factor within the Swat valley, it was prepared to cede some of the state's powers. The introduction of Nizam-e-Adl for the Malakand region should be seen as part of this attempt. If the state is unwilling to fight and is ready to cede its powers and responsibilities, the militants are only likely to expand their influence further.

Finally, for all the reasons mentioned above, the Taliban is likely to spread further into Pakistan. Suicide attacks, in particular, will increase, targeting military and security forces in Punjab and Islamabad. In the process, the jihadis of Punjab are likely to become the Punjabi Taliban. Swat is a good example of this process; much before the Taliban was born, there were armed jihadis in Swat and Malakand being led by Sufi Mohammad and his TNSM, who later became the Taliban of Swat led by Maulana Fazlullah. In the same way, Jaish-e-Mohammad, Sipah-e-Sahaba and Lashkar-e-Jhangvi, which consist primarily of Punjabis, are also likely to become the Punjabi Taliban.

There in lies the real danger to the future of Pakistan — Punjab becoming radicalised and violent.

5

J&K: From Militancy to Jihad?

Kavita Suri and D. Suba Chandran

A BRIEF HISTORY[1]

A distinction needs to be made between the 'conflict of' and the 'conflict in' Jammu and Kashmir (J&K). Ever since the 1920s, conflict in Kashmir has occurred at different levels; the nature and actors varying continuously. The perceived oppressive rule of the erstwhile Maharaja is the primary reason for the 'conflict in' Kashmir. The local population felt alienated and voiceless. At this juncture, the All Jammu and Kashmir Muslim Conference, one of the first political parties in J&K enjoying mass support, was founded by Sheikh Abdullah in 1932. The two decades immediately preceding Partition in 1947 witnessed a movement against the rule of Maharaja Hari Singh. This movement primarily aimed at better governance by the ruler and better representation of the ruled.[2]

Led by Sheikh Abdullah, this movement was peaceful and nonviolent. Later, Sheikh Abdullah changed the name of his party to All Jammu and Kashmir National Conference (NC). After him, the NC was headed by Farooq Abdullah, Sheikh Abdullah's son, and now by Omar Abdullah, his grandson. The NC was fighting for a representative government in J&K in the 1930s and early 1940s. After Independence and the accession of J&K to India, the 'conflict in' Kashmir

---

[1] This section on a brief history of armed conflict in Jammu and Kashmir is primarily drawn from D. Suba Chandran, 'J&K: Infiltration Declines Violence Persists', in D. Suba Chandran (ed.) *Armed Conflicts and Peace Processes in South Asia* (New Delhi: Samskriti, 2007).

[2] For the early political history of J&K before 1947, see Prem Nath Bazaz, *Inside Kashmir* (Srinagar: Gulshan Publishers, 2002) and *The History of Struggle for Freedom in Kashmir* (Srinagar: Gulshan Publishers, 2003).

continued at various levels and with differing intensity against the union government, demanding better governance and power-sharing between the union and the state.[3]

The 'conflict of' Kashmir began in 1947 between India and Pakistan, following the Partition of British India. In the pre-Independence period, Jawaharlal Nehru and the Indian National Congress came closer to Sheikh Abdullah due to his ideology, secularism and political outlook. At this time, Mohammad Ali Jinnah was campaigning for Pakistan and developed close ties with the Muslim Conference in J&K. Kashmir became significant for Jinnah and the Pakistan movement; its 'Muslim' character enabled Pakistan to put forward its claim to a Muslim-majority Kashmir. Pakistan, to date, refuses to accept the accession of Kashmir to India, considering it to be a fraud.

In 1947, J&K was one of 550 princely states and was ruled by a Hindu King, Maharaja Hari Singh, descendant of Maharaja Gulab Singh. The contemporary history of J&K can be traced to the Treaty of Amritsar, signed between the British Government and Maharaja Gulab Singh in 1846. According to Article I of the Treaty, 'The British Government transfers and makes over forever in independent possession to Maharaja Gulab Singh and the male heirs of his body, all the hilly or mountainous country, with its dependencies, situated to the eastward of the River Indus and the westward of River Ravi, including Chamba and excluding Lahul, being part of the territories ceded to the British Government by the Lahore State, according to the provisions of Article IV of the treaty of Lahore, dated 9 March 1846.'[4]

At the time of granting Independence, the 'conflict in' Kashmir was subsumed by the 'conflict of' Kashmir. On the eve of Independence, the Prime Minister of Kashmir sent identical telegrams, on 12 August 1947, to the governments of India and Pakistani suggesting a Standstill Agreement. According to him, 'the existing arrangements should continue pending settlement of details.'[5] Pakistan became proactive and started taking forcible steps to secure Kashmir's accession.

---

[3] For the initial problems between the Government of India and the J&K government during the 1950s and 1960s see Prem Nath Bazaz, *Kashmir in Crucible* (Srinagar: Gulshan Publishers, 2005).

[4] See the Treaty of Amritsar, 1846, signed between the British Government and Maharaja Gulab Singh.

[5] See 'Standstill Agreement with India and Pakistan', in Verinder Grover (ed.), *The Story of Kashmir: Yesterday and Today*, Vol. III (New Delhi: Deep and Deep Publications, 1995), p. 106

Pakistan sent both Pashtun tribesmen and its own troops to capture J&K by force. After the joint forces occupied Muzaffarabad on 22 October 1947,[6] Maharaja Hari Singh appealed to Lord Mountbatten, Governor General of Independent India, for help. Following the Defence Committee of India's decision that Indian troops could only be sent after Hari Singh acceded to India, the latter sent a letter to Lord Mountbatten, who, while[7] accepting his request, added a caveat that the accession should be ratified by the people of Kashmir.[8] On 25 October 1947, Maharaja Hari Singh signed the Instrument of Accession, which was accepted by Lord Mountbatten on 27 October 1947. Subsequently, Indian paratroopers were dispatched to Srinagar.

In November 1947, full-fledged fighting broke out between the Indian and Pakistani troops, which continued till December, with one-third of the territory remaining under Pakistan's control. On 20 December 1947, the Indian Cabinet decided to refer the case to the UN Security Council and lodged a complaint on 1 January 1948. Following this complaint, the UN Security Council adopted a resolution on 13 August 1948. It had three parts: the first called for a ceasefire between India and Pakistan; second, withdrawal of Pakistani troops from the disputed area; and, third, withdrawal of troops by India, except for a minimum force needed to maintain law and order; while the future of Kashmir would be decided 'in accordance with the will of the people'. Except for the first part of the resolution, there has been no progress on its other provisions, despite a series of successive resolutions passed by the UN. Since then, the 'conflict of' Kashmir has continued between India and Pakistan and has witnessed conflicts in 1965, 1971 and 1999'.

The 'conflict in' Kashmir started gaining momentum in the early 1980s. Several issues, including the problems of governance, narrow political interests of the union and state governments — especially the Congress and NC — social, political and communal mobilisation of Kashmiri society, converged in the late 1980s. What lit the spark was the 1987 election, widely perceived as the most unfair in Kashmir's history. The popular disaffection in the Kashmir Valley was exploited by Pakistan to initiate an armed conflict. Thus, after the 1987 elections,

---

[6] Lars Blikenberg, *India-Pakistan: The History of Unsolved Conflict*, Vol. I (Odense: Odense University Press, 1998), p. 76.
[7] Verinder Grover (ed.), *The Story of Kashmir: Yesterday and Today*, Vol. III, p. 108.
[8] *Ibid*.

the 'conflict of' Kashmir merged with the 'conflict in' Kashmir, leading to an armed conflict.

The armed conflict in Kashmir, however, was not monolithic. Initially led by the Jammu and Kashmir Liberation Front (JKLF), there was a rapid change in the principal actors and their objectives. The JKLF, led by Yasin Malik and Javid Mir, fought for an independent, but secular, Kashmir. The hedging of Kashmir with Pakistan was never its objective. As a result, the JKLF fell out of grace with its supporters across the border. The JKLF is divided into two major factions: one led by Yasin Malik in J&K (on Indian soil) and the other led by Amanullah Khan in Pakistan-occupied Kashmir (PoK). Amanullah's JKLF, even today, refuses to take part in the PoK elections and demands Kashmir's unification with Pakistan.

The second phase of the armed conflict, in the early 1990s, was overtaken by the Hizbul Mujahideen, the JKLF being the main casualty. During this period, realising Pakistan's objectives in Kashmir, the JKLF began distancing itself from Pakistan. Throughout this period, Pakistan sent many former Afghan mujahideen to fight in J&K. The mid-1990s saw the Hizbul Mujahideen and the Afghan mujahideen waging an intense war against the security forces. This phase also witnessed the militants, mainly Afghans, abusing local Kashmiris, especially Kashmiri women. This generated dissatisfaction among the local population with the militancy, the first positive turn of events since militancy began in the late 1980s.

In 1996, the situation improved considerably and elections were held for the first time in a decade. The NC formed the government in J&K; however, neither the union nor the state government seemed to have learnt any lesson. Both governments failed to take advantage of the situation on the security and administrative fronts. Two processes, initiated by Pakistan during this period, transformed the nature of the armed conflict in J&K. First, Pakistan allowed the Lashkar-e-Toiba (LeT), with its puritanical beliefs, to take over the militancy. Since then, the armed conflict has acquired a fundamentalist and jihadi streak, with the Hizbul Mujahideen playing a secondary role. Second, it initiated the war in Kargil, partly with the objective of reviving militancy in J&K. This provided a new impetus to the armed conflict, which subsequently saw a series of *fidayeen* attacks. This trend continued till 2001–02. The military standoff in 2001–02 and the elections for the legislative assembly in 2002 introduced a new realism. While Pakistan was pressurised by both India and the international community to rein in its support for militancy, the Indo-Pak peace process, which began in October 2003, has contributed to the present thaw in the armed conflict. Much would depend on the success of the bilateral peace process and Pakistan's ability to exercise control over jihadi groups like the Lashkar-e-Toiba and Jaish-e-Muhammad (JeM).

THE PRINCIPLE ACTORS[9]

The principal actors in the armed conflict of J&K include both state actors — India and Pakistan — and armed non-state actors (NSAs).

State Actors

India

The union government is the principal actor in the conflict 'within' Kashmir and 'of' Kashmir. Since 1947, it has pursued multiple political and military policies. At present, it is pursuing a bilateral political process to resolve all its issues with Pakistan, including the Kashmir question. Internally, it has been pursuing political, economic and military approaches to resolve the conflict in Kashmir. The policies of the union government have been criticised for being ad hoc and incoherent. Ever since the outbreak of violence in the late 1980s, the union government's major emphasis has been on organising elections to the J&K state legislature and the union Parliament, supporting the state government, and engaging various political organisations and groups in a dialogue. This political approach, however, has not been consistent; being conditioned by the parties that have formed governments in New Delhi and Srinagar. Also, the union government is generally criticised for allocating more funds to J&K without proper scrutiny.

On the security front, the union government has deployed military and paramilitary forces since the outbreak of violence in the region. Until recently, counter-militancy operations were mainly led by these

---

[9] This section on the principal actors in the armed conflict in Jammu and Kashmir is also drawn primarily from the previous edition. See Chandran, 'J&K: Infiltration Declines, Violence Persists', pp. 30–66.

organisations, with the local J&K police providing only marginal support. Three groups need particular mention when evaluating the counter-militancy operations — the Rashtriya Rifles (RR), the Border Security Force (BSF) and the Central Reserve Police Force (CRPF). While the RR was created within the Indian army as a special counter-intelligence force and functions under the union Defence Ministry, the BSF and CRPF are paramilitary police forces functioning under the union Home Ministry. An increasing role is being assigned to the local police as well. The main objectives of the union government are to prevent cross-border terrorism and militancy in J&K, reach a permanent settlement with Pakistan on the Line of Control (LoC), and ensure the smooth functioning of the state government. Power-sharing between the state and union governments and the quantum of autonomy to be devolved are major issues for decision at the governmental level.

Pakistan

Pakistan is the second principal actor, both in the conflict 'of' and the conflict 'in' Kashmir. At the bilateral level, Pakistan has attempted to keep the conflict alive both politically and militarily. All the India–Pakistan conflicts (1947–48, 1965, 1971 and 1999) were initiated by Pakistan to achieve its objectives militarily. The 1971 war could be considered an exception to this rule, as it started primarily in Bangladesh, then East Pakistan. Politically, Pakistan has attempted to internationalise the Kashmir issue by bringing it up at all major international fora, and inviting external actors to intervene. Pakistan has also been party to many failed bilateral dialogues with India. At present, it is again engaged in a political discourse with India. Cross-border terrorism, as a covert policy in J&K, emerged in the late 1980s, following Pakistan's involvement in militancy in Punjab. Until then, Pakistan had only provided political support to the separatists. Pakistan's successes in Punjab, and in the Afghan jihad against the Soviet forces, played an important role in its adoption of proxy war as its main strategy in J&K. The fact that the Indian government failed on the political and administrative fronts in J&K caused immense disaffection and alienation among the Kashmiris against New Delhi, which helped Pakistan sustain its proxy war. Cross-border terrorism has now become the cornerstone of Pakistan's policy in Kashmir.

Pakistan's main objective in J&K is to use Kashmir as a means to bleed India; to force India to give up its claims, especially to the Kashmir

Valley, and also to annex J&K. There have been slow changes in these objectives. Today, Pakistan's primary objective is not to annex J&K, but to annex PoK permanently, and loosen India's control over the Kashmir Valley.

The Jammu & Kashmir Government

The state government is the third principal actor in the conflict. The successive state governments — formed by the NC, People's Democratic Party (PDP) and the Congress — have all been accused of misgovernance, corruption and lack of accountability. Three major policies pursued by successive governments in recent years have been the demand for autonomy (by NC) the 'healing touch' (PDP) and emphasis on cross-LoC interactions (Congress). Autonomy for J&K has been the main slogan of the NC, led by Farooq Abdullah, and now by his son, Omar Abdullah. In 2000, the government led by the NC passed a resolution in the J&K legislative assembly demanding autonomy. The union government, then led by the Bharatiya Janata Party (BJP), rejected the resolution without even discussing it. 'Healing touch' was the major political and social approach pursued by the PDP government, led by Mufti Mohammad Sayeed, from 2002 to 2005. It sought to provide good and humane governance. Ever since the outbreak of militancy, the state government has strengthened its police force, which now plays a significant role in countering militancy. The state police has a special counter-militancy unit — the Special Operations Group (SOG). The Congress government took numerous measures to improve the Cross-LoC interactions.

Non-State Actors (NSAs)

The armed NSAs are not homogeneous and are divided into various groups based on their objectives, orientation, beliefs and support — both internal and external. Broadly, these armed NSAs could be classified under two categories — militants and jihadis. The Hizbul Mujahideen is the main militant organisation, while Lashkar-e-Toiba the main jihadi group.

Hizbul Mujahideen

Hizbul Mujahideen, the principal militant group, fights for political objectives and its focus is limited to J&K. Widely perceived as an indigenous organisation, Hizbul is mostly comprised of and led by ethnic Kashmiris. The LeT and JeM, on the contrary, are led by Pakistanis, and their top leadership hails from Pakistan. Differences exist among scholars on the main objective of the Hizbul — some argue that it fights for an independent Kashmir, whereas others believe that it wants to annex J&K to Pakistan. However, the political nature of the organisation's objectives is proven beyond doubt; therefore it is classified as a militant and not as a jihadi group. Moreover, objective is limited to J&K and it does not seek the destruction of 'Hindu India', openly sought by some other jihadi organisations. Until now, Hizbul's operations were limited to J&K and there has been no single militant act outside the state. On the contrary, the Lashkar is known for its attacks outside J&K'.

Finally, the Hizbul, at least a section of it, has shown a willingness to pursue a political path to resolve the conflict. In July 2000, the Hizbul announced a unilateral ceasefire and entered into a dialogue with the union government. Abdul Majid Dar, who was later killed in an internal power struggle within the Hizbul, had stated that the outfit would co-operate in a peace process with the Indian government;[10] he was also quoted as saying, 'Our [Hizbul's] activities will lessen in proportion to both countries [India and Pakistan] giving up their rigid stand to solve the Kashmir problem in a realistic approach'.

Lashkar-e-Toiba

The LeT is the main important jihadi group fighting for pan-Islamic objectives. For the Lashkar, Kashmir is a means to achieve their broader objective of establishing their version of Islam, both in the subcontinent and outside it. They fight against the Indian security forces and also against those Kashmiris who do not agree with their religious views. A poster of Al Badr, one of the jihadi groups, claimed, 'We have left our country to fight for your freedom. But still you people feel no sense of gratitude. We urge you to stop helping the Kafirs [unbelievers]. After this, no one who does so will be spared. He who helps a Kafir is also a Kafir. If you still do not pay heed, Allah has given his soldiers enough strength to finish you as well as the Kafirs.'

---

[10] 'Hizb will Cooperate in Peace Initiative', *The Hindu*, 25 May 2001; 'Hizb to Halt Hostilities if India, Pak Act Realistic', *The Asian Age*, 4 June 2001; 'Hizb Rules out Role for Foreign Militants', *The Hindu*, 21 November 2001.

MAJOR TRENDS IN CONFLICT IN 2008

Among the numerous trends that one could identify in J&K during, three in particular are important. First, there has been a considerable overall decline in the level of violence in J&K, creating a domino effect on certain other issues. Second, at the political level, the regional fault-lines between Jammu and Kashmir have become very pronounced. Third, there are serious signs of a communal and tribal divide in parts of Jammu. In addition to these, in 2008, one could also witness some of the other trends either continuing or declining.

An Overall Decline in Violence

There was an overall decline in violence in the armed conflict in 2008; this decline was comprehensive and not limited merely to infiltration or terrorist attacks. Consider the following numbers, based on State police sources.

First, when compared to 2007, there has been a remarkable decline in violence — by 40 per cent. For the first time since the militancy started and violence became in a norm in the last two decades, the number of militancy-related incidents have come down below four digits, around 700 in 2008. Since 1991, violence related incidents always stood above 1,000. It has been declining considerably in the last few years; in 2007, it came down to 1,090, which further got reduced to 708 in 2008.[11] The significance of this number will be clear if one takes into account the cumulative violence figure in J&K since 1990. There have been over 67,000 incidents of militant violence, killing more than 21,000 militants, 16,600 civilians, and 5,200 security personnel. Besides, the J&K Police has seized about 12.5 tonnes of RDX and more than 31 tonnes of other explosives besides 6,000 grenades and recovered more than 30,000 AK rifles from terrorists.[12]

When compared to previous years, the number of militants operating in J&K has also come down considerably, a fact which can also be surmised from the decline in the number of militants killed.

---

[11] Kavita Suri, 'J&K Militancy Down for the First Time in 20 yrs', *Statesman*, 26 December 2008.

[12] According to data provided by the Jammu and Kashmir police headquarters in 2008.

According to the Jammu and Kashmir police statistics, in counter-terrorism operations across the state, 102 militants were eliminated, including some top-ranking commanders. In the Valley, while a total of 64 militants were killed, including 43 top commanders, the figure for Jammu was 38, including 24 commanders.[13]

A district-wise analysis of terrorist violence in 2008 brings to light interesting statistics. Baramulla, Trehgam, Handwara, Sopore, Bandipore, Srinagar, Pulwama, Awantipura, Shopiyan, Bijbehara, Anantnag, and Budgam in the Kashmir Valley and Mahore, Gool, Surankot, Kishtwar, Doda, and Thatri have been the traditional hotbeds of terrorist activities. In 2008, Sopore, Baramulla, Bandipore and Srinagar witnessed substantial violence, with sporadic violence seen in Kupwara, Handwara, Pulwama, Shopiyan, and Tral. Out of the 242 terrorists killed in 127 terror attacks, 90 per cent were accounted by Sopore, Baramulla, Bandipore, and Srinagar. One could clearly see a divide across the Pir Panjal.[14] South of this range, the traditional regions of militancy accounted for very few terror activities and resulting in only 43 incidents and 93 casualties.

The second major trend relating to violence, based on the above analysis is that armed conflict in J&K today has become regionalised within the State. One can safely conclude that in many districts in Kashmir, armed conflict has almost died down. Even within the Kashmir Valley, for example in south Kashmir, considered to be the bastion of Hizbul Mujhadeen, militancy has declined considerably. In particular, the twin districts of Anantnag and Pulwama in south Kashmir have always witnessed a high degree of terrorist violence; in 2008, there was virtually no violence in Budgam, Bijbehara and Anantnag. In the Jammu region, the twin districts of Rajouri and Poonch have been very peaceful, being witness to only a few violent incidents.[15] In Doda, Bhaderwah and Kishtwar regions too similarly, one could see a visible decline in militancy in 2008.[16]

Third, in 2008 there was a dramatic fall in the number of civilian casualties. For the first time, since militancy took root in the state,

---

[13] *Ibid.*
[14] Pir Panjal range of the Himalayas divide J&K, into two district regions — to the north lies the Kashmir Valley, and to the south lies Jammu, along with the districts of Doda, Ramban and Kishtwar.
[15] Interactions with military, paramilitary and police officials in these two regions.
[16] Interactions with security forces and other people, and personal observations.

the civilian death toll come down to two digits — 89 — the lowest in the last two decades. 2007 had seen 164 civilian deaths. Of course, it was in 1996 that J&K witnessed the highest number of civilian casualties; 1,413 people were killed that year when elections to the state assembly were conducted for first time in over six years. In the same period, between 2006 and 2008, the number of civilians killed in Kashmir were 335 and 218 in the Jammu region. In Kashmir, north and south Kashmir suffered 45 per cent of the deaths and Srinagar around 10 per cent. In Jammu region, Doda, Kishtwar suffered 60 per cent deaths while Gool, Mahore, Budhal had 40 per cent deaths.

Fourth, there has also been considerable decline in the number of militants operating in J&K. According to Kuldeep Khoda, Director General of Police, J&K, for the first time, the number of terrorists operating in the state has fallen below 1000. In Jammu and Kashmir, according to the police estimate, there are around 800 plus militants, amongst with 570 plus are considered to be local and the rest foreign.

Fifth, 2008 also witnessed the lowest number of political killings. Only three political leaders were assassinated this year, compared to 101 in 2002 and nine in 2007. The significance of this number will become clear if we take into account that the year also witnessed elections for the J&K State Legislative Assembly. During the previous elections in 2002, 48 political activists, including a minister, were killed by terrorists during election campaigning. In fact, when compared to the 2002 elections, there has been a decline of more than 80 per cent in terms of violence witnessed during the 2008 assembly elections.

Finally, perhaps for the first time since militancy broke out in the region, there was no complaint of 'custodial disappearance'. However, there was one case relating to custodial death that was registered in Shopian, in the Kashmir Valley, against the Rashtriya Rifles.

Return to a Political Process?

In 2008 elections took place, hinting at both state and society resorting to a political process rather than a militant approach. Elections to the State Assembly were organised in six phases in 2008 and are considered to have been free and fair. They were conducted smoothly, with no complaints or allegations of rigging, bogus polling and forcing people to vote in this or that way. In the previous elections, there were always complaints of the security forces pressurising the people to vote and the militants warning and threatening people against it.

The elections were truly remarkable because of the unexpected levels of participation — in terms of the number of people contesting and voting; there were 1,353 contestants for 87 assembly seats in J&K and 61 per cent of the people voted.

More importantly, the response of the people and political parties before, during and after the elections marks a significant change in approach. While the Hurriyat Conference gave a boycott call, it did not enforce it by resorting to a door-to-door campaign. Militant groups too did not attempt to sabotage the electoral process. As a result, there was no violence during or leading up to the polls. Two reasons could be identified for this; first, perhaps, the Hurriyat, buoyed by the amazing response to its call during the Amarnath Shrine Board Crisis, did not expect that, there would be such popular participation in the elections. The Hurriyat perhaps believed that a low voter turnout, with no violence, would be a clear indication to the international community that New Delhi's perspectives are completely wrong. A second reason possibly is that, the elections also took place during and after the Mumbai terrorist attacks October 2008; Pakistan was clearly under pressure, and perhaps did not want to encourage any more militant attacks in Kashmir during the elections.

Declining Local Recruitment

A significant trend in recent years, which was reflected during this year as well, has been the decline in recruitment of local youths by militant groups. This phenomenon could be observed all over J&K, irrespective of the different regions within. While there are no concrete numbers available to prove this point, interactions with security forces, surrendered militants and local populations substantiate this trend.

Militants groups are finding it difficult to get fresh recruits. The youth of almost all the major districts of Jammu and Kashmir are not joining the militant groups voluntarily as was seen in the initial years of militancy. Instead, hundreds of Kashmiri youth are increasingly joining the Indian army and the State police. During the peak period of militancy, from 1990 to 2005, security forces could not even dare think of a recruitment camp in Kashmir, not to talk of north Kashmir, the stronghold of terror groups. The army ventured to hold its first recruitment drive in 2005, when 1,126 people responded with 127 qualifying after the screening. But now there is an overwhelming response to army recruitment camps in Kashmir. In north Kashmir, while in 2005 over 2,300 youth had applied, the numbers rose to 2,900 in 2006–07. In 2008, in only one camp held in Kupwara, 1,100 youth applied. These increased numbers, especially during the last two years, are indicative of the reduced levels of violence and aspirations of the youth to join the army, whose perception has changed among the people.

Declining Popular Support to the Armed Conflict

Active local support to armed conflict has also declined. There is a visible change all over J&K; at the ground level, the ordinary population does not support violence and prefers a political settlement. This change in mindsets, though not uniform in its intensity all over J&K, is prevalent. For example, in Rajouri, Poonch and Doda regions, there is no support for the militant movement, either covert or overt; in Kashmir Valley, even today there is an element of support, which is clearly evident from the massive voter turnout in the J&K assembly elections of 2008.

There were no serious allegations against the security forces of using coercion to make people vote. Nor was there any serious threat from the militants of imposing a boycott call. The Election Commissioner in fact acknowledged that the higher voter turnout was due to the lack of a fear factor.

Hizbul's Continuing Decline

The 2008 edition of *Armed Conflicts in South Asia* considered the decline of Hizbul Mujahideen as a major trend in 2007. In 2008, this trend continued; Hizbul Mujahideen today is no more the most powerful militant group in the Kashmir Valley. Several reasons could be cited to explain this:[17] surrenders, criminalisation, fatigue and better counter-militancy efforts. Surrenders by the Hizbul Mujahdeen cadres continue;

---

[17] See D. Suba Chandran and Kavita Suri, 'J&K: From Militancy to Jihad?', in D. Suba Chandran and P.R. Chari (eds), *Armed Conflicts in South Asia 2008: Growing Violence* (New Delhi: Routledge, 2008).

in the past three years, most of the militants who have surrendered and given up arms belonged to the Hizbul Mujahideen. Besides, developmental funds, allocated for various projects in Kashmir Valley are pouring in and reaching militant hands; many Hizbul commanders have improved their financial conditions, in addition to being bribed by the intelligence agencies. For example, the railway project in Kashmir Valley, starting from Qazikund to Baramulla, has been of great monetary benefit to many Hizbul militants. Third, security forces today have much better intelligence, especially about the hideouts and the movement of Hizbul cadres. This has resulted in Hizbul facing the brunt of counter-militancy operations in the last two years. More Hizbul commanders have been eliminated as compared to the Lashkar or Jaish. However, the above decline in the Hizbul should not be read as a necessarily positive development; their decline has left a void which is today being filled by the Lashkar.

Renewal of Political Slogans Demanding Independence

The agitation over the issue of transfer of land to the Shri Amarnath Shrine Board (SASB) in May 2008 resulted in a full-blown violent movement that engulfed the entire state of Jammu and Kashmir in July–August and resulted in an increase in violence. Kashmiri separatists, who had been lying low in the first few months of the year finding no takers for their agendas,[18] got a boost from this as they tried to take maximum advantage of the situation which slowly and gradually seemed to be slipping out of their hands.

Many Kashmiri youths came out in protest; Srinagar and many district headquarters witnessed anti-India slogans and demands for *azadi*. Big protest demonstrations were held throughout the Valley against the government's order for transfer of land. The separatist leaders provided leadership to the agitation, which was principally motivated by an anti-Jammu sentiment, and divert it to a movement for self-determination and *azadi*. In this agitation many people lost their lives in clashes with the security forces.

---

[18] Balraj Puri, 'Lessons from the Jammu and Kashmir Elections', *Mainstream*, 26 January 2009.

CONFLICT MANAGEMENT

The following measures could be understood as part of conflict management in J&K in 2008. They can be broadly divided into internal and cross-LoC measures. Organising elections for the State Legislative Assembly was the biggest effort of 2008, followed by the management of a self-induced crisis relating to the transfer of land to the SASB. Across the LoC, India proceeded to further strengthen border fencing, alongside opening the same for trade for the first time in many decades.

Elections for the Legislative Assembly

In 2008 the union government went ahead with organising elections for the State Legislative Assembly in a politically charged atmosphere in Jammu and in Kashmir Valley, following tensions between the two regions over the transfer of land to the SASB.

Elections were organised for all 87 seats; as mentioned earlier, there was 61 per cent polling, which produced the following results (see Table 5.1): the NC was able to retain its 2002 position by winning 28 seats, while the PDP performed better by securing three more seats than what it achieved in 2002. The Congress lost three seats compared to its previous tally, but still managed to win 17 seats. The BJP succeeded in winning 11 seats; compared to 2002, when it secured only one seat, its performance was considerably better.

Table 5.1: Party Performance in 2008 State Legislative Assembly Elections

	Valley(46)		Kargil and Leh(04)		Doda, Ramban and Kishtwar(06)		Jammu(24)		Rajouri and Poonch(07)	
NC	20	19	02	01	01	03	02	02	03	05
PDP	19	16	Nil	Nil	Nil	Nil	Nil	Nil	02	Nil
Cong	04	04	01	Nil	05	01	06	12	02	01
BJP	Nil	Nil	Nil	Nil	Nil	Nil	11	01	Nil	Nil
NPP	Nil	Nil	Nil	Nil	Nil	Nil	03	04	Nil	Nil
CPM	01	02	Nil	Nil	Nil	Nil	Nil	Nil	Nil	Nil
Others	02	05	01	03	Nil	02	02	05	Nil	Nil

Source: Praveen Swami, 'Rajouri Witnesses Taliban-type Terror as the Islamic Right Launches its Burkha Campaign', *Frontline*, 20(1), 2003, pp. 18–21.

One important issue that needs to be analysed further for its implications relates to the performance of the PDP and BJP, in terms of where they secured their seats. Most of the seats that the PDP was able to win were from Kashmir Valley, while all of what the BJP won came from Jammu — hinting not only at a regional, but also a communal divide.

An important positive result of the elections has been in the role of governance. The Congress performed better in those regions where there was better governance. During the previous Congress government Chief Minister Ghulam Nabi Azad succeeded in developing the infrastructure in the Doda–Kishtwar–Bhaderwah belt, which was translated into the Congress winning five out of the six seats from this region. South Kashmir also witnessed the same trend; owing to better administration of this region, the PDP was able to perform better here. Out of the 21 seats in the districts of Budgam, Pulwama, Sophian and Anantnag in South Kashmir, the PDP was able to win 14. In the border districts of Jammu, wherever, the previous Congress legislators have performed badly in terms of improving the governance, they were wiped out during this election.

Cross-LoC Fencing

The Indian Army sincerely believes that fencing the LoC can arrest infiltration. The army has nearly completed the process and is now in the process of upgrading it. An Anti Infiltration Observation System (AIOS) is part of this process. Since the beginning of its construction in 2003, fencing has undergone substantial design changes, based on experience, in terms of construction and maintenance over mountains, river beds and streams, snow-capped summits, etc. According to the Army, it is the AIOS that has been mainly responsible for the substantial decline in infiltration.[19] The army is in the process of further expanding this initiative, in terms of installing lighting, sensors and other related high-tech equipments.

Unfortunately, fencing has not been able to completely arrest cross-border infiltration, though it has considerably reduced it. Many security officials of the military and paramilitary forces agree that fencing

---

[19] Interactions with Indian Army personnel along the LoC.

can only reduce infiltration and cannot stop it.[20] Despite fencing, militants continue to cross the LoC, using different techniques, such as rubber ladders and, of late, a chemical powder which is being used to melt the LoC fence.

Cross-LoC Trade

Another major initiative that the Government of India undertook in 2008 was related to the opening of the LoC, allowing trucks to ply between the two parts of Kashmir. Ever since the LoC was opened for the movement of divided families in the Poonch and Uri sectors, there has a huge expectation from both sides that the LoC will be opened for trade as well.

Although cross-LoC trade has started, both countries have a long way to go to make this exercise fruitful. Traders from both sides are upset with the trade basket, which is limited to less than 40 items. Second, there were huge expectations, underscored by an emotional upsurge, regarding the opening of the LoC for trade; however, neither the state nor the traders had done any homework. On both sides of the LoC, many had simply assumed that trade between two parts of Kashmir will greatly benefit people on both sides. There was little or no understanding of the size of the markets and the nature of goods needed in Mirpur and Muzaffarabad among the traders of Jammu and Kashmir. Third, for political reasons, the traders did not want to use an international currency to trade. Especially in Kashmir Valley, they feared that any use of an international currency would create the impression that the trade was taking place between two countries and not two parts of Kashmir.

CONCLUSIONS

Lessons Not Learnt

New Delhi should understand two important issues — a decline in militancy does not mean that Pakistan has changed its strategy of supporting militancy to achieve its objectives in Kashmir. One should

---

[20] Interviews with military and paramilitary officials.

remain cautious and try and predict what is likely to be Pakistan's strategy in the changed atmosphere and how India can achieve its objectives. The parameters of terrorism, based on the number of infiltration bids, terrorists killed and figures regarding their presence, have shown a remarkable decline. However, it is pertinent to individually map the prevalence or absence of terrorism in all the relevant districts. The frame of vision related to the security situation that is based on such empirical data needs to be expanded to also include inherent and intangible threats. According to Army Chief General Deepak Kapoor, at least 300 militants are waiting to cross over into J&K, and there are 30–40 militant training camps still active in P. K. He believes that the LeT was attempting the biggest-ever push of around 300 terrorists over the LoC into India. The J&K police chief Kuldeep Khoda believes there are about 700 to 800 militants operating in the State, with '40 per cent of them (being) foreigners'.

Nor should New Delhi understand the popular participation seen in the 2008 elections as a yardstick to be used to measure the freedom sentiments of Kashmiris in Valley. The elections produced curious results: PDP's political base today is in the Valley and the BJP's is in Jammu. How will these two political parties chart out their programmes in the next few years? Will the PDP align itself with the Hurriyat in the Valley? And will the BJP align more with the Hindutva forces in Jammu? New Delhi needs to take into account the changed atmosphere after the J&K elections, Mumbai 2008 and the consequent breakdown in the Indo-Pak peace process. There is clearly a need to infuse the political process with some concrete proposals at this stage.

Cross-LoC movement is likely to drag on slowly, in terms of movement of people and goods, if the focus is not enlarged. A good initiative is thus likely to go waste, unless steps are taken to expand the nature of engagement and enlarge the stakeholder group. Currently, only the divided families can travel, that too only in Jammu and Kashmir sectors. It does not include those, who don't have families on the other side; most of the PoK refugees, who happen to be Hindus, who have migrated completely from the other side do not have relatives to prove. As a result, this movement primarily addresses one community. Nor are the divided families of Kargil and Gilgit allowed to cross. Cross-LoC trade is another bold initiative, which is likely to drag unless the basket of goods and transactions is made bigger. New Delhi should ensure that cross-LoC trade in the Valley does not end up like trade in Nathu La between India and Pakistan.

Let the J&K Police Lead[21]

Currently, security in J&K is being handled by the army, the paramilitary forces and J&K police. They work under the union Home and Defence Ministries and the state government. There are also several intelligence organisations, including the Intelligence Bureau (IB) and Research and Analysis Wing (RAW). While in theory these forces and intelligence organisations work together, in reality there are significant differences in their attitudes, style of functioning, and the extent of local support they receive. Undoubtedly, the J&K police enjoys more support than the others, although its Special Operations Group evokes the same negative feelings as the Rashtriya Rifles.

Second, the J&K police, being 'locals', are better equipped and suited to collecting intelligence. Filtering and analysing the inputs received can be handled better by the local police than the federal organisations. Often, the intelligence received by the military and paramilitary organisations is false or deliberately planted. Subsequent follow-up actions only end up worsening the situation instead of addressing it, thus damaging the state. Popular local reactions against high-handed operations are invariably exploited by anti-national and separatist forces. The local police are in a better position to handle this situation, thereby addressing another important issue that can be a cause for great embarrassment both at the national and international level, i.e., human rights violations. Incidentally, most cases of human rights violations involve the military and paramilitary forces, and not the local police.

Restart the Round Table Conferences and Make them Meaningful

In 2006–07, the Prime Minister undertook a serious initiative relating to the establishment of five Working Groups and organising three Round Table Conferences. It was a good effort, but was badly implemented. Unfortunately, the local population, in all three regions, perceived it to be meaningless and an eyewash.

With the Manmohan Singh-led government winning the parliamentary elections with substantial numbers, perhaps this is the time to restart the Round Table Conferences (RTC), and make Working

---

[21] The same suggestion was been given in the previous edition as well.

Groups more meaningful by expanding their scope and participation. Many groups, who perceive themselves as being direct and indirect victims of the conflict, have been left out of this process. For example, the PoK refugees, people of Kargil and Leh, the economic community and women feel that there should be adequate representation to include them and all other shades of opinion. Outside these groups which are willing to participate are the separatists, led by the two factions of the All Parties Hurriyat Conference (APHC) that have steadfastly refused to take part in this process. The moderate section of the Hurriyat, led by Mirwaiz Farooq, has laid down some preconditions before they take part in any process initiated by New Delhi. Unfortunately, there are groups that are willing to participate but have not been included in the process, and feel that the union government is more interested in roping in those sections that have been refusing to participate. If they are not willing to join the main process, there could be a separate process to address their concerns. On the other hand, those groups that are willing to take part should be included because their inputs will be significant.

A Debate on Demilitarisation

Demilitarisation was discussed in last year's issue as well. The ruling NC, opposition PDP and the separatist PDP have been demanding demilitarisation. Till a few years back, perhaps the situation was such that it did not warrant such an attempt. Is the atmosphere today better than what it was in 2004 or 2005?

Can India keep the military and paramilitary forces in Kashmir indefinitely? Is it in the interest of the Indian nation and the future of Kashmir? Is it in the interest of the military and paramilitary forces to remain deployed in counter-insurgency operations over extended periods of time? In the last edition, it was concluded that the present time may not be ripe to initiate demilitarisation and that it should be linked to positive developments in the ground situation. Today, after a successful election in 2008, perhaps the time is ripe to initiate a discussion on it.

6

Left-Wing Extremism in India: The Rule of the Maoists

Devyani Srivastava

A BRIEF HISTORY

Since its outbreak in March 1967 in Naxalbari village in West Bengal, the Maoist insurgency — also known as left wing extremism, Naxalite movement and people's war — has embodied a number of armed struggles that are striving for equitable socio-economic development. The formation of the Communist Party of India (Maoist) in September 2004 transformed the movement into an organised and co-ordinated insurgency. The security challenge posed by the insurgency, declared as the 'biggest internal security challenge' by Prime Minister Manmohan Singh, has spread from one state when it started, to at least 13 states now. Despite the fact that the insurgency has failed to achieve its broad goals, it continues to pose a security threat and is a challenge to the Indian state, enjoying support both among the masses and the intelligentsia.

The first phase[1] of the Naxal movement, starting with its outbreak in Naxalbari[2] was marked by the intellectual commitment of leaders like Charu Mazumdar, Kanu Sanyal and Jangal Santhal. Deeply inspired by the communist revolution in China and drawing lessons from the failure of earlier peasant uprisings, the revolutionary group of the

---

[1] The study of the movement under three phases has been suggested for conceptual clarity only, with periods of overlap between these phases as the movement evolved.

[2] Naxalbari is a village in Darjeeling district, in the State of West Bengal, India. The incident that precipitated the armed peasant struggle took place in Naxalbari in March 1967 when three share-croppers, with support from the Communist Party of India (Marxist) or CPI(M), seized the entire stock of 300 mds of paddy from the landlord's granary.

CPI(M), under the guidance of Mazumdar, sought to import Mao's principles of revolutionary armed struggles like area-wise seizure of political power in India. Through peasant committees, a number of activities like seizure of grains and paddy, land and weapons from landlords and plantation owners, ambushing of the 'reactionary' troops and the police, and attacks on local tyrants were carried out throughout West Bengal. Expectedly, the movement received the full backing of the Communist Party of China in terms of guidance, financial support and training of the leadership; however, the movement petered out by the early 1970s with the arrest and death of Charu Mazumdar in July 1972. Apart from strong police action, another factor held responsible for its decline is the deviation of its leaders from the classic revolutionary path, with an overemphasis on the annihilation of class enemies without due attention being paid to mass activity and the deliberate use of primitive weapons easily available to the peasants. Mazumdar was also accused of setting himself as the oracle of the Indian revolution and elevating himself above the party.[3] The Naxalite movement, therefore, remained leadership-centric instead of focusing on building party discipline, training guerilla squads or even addressing systemic problems as land reforms and such.

The second phase of the movement, starting in 1980, witnessed a more organised armed struggle across several states in Central India, despite being led by splinter Naxalite groups. The most prominent were the People's War Group (PWG), formed in April 1980 in Andhra Pradesh under the leadership of Kondapalli Seetharamaiah, and the Maoist Communist Centre (MCC), formed in 1975 in Bihar, which became a formidable force in the late 1980s under Pramod Mishra and Sanjay Dusadh. Rectifying the shortcomings of the first phase, these two groups discarded the policy of total annihilation of class enemies and considered mass mobilisation to be a prerequisite for any armed action, while focusing on strengthening their organisational network and upgrading their weaponry. The government's response once again emphasised police action, while the movement itself fell victim to internal rifts driven partly by opposing ideological considerations and partly by power struggles. Seetharamaiah was also accused of authoritarianism, suggesting the failure of the movement yet again in being able to rise above the leadership.

[3] Prakash Singh, *The Naxalite Movement in India* (New Delhi: Rupa, 2006), p. 102.

The current phase of the Naxal movement commenced with the holding of the Ninth Congress of the People's War in 2001 and received an impetus with the merger of the Communist Party of India (Marxist-Leninist), the PWG and the MCC, forming the united Communist Party of India (Maoist) (CPI [Maoist]) on 21 September 2004 following years of negotiation. The current phase is marked by two qualitative changes, military and political. The movement that earlier used local weapons, small groups and isolated attacks is today 'characterised by growing militarisation, superior army-style organisation, better trained cadres, attacks on large targets through large-scale frontal assaults, better co-ordination and possible external links'.[4] In political terms, the movement has altered its path from 'revolutionary democratic' activities to broad-based 'peoples democratic' mass agitations.[5] With the formation of the CPI (Maoist), the Maoists were ready to expand their struggle into newer areas and strengthen their protracted armed struggle.

THE PRINCIPAL ACTORS

CPI (Maoist)

Although there are at least 28 Maoist insurgent groups operating in India, the CPI (Maoist) is the most powerful and lethal, and has been leading the Maoist insurgency spread across 159 districts in 13 states of India. The aim of the CPI (Maoist) group is to establish a contiguous revolutionary zone stretching from Nepal to Bihar to Andhra Pradesh and beyond. While pursuing their goal of people's democracy, the ultimate goal of the CPI (Maoist) group is to seize power through a protracted armed struggle. The General Secretary of the PWG's Central Organising Committee, Muppala Laxman Rao *alias* Ganapati, is the General Secretary of the new party. The party's organisational structure remains the same, with a Central Committee, followed by Zonal/Regional Committees, State Committees, District Committees,

---

[4] 'Concluding Remarks at the 2nd Meeting of the Standing Committee of Chief Ministers on Naxalism', Press Information Bureau, 13 April 2006, http://pib.nic.in/release/rel_print_page.asp?relid=17128 (accessed on 20 March 2009).
[5] Venkitesh Ramakrishnan, 'Naxal terror', *Frontline*, 24(18), 8–21 September 2007, p. 5.

Divisions and Squads. At present, there are at least five Regional Bureaus, 13 state Committees, two Special Area Committees and three Special Zonal Committees in the country.[6]

Over four years of functioning the party has displayed great organisational unity and capability. A case in point is the 9th Unity Congress of the party held in the forests of Dandakaranya in early 2007 in complete secrecy despite a high security alert of the state. Held after 36 years, the Congress further consolidated the organisational unity and ability of the party to lead the struggle. Last year, however, the involvement of the Maoists in the killing of Laxamanananda Saraswati in Orissa is reported to have been condemned by the Central Committee, suggesting that the southern Orissa division of the CPI (Maoist) might have taken this step without consulting the central leaders.[7] Such reports, if true, could affect the organisational unity of the party in the days to follow.

Government Actors

Government actors include the central government, the state governments, police forces and the central paramilitary forces. With law and order being a state subject, the central government carries out its task of harmonising and co-ordinating the various strategies of the states through its committees, including the Task Force on Naxalism set up in October 2004, the Standing Committee of the Chief Ministers of the Naxal-affected states set up in April 2005, the Empowered Group of Ministers (EGoM) set up in September 2006, headed by the Home Minister, which includes select Union Ministers and Chief Ministers of Naxal-affected states; and the Naxal Management Division created in October 2006 to 'monitor the Naxal situation and counter-measures being taken by the affected States'.[8] At the state level, individual states have established their respective cells for dealing with the Naxalite problem. Chhattisgarh, for instance, set up a Unified Command Structure in February 2008, headed by the Chief Minister and comprising

---

[6] Annexure III, 'Organisational Hierarchy: Communist Party of India (Maoist)', in P.V. Ramana (ed.), *The Naxal Challenge: Causes, Linkages, and Policy Options* (Delhi: Dorling Kindersley, 2008), p. 198.

[7] 'Rifts among Orissa Maoists?', *The Times of India*, 21 January 2009.

[8] http://mha.nic.in/uniquepage.asp?Id_pk=277 (accessed on 20 March 2009).

both central and state officials, to address the Naxal problem. The Anti-Naxal Operation Cell of the Maharashtra Police is responsible for monitoring Maoist activity and carrying out anti-Naxal operations. In addition, the states are assisted in their fight by 36 battalions of central paramilitary forces (Andhra Pradesh [AP]–4; Bihar–4; Chhattisgarh–16 +1; Jharkhand–6; Orissa–4; and West Bengal–1) and 29 India Reserve Battalions sanctioned for the states, out of which 15 have been raised so far (AP–6; Bihar–2; Chhattisgarh–4; Jharkhand–1; Orissa–1; and West Bengal–1).[9]

Salwa Judum

Since its formation in June 2005 in Dantewada district of Chhattisgarh, the controversial anti-Naxal Salwa Judum campaign, premised on arming the tribals to fight against the Naxalites, has resulted in a spurt of violence in the southern belt of Chhattisgarh. Although the campaign was officially suspended in April 2006, the relief camps created as part of the campaign to separate the civilian population from the Naxalites continue to exist with close to 47,000 people inhabiting these camps. Since its inception, the campaign has received the full backing of the state that refers to it as a people's movement even while it came under severe criticism by human rights organisations for its gross violations of human rights and excesses committed against the tribals. Quashing the claims of the government, the Supreme Court, responding to a petition filed by a group of activists against the campaign, expressed its disapproval of the Salwa Judum and called for an independent inquiry into its formation and condition of the camps. The National Human Rights Commission (NHRC) investigated the activities of the Salwa Judum and found many atrocities being committed under the guise of countering Naxals. Despite this clear stand of the Supreme Court, P. Chidambaram, on taking over as Home Minister, has upheld the role of Special Police Officers, select armed members of the campaign trained in guerilla warfare, in fighting Naxalism, and approved their appointment 'wherever required'. It is reported that the Orissa government has already approved a similar

---

[9] Status Paper on Internal Security Situation as on 1 September 2008, Ministry of Home Affairs, Government of India, p. 38.

scheme for deploying 2,000 armed tribal youths in the age group 18–25 as Special Police Officers in five of its Maoist-infested districts to fight the Naxals.[10] They would be appointed on a contractual basis for three years and would undergo training in arms like the regular police force.

CONFLICT IN 2008: MAJOR TRENDS

The year 2008 reflected a further consolidation of the Maoist insurgency across the Indian heartland. Central to the continuing growth of the Maoists is their effective implementation of a revolutionary strategy which broadly encompasses three stages: the organisation stage, which focuses on mobilising public support through front organisations and propaganda work around exploitative structures of society; the guerilla warfare stage, in which the Maoists engage the state in a fight over control for a particular area; and the mobile warfare stage, where the revolutionaries have defeated the state and established their complete control.[11] Using this standard, the organisation stage can be said to be proceeding in most districts of Jharkhand, Bihar, Orissa, Chhattisgarh, the eastern districts of Maharashtra; the guerilla warfare stage prevails over at least three districts of Chhattisgarh, namely Bastar, Dantewada and Kanker, the border districts of Bihar–Jharkhand including Gaya, Nawada, Jamui, Rohtas and Aurangabad in Bihar and Chatra, Hazaribagh, Palamu districts in Jharkhand, Gadchiroli and Gondia districts in Maharashtra and the Jharkhand–Orissa border areas (see Table 6.1). There are no confirmed reports on the prevalence of the mobile warfare stage of the Maoists. With the use of different strategies in different areas, based on an understanding of the social conditions, coupled with the state's response, the Maoists have been able to advance their revolution both politically and militarily.

---

[10] 'Orissa to Launch its Own Salwa Judum to Fight Naxals', *Indian Express*, 31 October 2008.

[11] K. Srinivas Reddy, 'Revolutionary and Counter-Revolutionary Strategies of the Naxalites and the State', in P.V. Ramana (ed.), *The Naxal Challenges: Causes, Linkages and Policy Options*, p. 92.

Table 6.1: State-Wise Details of Maoist Violence and Activity, 2008

	Casualties[12]				Districts affected[13]	No. of police stations affected (2003–07)[14]
	Security Forces	Civilians	Naxals	Total		
AP	1	28	37	66	8	1635
Bihar	21	35	15	71	19	834
Chhattisgarh	67	35	66	168	11	307
Jharkhand	39	74	50	163	23	310
Orissa	76	24	32	132	22	464
Karnataka	1	3	3	7	–	–
Uttar Pradesh	0	0	2	2	–	1432
Maharashtra	5	2	7	14	8	923
Tamil Nadu	0	0	1	1	–	–
West Bengal	4	19	1	24	–	411
Total	214	220	214	648	–	–

Source: Compiled by author based on data sourced from South Asia Terrorism Portal (www.satp.org) and the Ministry of Home Affairs, Government of India.

Assessment of Geographical Spread

The three southern districts of Chhattisgarh in the guerilla warfare stage continue to be dominated by intense violence unleashed by both the Maoists and the state. These areas, which went through the organisation phase through the 1990s, entered the guerilla warfare stage with the launch of the Salwa Judum campaign in June 2005. Indiscriminate killings, torture of innocents, and massive displacement followed suit. However, last year the state recorded a dip in violence by 52 per cent as compared to 2007, despite accounting for the highest casualty rate among the states. This dip in violence is primarily due to the wanton violence following the launch of Salwa Judum by both the state and the Maoists being replaced by more specific and

---

[12] 'Fatalities in Left Wing Extremism', Maoist Insurgency, Data Sheets, South Asia Terrorism Portal, http://www.satp.org/satporgtp/countries/india/maoist/data_sheets/fatalitiesnaxal.htm

[13] 'Maoist Insurgency Assessments', Maoist Insurgency, South Asia Terrorism Portal, http://www.satp.org/satporgtp/countries/india/maoist/Assessment/index.htm

[14] Naxal Management Division, Ministry of Home Affairs, Government of India.

targeted attacks. With the suspension of the campaign in 2006 by the state government, the heavy deployment of the Central Paramilitary Forces (CPMF) in Chhattisgarh (16 battalions) and the setting up of a Unified Command Structure headed by the Chief Minister to fight the Maoists, over the past two years the state has focused on combing operations in the jungles of Bastar and Dantewada. The Maoists have responded by intensifying their attacks on the security forces through landmine blasts, ambushes and firing. The high casualty rates among both the security forces and the Maoists reflects the intensity of the conflict. Owing to the densely forested terrain being used as a training ground by the Maoists and the concentration of minerals providing a source of explosives (primarily through theft), the conflict is unlikely to diminish in these areas with the Maoists displaying their intent and ability to engage the Indian state in a pitched battle. Low voter turnout in Naxal-affected constituencies like Dantewada during the state assembly elections despite less violence, and the continuing attacks on mining activities are a further indication of the dominance of these rebels in the region.

The Naxal conflict in Bihar and Jharkhand remained intense during 2008 with the Maoists using terror to spread fear and intimidation among the population, along with guerilla warfare strategies. A series of killings — of suspected police informers, local panchayat leaders, attacks on construction works/companies by the Maoists, encounters between security forces and extremists and factional clashes between various Naxal groups have created a situation where violence reigns supreme. Dominated by the scheduled castes and governed by weak administrations, the two states constitute an important social base for the Maoists. By disrupting the smooth functioning of the administration, the Maoists are trying to create a political vacuum that can then be filled by them. In addition, the two states also provide a large percentage of the Maoists revenue through levies and extortion that have become a menace. According to reports, Bihar itself provides at least Rs 300 million annually. The increasing criminalisation of the Maoists in the State, however, has not only created several splinter caste-based extremists groups, but also stripped the rebels of their ideological appeal. These factors, together with the strengthening of state capacities, can play a crucial role in containing the Maoists.[15]

---

[15] Satish Kumar, 'Changing Face of the Naxalites in Bihar: From Homelessness to Real Estates', Article No. 2608, Institute of Peace and Conflict Studies (IPCS), 1 July 2008.

The most significant development in 2008 was the graduation of Orissa from the mass mobilisation stage to the guerilla warfare stage with a 47 per cent increase in violence. The transformation, though intense, was not surprising given the gradual consolidation of Maoists in the state around issues like the agitation against industrial projects, oppression of the tribes and forest-dwellers mainly in the southern districts, and the revenue derived from ganja cultivation. From sporadic incidents of violence, mostly in Orissa's border districts, the state witnessed the most daring attacks last year against the security forces, including in hitherto peaceful districts like Nayagarh. While the growth in violence has been attributed to the heavy influx of Maoists from the bordering districts of Andhra Pradesh and Chhattisgarh, the role of Sabyasachi Panda, the secretary of the Maoist Orissa committee, must not be overlooked. The brutal Nayagarh attack for instance is believed to have been masterminded by him. Another issue, which emerged as a rallying point for the Maoists under Panda, was the alleged campaign for conversion to Hinduism being carried out by the Rashtriya Swayamsevak Sangh, Bajrang Dal and Vishwa Hindu Parishad leaders in the Kandhamal district of Orissa, resulting in the murder of Saraswati Lakshmanda in August 2008. The communal riots that followed the assassination resulted in the death of at least 37 Christians. Although the Maoists claim to have taken this step to protect the rights of the Adivasis and Dalits, Panda's role in the killing of Saraswati has come under criticism both from the Maoists leaders and other sympathisers for provoking large-scale violence against Christians. While the local population remains sympathetic to the Maoists, who have a base in the district, it remains to be seen how this development will impact the future course of the movement in the state.

In the state of Andhra Pradesh the Maoist decline continued further with only eight of the state's 25 districts recording Naxal activity during the year. Despite sporadic incidents of attacks by Maoists, the state recorded a 9 per cent decline in violence compared to last year with the death of only a single policeman. Moreover, sustained police operations resulted in the further neutralisation of at least 621 cadres, including some of their leaders and commanders.[16] However, recent reports have pointed to an increase in Maoist activity in the Telangana districts of Andhra Pradesh, reported to be in preparation

---

[16] Andhra Pradesh Assessment 2009, Maoist Insurgency, South Asia Terrorism Portal, http://www.satp.org/satporgtp/countries/india/maoist/Assessment/2009/andhra.htm

for the upcoming general and state elections. One issue of concern among the police force is that of redeployment of cadres from Orissa and Chhattisgarh, particularly during election time. According to reports, at least three Maoist guerilla platoons are believed to be moving around in the forest areas of Karimnagar, Khammam and Visakhapatnam. Moreover, reports also indicate a Maoist recruitment drive in Visakhapatnam district. In light of these developments, the possibility of a revival of Maoist activity in the state cannot be ignored.

Other States affected by the Maoist insurgency, including Maharashtra, Uttar Pradesh, West Bengal and Karnataka, witnessed varying degrees of conflict last year. In Maharashtra, despite the sustained counter-Naxal operations in the state, the eastern districts of Gadchiroli, Gondia and Chandrapur witnessed a further intensification of mobilisation activities by the Maoists, apparent through recruitment drives and expansion of front organisations. In addition, the Maoists also used the tactic of terrorising people through a series of killings of suspected police informers and Naxals who had surrendered. With poor human development indices, caste divisions, forest terrain, loopholes in the government's measures (low level of rehabilitation of the surrendered Naxals, for instance) and the inflow of cadres from neighbouring areas in Chhattisgarh and Andhra Pradesh that are witnessing intense counter-Naxal operations, the conflict in these areas is likely to intensify in 2009. In West Bengal, the Maoists are rallying their struggle against the dominance of the left parties — CPI (M) and CPI (ML) — that are labelled fascist parties. A series of killings of Marxist leaders was carried out last year to achieve this purpose. The end of the year saw an endorsement by the Maoists of the tribal agitation in the Lalgarh area of West Midnapore district against police atrocities, which could provide a platform for the Maoists to strengthen their mass activity in the state. A number of arrests of Maoists along with seizure of explosives and weapons in the eastern districts of Uttar Pradesh, mainly Sonebhadra and Chandauli, indicates the presence of the Maoists in these areas for shelter. Maoist activity was also noticed in four coastal districts of Karnataka namely Chikmagalur, Mangalore, Udupi, and Shimoga.

Violence Against Security Forces

The main tactic of the armed struggle by the Maoists has been to attack security forces, including police stations and the police or the paramilitary patrol teams. According to the Ministry of Home Affairs

(MHA) data given below (Figure 6.1), the casualties among the security forces have registered a dramatic increase in the past few years. Last year, the attacks on security forces went up dramatically — in Orissa by approximately 35 per cent, and in Jharkhand by 16 per cent. A notable development in the past two years has been that the fatalities of security forces exceed that of the Maoist extremists, reversing the trend in the first two years of the CPI (Maoist) operation (2005–06). With the heavy deployment of security forces in Naxal-affected areas and the intensification of combing operations, the security forces are increasingly coming under Maoist attack. The other equally important reason is the use of new tactics by the Maoists in targeting the security forces, as demonstrated in the attack carried out on a motor launch carrying 66 policemen in a water reservoir in the Malkangiri district of Orissa killing 34 men on 29 June 2008. The Maoists have reportedly raised a Boat Wing to facilitate faster movement of their cadres and weapons in this region. This reflects clearly the edge that the Maoists possess over the state in guerilla warfare.

The Maoists have continued to effectively use the method of swarming attacks to target security forces, be it in Bihar, Orissa, Jharkhand or Chhattisgarh, apart from ambushes and gunfire during encounters. Landmine blasts too have become a frequently used method of attacking security forces. In a massive seizure, the Jharkhand police recovered as many as 80 landmines from a 1.5–2 km stretch in Bokaro

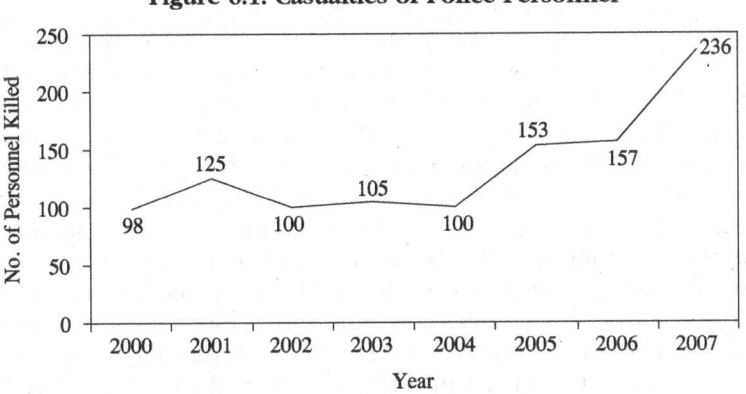

Figure 6.1: Casualties of Police Personnel

Source: 'Trends of Overall Naxal Violence', Status Paper on Internal Security Situation as on 1 September 2008, Ministry of Home Affairs, Government of India, New Delhi, p. 25.

district in April. In Orissa, the use of anti-landmine vehicles by the Special Operation Group (SOG) proved ineffective in preventing landmine blasts on 16 July that killed 17 security personnel.

It has been noticed that there is a high probability of security forces being attacked while on their return from a combing operation. The meticulous planning and execution of these attacks gives the impression that the rebel group had prior information about the operations. After any major ambush, the Maoists issue warnings to the government against taking repressive action against the people and threaten to step up attacks on the police. Notably, the Balimela attack of 29 June in Orissa had forced the state into intensifying its combing operations, which was followed by a landmine attack in Malkangiri district in Orissa that killed 15 police personnel. This reflects the aim of the Maoists to reinforce their success in counter-offensive operations against security forces, instead of maintaining the status quo. Another objective for attacking police stations and police patrol teams is to get hold of their weaponry. Many of the attacks were accompanied by incidents of looting arms and ammunition, the most daring being the Nayagarh attack in Orissa. The railway guards in particular are frequently targeted for this purpose.

Attacking Development Projects and Infrastructure

In a bid to disrupt public life and undermine the writ of the state administration, the Maoists continued to target public infrastructure, including railway tracks, construction companies, telecommunication and power transmission centres. In many such attacks, a large group of Maoists raided project sites and threatened the workers to stop work. According to one estimate, 2008 witnessed the largest number of attacks on communication towers.[17] While Bihar and Jharkhand witnessed the highest number of attacks on the railways, Chhattisgarh witnessed some daring attacks on communication towers. In Khammam district of Andhra Pradesh, Maoists reportedly imposed a ban on the use of mobile phones and used coercive means to take away mobile phones in the Bhadrachalam division. The Maoists also used their trademark method of strikes and bandhs to disrupt life. However, these remained localised in 2008, as opposed to the economic

[17] P.V. Ramana, 'Maoists Attack on Infrastructure', *IDSA Strategic Comments*, 20 February 2009.

blockades imposed by the Maoists across various states in the past two years.

Violence Against Civilians

In a bid to further consolidate their position, the Maoists continued to target civilians suspected to be 'exploiters' and 'state agents', including suspected police informers, traders, local political leaders and government officials. Such attacks tend to be very brutal and are concentrated in areas with a heavy presence of security forces, and are intended to deter people from any resistance to the Maoist authority. Apart from killings, extortion demands and threats constitute another form of terrorising people, particularly local contractors and businessmen. This problem is particularly acute in Jharkhand where the contractors are reportedly paying as much as 30 per cent of the total estimated value of their job as their levy. According to police statements, the Maoists set a target for earning Rs 1,125 crore in 2008, a 25 per cent increase from 2007, when they collected Rs 1,000 crore. Notably, apart from Bihar, Jharkhand and Chhattisgarh, the other states contributing to this fund-raising were Tamil Nadu, Karnataka and Maharashtra.

Elections in the Maoist Heartland

The state assembly elections held in Chhattisgarh in November last year clearly demonstrated the sway of the Maoists in its southern belt. For one, Naxal violence marred the campaigning of many leaders, resulting in the death of at least 10 security personnel and three political activists. In addition, abortive albeit spectacular strikes carried out by the Maoists including one against the chopper of a BJP parliamentarian in Antagarh assembly constituency in Kanker district, and another on the vehicle of former Chief Minister, Ajit Jogi, in Bilaspur district, further displayed their militant capabilities. Second, the voter turnout in two heavily affected assembly constituencies of Dantewada district, Bijapur and Konta, remained very low at 29 and 43 per cent respectively, as compared to the state's average of 70.66 per cent.[18] The low voter turnout was partly due to the Maoists

---

[18] Past Elections, 2008, Chhattisgarh. Election Commission of India, Government of India, available at http://eci.nic.in/StatisticalReports/ElectionStatistics.asp

boycott, and partly because at least 1 lakh refugees from the area have fled to neighbouring Andhra Pradesh to escape the atrocities of the Salwa Judum.[19] Relating to this is the defeat of Mahendra Karma, the Congress MLA from Dantewada for ten years, who is also associated with being at the forefront of the Salwa Judum movement. This punctures the claims of the BJP government that was re-elected in touting their victory as a vindication of the Salwa Judum campaign and its counter-Naxal policies. Also, the fact that many affected by the Salwa Judum were unable to cast their votes because of their escape to neighbouring states renders any assessment of the verdict in favour of the campaign as untenable. Moreover, the electoral politics of the state is such that the three Naxal-affected districts of Bastar, Dantewada and Kanker contribute only 12 out of 90 seats in the Legislative Assembly and do not play a major role in the elections. This is further proven by the fact that issues affecting the tribal population in these districts include land displacement and forest mismanagement, were not raised during campaigning by any party.

Operational Capabilities

The main source of funding for the Maoists remain abductions, extortions and looting. The arms and ammunition used by them, as evident during a number of seizures, range from RDX, cable wires, gelatine sticks, detonators, country-made weapons, INSAS rifles, AK-47s, SLR and improvised explosive devices. As per reports, the maximum yield in terms of ammunition and explosives seized has been from Bihar and Jharkhand, followed by Chhattisgarh. According to MHA reports, the Central Reserve Police Force (CRPF) seized over 6000 kg of explosives in Bihar and 893 kg in Jharkhand till October 2008. Notably, the force also recovered codex wire in Jharkhand for the first time, a lethal explosive that can cause a blast up to 720 m, and has so far only been used by the armed forces in wars.[20] A large amount of the explosives seized have been found to come from Andhra Pradesh Explosives at Nalgonda in Andhra Pradesh and Haryana Explosives. In addition, the looting of explosives from large mining companies particularly in south Chhattisgarh is another prominent source. A major

---

[19] Interview with Dr Nandini Sundar, Professor of Sociology, Delhi School of Economics, New Delhi, 10 December 2008.

[20] 'Gelatine, Detonators Seized in Giridih', *The Telegraph*, 16 October 2008.

source of funding for the Maoists allegedly comes from poppy cultivation, reported from the Ghagra area of Gumla district in Jharkhand, and parts of Kishanganj and Purnia districts in Bihar. Police sources claim that the opium fields are being concealed by growing maize on the sides. The Naxals are also believed to be patronising hemp cultivation to fund their activities. This has been reported form Debagarh district in Orissa.

CONFLICT MANAGEMENT

The counter-Naxal policy of the Indian state has come to revolve around a multi-pronged strategy combining political, socio-economic and security measures. Central to this policy is the emphasis on the need to 'provide security of life and property and provide a secure environment for development and economic growth'[21] (as stated by the Naxal Management Division of the MHA). The year 2008 began with sincere efforts by the government to implement this policy. A case in point is the number of reports prepared by government bodies, including the Expert Committee of the Planning Commission's report on *Causes of Discontent, Unrest and Extremism* which sought to explore the correlation between human development indicators and social unrest, or the seventh report of the Administrative Reforms Commission on *Capacity Building for Conflict Resolution* which stressed the need for a multi-pronged strategy for conflict resolution. In situating the injustice of the economic and social systems at the core of the Naxalite problem, these reports reflect a significant shift from the dominant perception of the Naxalite problem as merely being a law and order problem.

As the year progressed, however, the frequency and lethality of the Maoist attacks prompted the government to adopt a harsher stand. Upon assuming office as the Home Minister after the Mumbai attacks, Chidambaram stressed upon a zero-tolerance policy towards Naxalite extremism and called upon the states to prepare for a long and hard struggle. The National Investigative Agency Bill tabled in Parliament post the Mumbai attacks extended the definition of terrorism to

---

[21] Naxal Management Division, Ministry of Home Affairs, Government of India, http://mha.nic.in/uniquepage.asp?Id_Pk=540 (accessed on 20 March 2009).

include left-wing extremism, thereby allowing for augmenting the powers of the state to address the Maoist threat. Despite the long-term thrust of counter-Naxal policies, 2008 saw a heavy focus on a security response.

Counter-Guerilla Warfare

The key feature of the government strategy is counter-guerilla warfare, i.e., fighting the Maoists in their den with the use of specially trained commandos. A number of combing operations, including joint operations between the states (except for West Bengal which does not allow police from other states to enter its territory) were carried out against the Maoists. Following the success of the Greyhounds, the elite commando force in Andhra Pradesh, the government seeks to replicate this model in other states also. For this purpose, in August 2008, the union government has approved the formation of a specially trained Combat Battalion for Resolute Action (COBRA) force, consisting of 10 battalions to be trained along the lines of the Greyhound force for deployment in Naxal-affected states. In addition, six Maoist-affected states, including Chhattisgarh, Jharkhand, Orissa, Madhya Pradesh, Bihar and Maharashtra, are developing Special Forces on the lines of the Greyhounds to tackle the red terror.

In implementing its counter-guerilla warfare strategies, the government, however, faces several challenges. For one, the modernisation of the police force which this strategy requires is wanting in the heavily-affected states. The dismal utilisation of funds by three states selected under the Modernisation of State Police Force Scheme illustrates this lacuna in the system. The data given in Table 6.2 shows that while the amount provided has increased with each passing year, the percentage utilisation has declined concomitantly. In terms of the actual police strength as against the sanctioned strength too, data till 2007 reveals glaring discrepancies in most states: in Chhattisgarh, the actual strength of the civil police, including district armed police, was 18,710 as against the sanctioned 25,716; in Jharkhand, it was 29,198 as against 38,785; in Orissa it was 27,408 as against 31,367; and in Bihar, it was 45,670 as against 65,219.[22] These facts highlight the fact that the problem lies in the implementation of policies at the

---

[22] 'Police Strength, Expenditure and Infrastructure', *Crime in India-2007*, National Crime Records Bureau, Ministry of Home Affairs, Government of India, available at http://ncrb.nic.in/cii2007/cii-2007/CHAP17.pdf

grass-roots level, rather than in policy formulation. It must be noted that the success of the Greyhounds in Andhra Pradesh was greatly occasioned by other enabling factors, including the fortification of every police station and checkpost in the state, modernisation of weapons, communications, transport and support technologies, and enhanced co-operation between intelligence and operation wings, among other factors.

Table 6.2: Scheme for Modernisation of State Police Forces — Central Funds Released/Utilisation Position as on 30 June 2005 for Chhattisgarh, Jharkhand and Orissa

	Chhattisgarh		Jharkhand		Orissa	
	Funds released (in Rs crore)	Percentage utilisation	Funds released (in Rs crore)	Percentage utilisation	Funds released (in Rs crore)	Percentage utilisation
2000–01	20.57	99.95	40.15	83.25	30.58	98.16
2001–02	21.97	96.18	28.93	95.85	30.5	93.1
2002–03	16.7	94.4	12.73	97.53	16.76	91.13
2003–04	17.47	75.9	8.5	63.02	21.91	72.74
2004–05	32.72	38.97	22.23	7.33	27.66	51.37

Source: Development Initiatives, Ministry of Home Affairs, Government of India, http://www.nha.nic.in/uniquepage.asp?Id_Pk=293 (accessed on 25 March 2009).

Apart from counter guerilla operations, poor state resources also impede the effective implementation of other strategies to supplement hot pursuit. A good example is the surrender policy implemented by individual states. The central government provides them assistance by reimbursement of expenditure upto Rs 10,000 for a surrenderee, without arms, and up to Rs 20,000 with regular weapons under the Security Related Expenditure scheme.[23] In reply to a Lok Sabha question, Minister of State for Home Affairs, Sriprakash Jaiswal, said that out of 1,550 militant surrenders last year, 197 occurred in Andhra Pradesh and 150 in Maharashtra. However, the rehabilitation of the surrendered militants remains of primary concern and a weakness in

---

[23] '1,550 Naxalites, Militants Surrendered in 2008', *ZEE News*, 24 February 2009.

the surrender policy. This problem is particularly acute in Maharashtra where the surrendered Naxals have come under repeated attacks. Since August 2005, when the surrender scheme was implemented by the Maharashtra police, 282 Naxalites have surrendered, but only 18 have been rehabilitated so far.[24] The problems include the failure of distribution of funds to the surrenderee and delay in the rehabilitation process.

Besides, the training imparted to the police has been limited to 'military' aspects for neutralising the cadres as opposed to 'civic' aspects like strengthening ties with the local population. Recognising the limitations of this approach, the states are expanding their civic action programmes by initiatives like holding health camps, distributing food and clothes, holding sports tournaments and tribal festivals, but much more will need to be done to overcome the years of distrust of state institutions and policies. Increasing accountability and transparency in the police force by carrying out proper investigation of reported incidents, enhancing consultation with the people, and developing mechanisms for the redressal of public grievances are some of the measures that can play a pivotal role in overcoming the trust deficit among the people.

Socio-Economic Development

Moving beyond a law and order approach, emphasis is also being laid on improving the development of Naxal-affected areas, both by the centre and the States, that are most often also their most backward areas, The key schemes implemented by the centre include the Backward Districts Initiative (BDI) component of the Rashtriya Sam Vikas Yojana (RSVY); the Pradhan Mantri Gram Sadak Yojana (PMGSY) and the National Rural Employment Guarantee Act (NREGA) that has now been extended to all the districts in the country. In addition, a new scheme has been introduced in the Eleventh Plan, with an allocation of Rs 500 crore, to cater to critical infrastructure gaps that could not be covered under the existing schemes. The efforts of the centre are supplemented by area-specific programmes implemented by the individual states. The Orissa government, for instance, implemented several civic action programmes in the two districts of Malkangiri and Rayagada. Chhattisgarh's minerals policy provides

---

[24] 'Poor Rehab Hits Naxal Surrender Policy', *The Times of India*, 25 June 2008.

several incentives, including simple procedures and secure land rights, to attract domestic and international investors to its mineral-rich southern belt. The Maharashtra government approved an outlay of Rs 51.6 million to provide incentives to at least 170 villages in Gadchiroli and two villages in Gondia to undertake development work and deny entry to the Naxalites.

As the government seeks to focus on development to overcome the socio-economic grievances sustaining the Naxalite movement, it is confronted with several challenges. For one, a review of the implementation of these schemes in Naxal-affected districts highlights the challenges, including weak monitoring mechanisms, low awareness levels and frequent targeting by the Maoists, particularly of road construction efforts under the PMGSY, which impede the effective implementation of these schemes.[25] The most fundamental challenge however is defining the nature of development. The fact that the Naxalites are the strongest among poor people who inhabit some of the richest territory in India is indicative of the fact that development has eluded the original inhabitants of the land. A glaring example of this contradiction is the war being waged by tribespeople and forest-dwellers against the state in the mineral-rich territories of India. As the Government of India opens its mineral deposits for exploitation by private capital to meet the growing needs of a mineral-hungry economy, the adverse social, cultural and economic impact of this policy on the tribespeople and forest-dwellers is leading to violent protests across the country, be it against the ESSAR steel plant in Dantewada district, the TATA steel plant in Kalinga Nagar, or the POSCO steel plant in Jajpur and Jagatsinghpur districts of Orissa. Unless the government supplements its development policies with rehabilitation measures, land reforms, and the recognition of the rights and privileges of the tribespeople and forest-dwellers, this conflict will only provide further fuel to Naxalism.[26]

Seen cumulatively, the biggest drawback of the government's counter-revolutionary strategies lies in the definition of success. The tendency in the government to equate it with the elimination of armed

---

[25] For a review of the NREGA, see 'NREGA: Opportunities and Challenges', Natural Resource Management and Livelihood Unit, Centre for Science and Environment, New Delhi, 2008.
[26] For an assessment of the impact of India's mining policies on the tribals, see report 'Caterpillar and the Mahua Flower: Tremors in India's Mining Field', Panos South Asia, June 2007.

cadres and to exploit natural resources, rather than address the social base of the Maoists, will only be able to achieve a short-term reprieve rather than long-term peace.

CONCLUSIONS

In the year 2008, the Maoists consolidated their armed struggle across India. From Chhattisgarh in 2005–06 to Bihar–Jharkhand in 2006–07, the last year witnessed an intensification of the armed struggle in Orissa. Besides carrying out successful offensives against the security forces, the Maoists were able to disrupt commercial activity in many parts of the state. That left-wing extremism has intensified and spread across the country was confirmed by the Prime Minister speaking at the Chief Minister's conference on internal security held on 6 January 2009.[27] The Prime Minister emphasised the changing nature of left-wing extremism 'from an ideologically driven movement into one in which the military ethos has become predominant' laying the grounds for a military response to the problem.

Consequently, the Maoist conflict is likely to intensify in the foreseeable future with the Maoists utilising new strategies and technology, and the state focusing on augmenting and modernising the police forces. Going by the past trajectory of the movement, the conflict has tended to decline following a period of intense violence, with the Maoists not being able to counter the crackdown by the state. By this logic, the current phase of the insurgency, marked by intense violence, can be presumed to represent the beginning of their decline. However, through a process of introspection, rectification and implementation of new strategies, the Maoists have been able to revive the insurgency in different parts of India at different times. The real danger, therefore, lies not so much in its sustenance, but its changing nature over the last four decades. Moreover, the preference given to a police response to the Maoists, while successful in controlling the movement at a particular time can be held partly responsible for the periodic resurgence of the Naxalite movement. This has allowed a neglect of other components of counter-insurgency, as evident in the

---

[27] 'PM Inaugurates Chief Minister's Conference on Internal Security', Speeches, Prime Minister Office, Government of India, 6 January 2009.

case of Chhattisgarh, which responded to the Maoist threat by greater use of force through the Salwa Judum in its southern belt, without addressing the basic issues affecting tribals like land acquisition and forest mismanagement. The state has thereafter witnessed a dramatic escalation in violence. The decline of Naxal activity in Andhra Pradesh is often cited as a success of the state's counter-revolutionary strategy using its Greyhounds, but this must be assessed from a broader perspective of addressing the insurgency rather than neutralising the Naxalites in the region. It needs to be understood that the success of the Greyhounds has not translated into successfully dealing with the root causes sustaining the insurgency in the area.

From this standpoint, the long-term sustenance of the movement depends as much on how the Maoists shape their ideology and actions in the coming years as on the urgency with which the state responds to the grievances that motivate their movement. The Maoists need to move beyond spearheading various issues of the deprived sections of society to effectively replicating the functions of government in areas controlled by them. Without this, the increasing use of violence against civilians by them would only alienate the support for the insurgency. The example of Orissa is instructive here where the violence against religious leaders by the Maoists has earned it the wrath of many of their sympathisers. Another crucial dilemma that the Maoists face is that of defending their image as saviours of the poor while, at the same time, prohibiting any development work being carried out in areas controlled by them. As the government expands the development of backward regions as a core component of its counter Naxal policy, the Maoists are likely to face questions about their own legitimacy.

The Indian state needs to be more proactive rather than reactive to stay one step ahead of the Maoists. In formulating its counter-revolutionary strategy, the Indian state needs to focus on strengthening the civil administration, social and economic institutions to make them more inclusive to meet the interests of the backward classes. Above all, while social and economic deprivations provide fodder to the movement, the Maoist revolution is a political movement with the basic goal of overthrowing the state government and gaining power. In countering the Maoists politically, therefore, the instruments of change used by the state assume critical significance in setting it apart from the extremists. The state must ensure that in protecting people from violence, it does not compromise its democratic fundamentals of liberty, equality and justice, the absence of which creates the very conditions that fuel and sustain the insurgency.

7

North-East: Minimal Gains of Counter-Insurgency Operations

Bibhu Prasad Routray

For the seven states of north-east India, their tryst with insurgency is almost six decades old. Starting with an armed rebellion by the Nagas in the 1950s, almost all the states in the region have become theatres of armed conflict. The insurgents have several demands, ranging from secession, sovereignty, autonomy to greater rights over resources. While many small and fringe groups perished within a few years of their origin, the major ones continue to exist, defying the politico-military counter-measures of the Indian state. The official counter-insurgency campaigns have only few silver linings. Barring Mizoram, where insurgency ended in the 1980s and the Bodo heartland of Assam, where insurgents gave up arms to settle for an autonomous administrative structure, the government's achievements to end these conflicts by military interventions, peace talks or ceasefire agreements have been abysmally low. Despite temporary reductions in insurgent violence, the northeastern region remains a challenge for the nation-building exercise in India.

This survey of armed conflicts in the northeast covers four states — Assam, Manipur, Nagaland and Tripura, where the violence has been greatest. These four encompass all the counter-insurgency approaches of the Indian state and are representative of the chaos and fear that the civilian population faces.

A BRIEF HISTORY

Nagaland, arguably the oldest conflict theatre in the north-east, arose in revolt before India's independence. Claiming that it had been independent and unconquered by anyone, the Naga National Council (NNC) appealed to the Indian National Congress for delinking with the Indian state. This was rejected, leading NNC general secretary, A.Z. Phizo, to declare the independence of Nagaland. The NNC went on to initiate an insurgency movement and the Government of India moved the army into the Naga hills. The insurgency was sought to be ended by the Shillong Accord of 1975 between the NNC and Government of India. The NNC's unconditional acceptance of the Constitution of India,[1] however, meant little as a section of the NNC rebelled against the accord and formed the National Socialist Council of Nagaland (NSCN) in 1980. Seven years later, in 1987, tribal differences split the NSCN into two groups: the Isak-Muivah faction (NSCN-IM) and the Khaplang faction (NSCN-K).[2] Both these outfits continued with the avowed objective of establishing a greater Nagaland comprising the Naga-inhabited areas of Nagaland, Assam, Manipur, Arunachal Pradesh and neighbouring Myanmar. In 1997, the NSCN-IM signed a ceasefire agreement with the Government of India. Both sides have held over 100 rounds of dialogue since then. The NSCN-K entered into a similar ceasefire agreement in 2001, though the two sides are yet to start a dialogue. These agreements have since been periodically extended.

Insurgency in Assam started with the birth of the United Liberation Front of Asom (ULFA) in 1979. Formed with the objective of establishing a sovereign socialist Assam, free from the 'colonial exploitation of India' as well as halting the illegal migrants from Bangladesh,[3] ULFA, apart from targeting the symbols of state structures and security forces, has also attacked the civilian population. Following the military operations — Rhino and Bajrang[4] — in Assam in the early 1990s, the outfit found refuge in Bangladesh, where it was patronised by the

---

[1] For the text of the Shillong Accord, see 'The Shillong Accord of 11 November 1975 between the Government of India and the underground Nagas', Naga International Support Centre, http://www.nagalim.nl/naga/history/shillong_accord.html (accessed on 24 March 2009).

[2] For details of the NSCN-IM's aims and objectives, see the outfit's well-maintained and regularly updated website, www.nscnonline.org. The NSCN-K does not have a website.

[3] Details of ULFA's aims and objectives can be found at the outfit's poorly maintained website http://www.geocities.com/CapitolHill/Congress/7434/ulfa.htm. For further details also see its fortnightly *Freedom*, which is electronically distributed to select media persons in Assam.

[4] Operation Bajrang was conducted between 27 November 1990 and 10 June 1991. The achievements of this operation were minimal. Subsequently, Operation Rhino was launched on 15 September 1991 and concluded on 13 January 1992.

ISI of Pakistan and the Directorate General of Forces Intelligence (DGFI) of Bangladesh. It has also maintained camps in Bhutan and Myanmar. In December 2003, the Royal Bhutan Army (RBA) launched a military operation against the outfit, clearing Bhutan's soil of the ULFA; however, it has managed to survive and continues to launch periodic strikes in Assam.

Apart from the ULFA, insurgency movements representing the Bodos, the largest plains' tribes in the State, in the 1980s started protesting against the dispossession of their tribal lands by Bengali and Assamese settlers. The National Democratic Front of Bodoland (NDFB) emerged in 1988, demanding an independent Bodo country. Another insurgent group the Bodo Volunteer Force (BVF) signed an accord in February 1993 with the union government. However, a section of the BVF rejected this Accord and formed the Bodo Liberation Tigers (BLT) in 1996. The BLT's terrorist acts ended with the ceasefire agreement of 29 March 2000. The Bodoland Territorial Council (BTC) was created in December 2003. The NDFB, however, continued to remain outside the ambit of the negotiations. In October 2004 it announced a unilateral ceasefire, which has subsequently been extended. Around 740 cadres of the NDFB are housed in three designated camps set up by the State government in Assam. The NDFB, however, is accused of having setting up three more illegal camps[5] at Tipkai, Kazigaon and Basbari in Kokrajhar district.

Assam has also been affected by fringe insurgent movements initiated by the Karbi and Dimasa tribes, the Adivasis and the Islamists. Karbis and Dimasas have demanded autonomy for their homelands, whereas the Adivasis have demanded greater recognition of their rights. The government entered into ceasefire agreements with the Karbi insurgent outfit, the United People's Democratic Solidarity (UPDS) and the Dimasa outfit, Dima Halim Daogah (DHD). But splinter groups of both these outfits, the Karbi Longri North Cachar Hills Liberation Front (KLNLF) and the Black Widow (BW) have continued their activities. The Islamist outfits are mostly led by the Muslim United Liberation Tigers of Assam (MULTA), whose activities, however, remain minimal.

The emergence of insurgency in Manipur is formally traced to the constitution of the United National Liberation Front (UNLF) on 24 November 1964. Issues like the alleged 'forced' merger of the

---

[5] 'Rebels Killed, Teacher Shot at in Assam', *Telegraph* (Guwahati edition), 30 April 2009.

Kingdom of Manipur with the Indian Union and the delay in the conferring full statehood on Manipur have been exploited by the insurgents to consolidate their position in the state. The People's Liberation Army (PLA), founded in September 1978, the People's Revolutionary Party of Kangleipak (PREPAK) founded in 1977 and the Kangleipak Communist Party (KCP) founded in 1980 have emerged in the valley areas of Manipur and demand independence.

In the hill areas of Manipur, several tribal communities have initiated their own insurgency movements, making a variety of demands. The Kuki tribals started their insurgency in the early 1990s, rising against the oppression of Naga outfits like the NSCN-IM. Following ethnic clashes between the Nagas and Kukis in the early 1990s, a number of Kuki outfits were formed. Similarly, Islamist outfits like the People's United Liberation Front (PULF) have been founded to protect the interests of the 'Pangals' (Manipuri Muslims). Most of these outfits have resisted government offers for negotiations. Manipur is one of the worst affected states in the north-east with at least 20 active militant outfits. Except for the Kukis, none of the them have demonstrated any desire for negotiation with the government.

Unhindered migration from Bangladesh (formally East Bengal) has transformed the demography of Tripura, once a tribal majority state. The migrants have managed not only to push the indigenous tribals to the hills and forests by grabbing their lands, but also dominated the politics and administration of the State. Insurgency started as a protest movement against the non-tribal domination. 'First organized-armed tribal movement was known as Senkrak which manifested itself in mid sixties ... as a reaction to settling down of non-tribal refugees in the Tribal Reserve Forest Areas. This movement was however, brought under control by 1968'.[6] Subsequently, the Tripura National Volunteers (TNV) was founded by B. K. Hrangkhawal with a similar objective in collaboration with the Mizo National Front (MNF). This outfit dissolved in December 1980, but was revived on 10 November 1982. TNV continued its activities till the signing of a tripartite agreement on 12 August 1988 paving the way for the surrender of its cadres. Another militant outfit, the All Tripura People's Liberation Organisation (ATPLO) remained active from December 1980 to July 1983.

---

[6] 'Militancy', website of the Tripura Police, http://tripurapolice.nic.in/amilitancy.htm#b1 (accessed on 20 January 2009).

Some disgruntled TNV cadres formed the National Liberation Front of Tripura (NLFT) in March 1989, led by Dhananjoy Reang. The NLFT has undergone several splits since then. However, the outfit, which is presently based in Bangladesh, remains one of the two most active groups in the State. The other outfit, in addition to the NLFT, which has steadfastly refused to be drawn into any peace deal with the government is the All Tripura Tiger Force (ATTF), founded in July 1990 as the All Tripura Tribal Force. In fact, the ATTF had signed a memorandum of understanding with the Tripura government on 23 August 1993. However, a faction led by Ranjit Debbarma decided to continue the armed campaign. Over the years it has found shelter in Bangladesh and indulges in hit-and-run campaigns inside Tripura. Effective police action since late 2002 has managed to bring about a significant reduction in fatalities.

THE PRINCIPAL ACTORS

Assam

ULFA continues to be the principal insurgent group in Assam, whose influence extends over 20 of the state's 27 districts. In June 2008, two of the three companies of the ULFA's primary strike force, the 28th battalion, came overground, seeking a negotiated settlement to their grievances. This weakened the outfit considerably. The outfit's activities in the easternmost districts of Assam, for which this Myanmar-based battalion was responsible, declined, giving rise to speculation that it might collapse due due to non-activity. However, the outfit has survived by revitalising its 709th battalion. This battalion, which was almost defunct after the December 2003 military operations in Bhutan, was brought under the direct command of the ULFA commander-in-chief, Paresh Baruah. ULFA, now consists of 200–250 armed cadres and these are mostly based in Sonari, Majuli and Dhemaji in upper Assam areas and Nalbari district in lower Assam.[7] In co-operation with NDFB cadres, it was responsible for the 30 October serial explosions that rocked four western districts of Assam.

---

[7] 'Ulfa Scare: Tight Security for Polls', *Times of India* (New Delhi edition), 22 March 2009.

The NDFB underwent a massive revamp on 15 December. Accusing the Bangladesh-based chief of the outfit, Ranjan Daimary, of involvement in the 30 October serial explosions, the Assam-based leaders and cadres of the NDFB expelled him from the outfit and elected vice president B. Sungthagra alias Dhiren Boro as the new 'president'.[8] The 'general body meeting' held in the Serfanguri camp in Kokrajhar district also elected a full set of office bearers. Ranjan Daimary, however, retains command over the 3rd battalion, which has been responsible for a number of attacks in the districts of western Assam.

Away from the hotbed of ULFA-led violence and removed also from the epicentre of counter-insurgency operations, the peripheral insurgencies, led primarily by the KLNLF and the BW, continued to thrive in the hilly southern districts of Assam throughout 2008. The BW, operating in the district of NC Hills since its formation in 2003, has grown enormously in lethality. Led by Jewel Garlossa, a former employee of the public health engineering department in the district, its estimated 200 cadres have access to sophisticated weapons, courtesy the Khaplang faction of the NSCN, with which it shares cordial strategic linkages. The All Assam National Liberation Army (AANLA), purportedly fighting for the rights of the plantation workers, whose ancestors were brought to Assam from northern India by British colonialists, saw its capacity being significantly dented by security force operations in 2008. Islamist militancy, led by the MULTA, remains dormant.

Manipur

As many as 20 insurgent outfits operate in Manipur, at least five of which operate in the valley areas of the state.[9] An assessment by the Manipur police in June 2008[10] estimated the strength of the armed

[8] An NDFB cadre Aghai Basumatary, who was arrested from the Goalpara district, told his interrogators that he had received instructions from Daimary to carry out the blast at Ganeshguri. The NDFB statement adopted at the 15 December conclave read as follows: 'The NDFB, in a unanimous decision of the national council, has expelled D.R. Nabla and his associates with immediate effect as a disciplinary action'. See 'NDFB expels Daimary', *Telegraph*, 2 January 2009.

[9] The valley-based militant outfits are People's Liberation Army (PLA), the United National Liberation Front (UNLF), the People's Revolutionary Party of Kangleipak (PREPAK), Kangleipak Communist Party (KCP), the Kanglei Yawol Kanna Lup (KYKL).

[10] 'Most Nabbed UG Cadres end up Released Without Trials: Official Report', *Imphal Free Press*, 16 June 2008.

cadres of insurgent outfits in the state. The list does not include the overground workers or cadres who have been stationed in designated camps. The valley-based UNLF has a strength of 300 to 350 cadres, the PLA has 120 to 130 cadres, PREPAK has 40 to 45 cadres and KYKL has a cadre strength of 70 to 80. In the hills, the NSCN-IM has a cadre strength of 350 to 380 cadres. The Kuki militants belonging to the Kuki Revolutionary Army (KRA) are about 45 to 50 in number, the United Kuki Liberation Front (UKLF) has 45 to 50 cadres, the Kuki National Army (KNA) has 200 to 225 cadres and the Kuki Liberation Army (KLA) has 30 to 40 cadres. Outfits like the KCP, Kuki National Front (KNF-Prithvi) and PULF have from 110 to 130 cadres.

Proximity to Myanmar and the porous Indo-Myanmar border continues to the facilitate unhindered movement of insurgents. The smuggling of small arms and narcotics takes place with little opposition from state forces. As a result, each of these outfits has ample funds and access to sophisticated weapons and explosives.

Unlike other theatres of conflict in the north-east, not many 'surrenders' have been reported from Manipur, indicating the tight control of the outfits over their cadres. Armed with an extremely efficient intelligence network and superior fire power, the militants have been able to carve out a number of liberated zones across the State. Security forces operations against these movements have achieved only limited success so far.

Tripura

Insurgent outfits in Tripura have been weakened over the years. On 25 November 2008 Chief Minister Manik Sarkar informed the State Assembly that the combined strength of the two principal militant formations operating in the State, the NLFT and the ATTF was less than 300. While the NLFT's cadre strength was estimated at between 180 and 200, the ATTF strength was believed to have fallen to an all-time low, with no more than 90 to 100 cadres.[11] During the last three years as many as 871 militants belonging to NLFT, ATTF and the Borok National Council of Tripura (BNCT) have surrendered.[12] It is significant

---

[11] 'Militants' Manpower Reduces to about 300', *Tripurainfo*, www.tripurainfo.in (accessed on 25 November 2008).

[12] 'Militancy Down, 871 Rebels Surrender in 3 yrs', *Tripurainfo*, www.tripurainfo.in (accessed on 11 March 2009).

that effective counter-insurgency operations have driven out a bulk of the remaining cadres and their top leadership to Bangladesh. Hit-and-run attacks from across the international border, and surreptitious movements by cadres in search of avenues for extortion, remain the dominant types of extremist activity in Tripura.

Nagaland

The NSCN-IM remains the most powerful outfit in the state. Reports have indicated that the ceasefire regime starting from 1997 has allowed the outfit to augment its cadre strength and the arms in their possession. A ceasefire reached with the government has allowed the outfit to continue operating with 'state sanction'; whereby, activities like extortion, defined by the outfit as 'tax collection' and gross interference in administrative matters continue unabated. Though the ceasefire ground rules restrict the movement of armed cadres of the outfit outside their designated camps, their cadres frequent the country-side in the state in search of finance and their rival NSCN-K cadres. The NSCN-IM is also present in the Tirap, Changlang and Lohit districts in the neighbouring State of Arunachal Pradesh. Large-scale extortion and recruitment activities by the outfit is reported from these districts.

The NSCN-K, in spite of its losses in clashes with the NSCN-IM, has managed to hold on to its areas of influence, primarily in districts like Mokokchung and pockets in Dimapur. The outfit's strength derives from its facilities in the Sagaing division in Myanmar, across the Mon district of Nagaland, despite periodic attacks by the Myanmarese army. The absence of a dialogue process with the government continues to deprive the outfit of vital popular support, but it remains steadfastly opposed to the initiation of a dialogue process, unless the government calls off its talks with the NSCN-IM.

The NNC, on the other hand, remains a poor shadow of its former strength when it had initiated the Naga insurgency. Split into three factions, the NNC has its share of supporters among the older generation, who were associated with the movement started by A.Z. Phizo. However, it is struggling to keep its identity, while being targeted by powerful outfits like the NSCN-IM.

CONFLICT IN 2008

The state of insurgency in the north-east registered a marginal improvement in 2008 over the previous year. According to official data, fatalities among 'civilians and security force personnel decreased to 506 upto December 15, 2008 as compared to 577 during the corresponding period in the previous year. 4139 militants were killed or surrendered/arrested during 2008 up to December 15, 2008 against 2975 in the previous year'.[13] This improvement apart, there is little to indicate that the region is emerging out of violence and chaos. The following analysis of the conflict situation in the separate states in 2008 would reveal that the region continues to be trapped in violence.

Table 7.1 : Security Situation in the North-Eastern States

Head	2004	2005	2006	2007	2008*
Incidents	1,234	1,332	1,366	1,489	1,077
SFs killed	110	70	76	79	26
Civilians killed	414	393	309	498	285
Militants killed	404	406	395	514	418

Source: Status Paper on Internal Security Situation as on 1 September 2008, Ministry of Home Affairs, Government of India, p. 11.
Note: *As on 31 August 2008.

Assam

In Assam, 209 fatalities were recorded in the first eight months of 2008 in 282 insurgency related incidents. All 27 districts of Assam reported insurgent violence.

The ULFA dominated the insurgency scenario in the State. The disintegration of its '28th battalion' in June 2008 resulted in a diminution in militant activities in the districts of Tinsukia, Sivasagar and Nagaon.

---

[13] 'Notable Improvements in the Law & Order situation in J&K and NE', Year End Review—2008, Ministry of Home Affairs, Government of India, 31 December 2008, http://pib.nic.in/release/release.asp?relid=46277 (accessed on 19 January 2009).

Table 7.2: Security Situation in Assam

Head	2004	2005	2006	2007	2008*
Incidents	267	398	413	474	282
SFs killed	17	7	32	27	10
Civilians killed	194	173	164	287	118
Militants killed	104	74	46	122	81

Source: Status Paper on Internal Security Situation as on 1 September 2008, p. 14.
Note: *As on 31 August 2008.

At the same time, the central and lower Assam districts emerged as the outfits primary battleground. The weakness of the ULFA has made it more subservient to the ISI in Bangladesh, whose anti-Indian designs, in these tentative phases, begin to reflect more prominently through ULFA's activities in Assam. ULFA's strikes then assumed more sophistication and lethality.

On 30 October 2008 the ULFA detonated nine near-simultaneous explosions within a span of one hour in four districts in the western part of the state, including state capital Dispur and conjoined Guwahati, killing 88 persons and injuring 540.[14] In this biggest ever terrorist strike in Assam, more than half the deaths were reported from Dispur–Guwahati alone, while the districts of Kokrajhar, Barpeta and Bongaigaon accounted for the rest. All the explosions were set off at crowded public places — including markets, courts and police stations — with the apparent intention of maximising civilian fatalities. ULFA's initial denial of involvement and the claim of responsibility by an unknown Islamic Security Force-Indian Muzahideen' (ISF-IM) did give rise to some confusion about its involvement in the attack. Subsequent investigations, however, concluded that the ULFA along with the NDFB was involved in the blasts. A chargesheet filed by the Central Bureau of Investigation (CBI) on 25 May 2009 named 19 persons including former NDFB chairman Ranjan Daimary[15] as the prime perpetrators of the explosions.

In the Bodoland region of Assam, the NDFB was accused by the Assam government of fuelling the week-long riots between Bodos

---

[14] Bibhu Prasad Routray and Shanthie Mariet D'Souza, 'Deconstructing the Assam Blasts', 7 November 2008, http://in.rediff.com/news/2008/nov/07column-deconstructing-the-assam-blasts.htm (accessed on 20 January 2009).

[15] 'CBI Names 19 for Oct. Blasts', Telegraph, 26 May 2009.

and immigrant Muslim settlers in the Udalguri, Darrang and Baska districts. Violence, principally over land resources, between the two communities, beginning on 3 October, had led to the death of over 50 persons and displaced over 150,000 from their villages. Till 2009, over 50,000 people, mostly Muslims continue to live in relief camps. The state government's deadline of 15 January 2009 for the return of all affected people to their villages was not met. The suspension of operations agreement with the NDFB, meanwhile, was extended on 6 January 2009 till 30 June 2009. On 4 July 2009, the agreement was extended once more for another six months.

The BW, operating in the hilly southern district of NC Hills, remained the most potent fringe militant formation in Assam, accounting for at least 40 civilian and 11 security forces lives in 2008. On 30 October, when the ULFA co-ordinated serial blasts in Assam, seven police personnel were killed in an ambush by BW cadres. Earlier, on 11 May, a group of around 10 BW militants shot dead eight labourers engaged in the construction of railway quarters at Thoibasti in the NC Hills district. These strikes followed the 22 March unilateral ceasefire declaration by the outfit. The state and central governments rejected the offer on the grounds that the declaration did not lead to cessation of violence by the outfit in the subsequent months. The BW has since carried out several attacks on security forces personnel and the train services passing through the district.

The KLNLF accounted for at least nine civilian casualties in the Karbi Anglong and neighbouring Nagaon districts. On a few occasions the outfit carried out attacks on the Hindi-speaking non-tribal civilians inhabiting these districts. On 30 December it declared a two-month ceasefire starting on 1 January 2009, primarily directed at putting a halt to counter-insurgency operations against the outfit launched in the later part of the year. The state government decided not to reciprocate the offer.

The railway network and properties in Assam, regarded by the insurgents as manifestations of India's exploitation of the region, have been the traditional targets of attack. On 24 December, the AANLA carried out a minor explosion on the tracks near Bokajan in Karbi Anglong district, five minutes after the Rajdhani Express crossed a nearby station. However, the capacities of this outfit were dented by security force operations in 2008.

Islamist militancy in Assam is linked principally to illegal migration from Bangladesh and remains an exaggerated phenomenon. Islamist groups did not carry out any acts of violence in 2008. MULTA's activities remained confined to acting as a subsidiary to the ULFA. Similarly, the Bangladesh-based HuJI, which has not participated in the terrorist acts in Assam, received two setbacks in the State. On 26 September, seven suspected HuJI militants were killed in an encounter with the army in Dhubri district. On 16 October, two more suspected HuJI militants were killed during an encounter with army personnel in Goalpara district.

Manipur

In 2008, Manipur was the most violent State in the north-eastern region. In the first eight months of the year, 314 militancy related fatalities were reported. Fatalities among civilians and security forces have been significantly reduced. Despite the fact that militant fatalities have been high in Manipur, there has been no impact on their capacities.

Table 7.3: Security Situation in Manipur

Year	2004	2005	2006	2007	2008*
Incidents	478	554	498	584	465
SFs killed	36	50	28	39	12
Civilians killed	88	158	96	130	96
Militants killed	134	202	187	219	206

Source: Status Paper on Internal Security Situation as on 1 September 2008, p. 15.
Note: *As on 31 August 2008.

Insurgency is spread over all the nine districts of the state, including four in the valley and five in the hills. The militants have not confined their influence to the remote corners of the state, but have displayed their potential in the fortified state capital, Imphal, by attacking the offices and residences of political authorities. On 8 March, for instance, PREPAK militants drove up to the heavily guarded Manipur Assembly complex and exploded a bomb; fortunately no fatalities were caused. Again, on 24 April, at least five persons, including a woman, were injured when a remote controlled IED (improvised explosive device), placed on a scooter, was detonated by unidentified militants at the Babupara VIP colony near the Chief Minister's bungalow in Imphal.

In the worst of these attacks, at least 17 persons were killed on 21 October and over 30 injured[16] when a bomb placed on a motorcycle was set off by the Military Council faction of the KCP in Imphal. Militant attacks are often related to the all-pervasive extortion activities. Places of worship, educational institutions, health centres and commercial establishments have been systematically subjected to extortion claims by almost all the outfits. On 30 March, Chief Minister Okram Ibobi Singh said that militant groups were extorting money out of donations given to various temples. Educational institutions are also being targeted by them. On 25 May 2009, unidentified insurgents shot dead Md Islamuddin, an economics professor of the Manipur University on the university campus.[17]

As has been the trend in previous years, the insurgent groups issued several 'decrees' in a bid to control the normal lives of the civilians and demonstrate their authority. On 31 January, the KYKL reiterated its 'diktat' of using the Meetei Mayek script on signboards in shops, offices and institutions in the four valley districts. Again, on 23 April, the KYKL 'banned' the *thabal chongba* (dancing ceremony) at Khongjom in Thoubal district. Similarly, on 29 April, the KYKL and UNLF ordered a halt on the hike in the price of kerosene oil in local markets. The PLA 'banned' the export of rice or paddy outside Manipur with effect from 12 December to discourage the cultivation of cash crops. With the state's ability to provide security to its citizens virtually non-existent, any refusal to fall in line with these diktats has proven fatal. On 17 March, at least seven non-Manipuri traders selling tobacco products and *mitha manna* (betel leaf), which was 'banned' by the PLA, were shot dead by PLA militants at Mayang Imphal Hanglun in the capital.

The media in the state has also been forced to walk the tightrope between presenting an unbiased narrative and becoming a mouthpiece for the militant outfits, who use the newspapers to announce their 'party programmes'. Both the English language and the vernacular media have been told to carry verbatim press releases by the militants and failure to do so is often followed by threats and/or actual reprisal attacks. On 4 August, the Military Council (MC) faction of the KCP imposed an 'indefinite ban' on the widely-circulated

---

[16] '17 Killed in Imphal Blast', *The Hindu* (New Delhi edition), 22 October 2008.
[17] 'Manipur Professor Shot Dead on Campus', *Telegraph*, 26 May 2009.

popular Manipuri daily *Poknapham*, after the newspaper published a statement issued by the outfit in one of its inside pages and not on the front page. On 17 November, a junior sub-editor of the English daily *Imphal Free Press*, Konsam Rishikanta, was killed by unidentified militants at Langol in the Imphal West district. The incident led to the suspension of publication of all newspapers in the State for over a week as a mark of protest.

The outflow of insurgency from neighbouring Nagaland has further aggravated Manipur's woes. As in earlier years, in 2008, major parts of Manipur's four hill districts — Tamenglong, Senapati, Ukhrul and Chandel — remained affected by the activities of the NSCN-IM. It carried out unceasing extortion and abduction activities. It also intermittently engaged in fratricidal clashes with its rival NSCN-K.

The conflict dynamics in Manipur have become even more complex after the intervention of a new player — the left-wing extremist Communist Party of India-Maoist (CPI-Maoist) — in the State. The PLA signed a three-point pact on 21 October with the CPI-Maoist.[18] Both groups called for a consolidation of 'mutual understanding and friendship' to 'overthrow the common enemy', which is the 'reactionary regime of India'. The actual ramifications of this agreement are yet to become manifest in Manipur.

Tripura

Tripura continues to reap the benefits of its highly successful police-led counter-insurgency policy. Starting in 2003, violence in this tiny state in India's north-east, surrounded by Bangladesh on three sides, has steadily declined. During the first eight months of 2008, only 18 fatalities were recorded in Tripura in 53 incidents (see Table 7.4). It included no security force fatality, indicating the domination of the men in uniform over the insurgents.

The 1 October serial explosions[19] in the capital Agartala remained the high point of insurgency in Tripura in 2008. Four explosions, two of

---

[18] 'Tight Vigil for Twin Festivals', *Telegraph*, 28 October 2008, http://www.telegraphindia.com/1081028/jsp/northeast/story_10027087.jsp (accessed on 30 October 2008).

[19] 'Several Injured in Serial Blasts in Agartala', *Economic Times* (New Delhi edition), 2 October 2008, http://economictimes.indiatimes.com/articleshow/3550572.cms (accessed in October 2008).

Table 7.4: Security Situation in Tripura

Year	2004	2005	2006	2007	2008*
Incidents	212	115	87	94	53
SFs killed	46	11	14	6	0
Civilians killed	67	28	14	14	6
Militants killed	51	21	22	19	12

Source: Status Paper on Internal Security Situation as on 1 September 2008, p. 19.
Note: *As on 31 August 2008.

them described by the state police as powerful, went off within a span of 45 minutes, in the Radha Nagar, Gol Bazaar, GB Bazaar and Krishna Nagar localities, killing none, but injuring 74 persons. Investigations indicted the ATTF and the HuJI in Bangladesh for orchestrating the blasts. On 12 October, Tripura Police personnel neutralised an ATTF hideout where the bombs used had been manufactured, Despite the steady erosion of militancy, however, incidents were reported from Tripura's four districts. The West district, where Agartala is located, reported the maximum number of insurgency-related incidents. Only 25 cases involving the ATTF were reported in 2008. At least 31 ATTF cadres were either arrested or surrendered. Only one ATTF cadre was killed during the year. On 14 September, Bangladesh Rifles (BDR) personnel handed over 18 ATTF militants to the Border Security Force (BSF) authorities at Khowai Immigration Centre in West district. All the militants were reportedly arrested by the BDR from their Satcherri hideout in Bangladesh in October 2004, and had served prison terms in that country.

Some activities of the BNCT, a shadowy insurgent group working primarily for the NLFT, were reported. The group, after its emergence in 1997, has been marginalised by police action. Since 2006, however, it has been revived by the NLFT, in an attempt to divert the focus of counter-insurgency operations. The BNCT mostly manages the NLFT's abduction and extortion activities, principally in the North and Dhalai districts. BNCT has also abducted tribal youth for forcible recruitment into the NLFT. At least 19 cases of abduction were registered against the BNCT cadres in 2008. Two BNCT cadres were killed in an encounter with the security forces and 45 BNCT cadres surrendered during the year. Another 10 cadres were arrested.

The improved security situation in Tripura was apparent in the largely peaceful elections to the State Legislative Assembly on 23 February. In earlier elections, the militants had unleashed a reign of terror, significantly affecting voter participation. About 92 per cent of the 2.03 million electorates exercised their franchise, which is an all-time high percentage of votes polled in any election in India.[20]

Nagaland

In spite of a 11-year-old ceasefire between the Government of India (GoI) and the NSCN-IM and a similar eight-year-old ceasefire between the GoI and the NSCN-K, Nagaland remains the theatre of endemic fratricidal clashes and pervasive extortion violating the ground rules of the ceasefire. Nagaland not only registers higher levels of insurgent violence than many states with an 'active' insurgency, but the situation appears to be progressively worsening over the years. According to the MHA, 175 fatalities were reported in the state in 244 incidents in the first eight months of the year. Insurgents constituted over 63 per cent of the total fatalities and civilians 34 per cent of the dead. At least 10 of the 11 districts in Nagaland reported insurgent violence in 2008, mostly from the state's commercial township Dimapur and capital Kohima (see Table 7.5).

Table 7.5: Security Situation in Nagaland

Year	2004	2005	2006	2007	2008*
Incidents	186	192	309	272	244
SFs killed	0	1	2	1	3
Civilians killed	42	28	29	44	61
Militants killed	55	70	116	109	111

Source: Status Paper on Internal Security Situation as on 1 September 2008, p. 17.
Note: *As on 31 August 2008.

The NSCN-Unification (NSCN-U) formed in November 2007 vanished from the scene of conflict after the first week of August 2008. However, it left behind a trail of bitter fratricidal clashes and deaths. There is reason to believe that the Indian intelligence agencies played a role in the creation of NSCN-U to weaken the NSCN-IM. This NSCN-U, consisting of the Sema Naga tribals defecting from the NSCN-IM, simply took over the role of NSCN-K in its area domination duel with the NSCN-IM. It was, however, a losing battle against the

[20] 'Tripura Makes Electoral History with 92 Percent Polling', http://www.thaindian.com/newsportal/politics/tripura-makes-electoral-history-with-92-percent-polling_10020865.html (accessed on 28 February 2008).

better armed and organised NSCN-IM and maximum fatalities in these clashes were caused to the NSCN-U, whose cadres have since rejoined the NSCN-K.

The thriving insurgency economy is one of the principal motivating factors behind the continuing conflict in Nagaland. Extortion activities by the insurgents keep the wheels of this economy moving. In the first seven months of 2008, the three factions of the NSCN had collected over Rs 200 crores through their extortion drives in Nagaland's commercial township of Dimapur alone. A conservative estimate of the annual budget of the NSCN-IM alone is in the range of Rs 200 to 250 crores. The insurgents target the civilian population in the state, but also the transit traffic and travellers bound for neighbouring Manipur, on the national highways passing through Nagaland. The Union Ministry of Home Affairs on 29 January, wrote to the Nagaland government, broadening the definition of ceasefire violations to include, among others, extortion in the garb of collecting 'taxes', as well as abductions and killings to extract ransom. Over 20 non-Naga businessmen were abducted and killed in Dimapur alone by elements having alleged links with militant outfits operating in Nagaland. Over 200 affluent non-Naga traders have fled the state fearing for their lives.[21]

Nagaland is flush with small arms since it shares its borders with Myanmar. The insurgent groups smuggle them in from Myanmar. A bulk of these is kept to enhance the capacities of their cadres while the rest are sold to outfits operating in other states of the north-east. In October 2008 a consignment of arms and ammunition consisting of M-series rifles, AK-47 rifles, rocket launchers, RPGs and other ammunition landed in Nagaland. The NSCN-K captured a part of the consignment consisting of 30 AK-47 rifles, about 40 M-Series rifles and 200 grenades and put them up for a display in Zunheboto district. It blamed the NSCN-IM for being in league with Thai arms smugglers to bring these tools of terror into the state.

CONFLICT MANAGEMENT

Assam

Nearly 70 cadres came over ground in June 2008 following the decision of the 'A' and 'C' companies of the ULFA's 28th battalion to

---

[21.] 'Abducted Non-Naga Trader Dies of Torture', *Telegraph*, 24 April 2009.

initiate peace talks with the government. Subsequently, these cadres, led by Mrinal Hazarika, Dibakar Moran, Prabal Neog and Jiten Dutta organised public meetings and addressed rallies, galvanising public opinion to peacefully settle the decades-long conflict.[22] Hopes were generated by both the pro-peace ULFA leaders and the security forces establishment in Assam, who predicted the imminent surrender of many more ULFA cadres, threatening the outfit with near extinction. This even prompted the state government to ask New Delhi to halt counter-insurgency operations by the army and paramilitary forces, a request that did not find favour in New Delhi. However, neither the Bravo 'company', the sole remaining formation of the '28th battalion', nor the 27th, active in the hilly southern district of Karbi Anglong and the '709th battalion', active in western Assam districts come overground.

Some sense of despondency has also started creeping into the pro-talk faction of the ULFA, due to the lack of progress on peace talks with the government. Their demand of autonomy for Assam, in contrast to the demand of independence by the parent outfit, remains too radical for New Delhi. Meanwhile, senior cadre of the outfit, Rabin Gogoi and his security guard Luit Baishya were killed by suspected ULFA cadres on 24 March 2009 at Sadiya in Tinsukia district.

Following a succession of terrorist strikes, especially after the 30 October serial explosions, the Assam government declared a 'zero tolerance' policy towards militancy. On 3 December, it replaced its Police Chief R.N. Mathur with G.M. Srivastava, who is credited with executing a highly successful counter-insurgency campaign in Tripura. On 10 January 2009, the Assam Legislative Assembly passed the Assam Preventive Detention (Amendment) Act, 2009, raising the maximum period of preventive detention of terrorist suspects from six months to two years. 22 companies of security forces were additionally allotted to the State, taking the overall strength of central forces in the State to 142 companies. A 'comprehensive security plan' for State capital Dispur and conjoined Guwahati was also put in place.

The state police are also believed to have played a role in the massive change in the organisational set-up of the NDFB. Vice-President B. Sungthagra *alias* Dhiren Boro, who replaced Ranjan Daimary as the new 'president', had been released from prison in the earlier part of 2008 after his arrest in Gangtok the capital of Sikkim in January

---

[22] The pro-talk faction of the ULFA maintains a website, http://sandhikhyan.org/, which is regularly updated to include the outfit's demands and views on the conflict.

2003. He promised to carry the peace process forward, a break from the logjam over which Ranjan Daimary presided over for nearly four years. However, as evident from the 30 October serial explosions in Assam, Ranjan Daimary retains significant support of NDFB cadres and would prove to be a spoiler in the future. The new leadership's ability to rein in wayward cadres of the outfit, who have not only engaged in intermittent clashes with erstwhile BLT cadres and in extortion activities, but also, on occasions, served as mercenaries for the ULFA, would be seriously tested.

Manipur

Counter-insurgency operations in Manipur have been primarily led by the army and the central para-military forces, with the state police playing a subsidiary and marginal role. The lack of adequate support from the police, however, affects the objective of reducing the areas under the domination of the insurgents. These operations have failed, allowing the insurgents to retake these liberated zones. For example, the army, in January 2008, claimed to have dislodged the UNLF from its last bastion in the State, the New Samtal area spread over 1,000 square kilometres in the south-western Chandel district. Within the next three months, however, the UNLF cadres, who had simply vacated the villages and retreated into the forest areas, or had crossed over to the safety of adjoining Myanmar, returned to the area, and started ambushing security force contingents.

The Manipur police's irrelevance in the counter-insurgency operations has persisted, despite the fact that the State boasts a police–population ratio of 627, much higher than Nagaland (475), Assam (176) and the Indian average of 125. Manipur's policemen per 100 square kilometre area ratio of 73.2, is far in excess of Assam (66.4), Nagaland (62.2) and the national average of 45.

Manipur has consistently failed to take advantage of the popular discontent against the insurgents. In May 2008, the state government, responding to an appeal by the people of Heirok in Thoubal district to arm them against the militants, recruited 300 Special Police Officers (SPOs). However, due to a clampdown by the UNLF and KYKL militants, who clearly dominated the area, the programme was abandoned. The UNLF and KYKL cadres stopped the people of Heirok from moving out of their villages and, on occasion, carried out attacks on them.

The only silver lining in Manipur has been the August 2005 Suspension of Operations (SoO) agreement between 19 Kuki militant groups, consisting of about 1,745 cadres, and the union government. Although little progress has been achieved in terms of solving the problem of Kuki militancy in the Hill districts, the agreement continues to hold. The three-year-long ceasefire agreement, however, has not prevented the abduction and extortion activities of these outfits. Three rounds of talks — two in New Delhi (on 19 May and 22 August) and one in Imphal (on 19 December) — have been held. Valley-based civil society groups, however, complain that the SoO is leading to a rise in crime and unchecked violence in some parts of the state.[23] The Joint Monitoring Group (JMG), following the third round of meetings, issued instructions to the Kuki groups to refrain from abduction and other unlawful activities.

Tripura

Despite setbacks, both the NLFT and ATTF continue to resist starting a process of negotiation with the government. On the other hand, the state government is keen to neutralise these insurgents through counter-insurgency operations and has not pressed for a peace process. Backed by the ruling left-front regime, the counter-insurgency grid in Tripura has crippled the capacity for operations and recruitment among insurgent formations. Strategic deployment of security forces personnel in the hills, plugging militant routes into the state, has been a key component of the counter-insurgency operations. There has also been a continuous improvement in security forces' capacities. crucially, the retreat of militancy has ensured the presence of state structures and the initiation of developmental activities in the most remote parts of Tripura that were being preying upon by the militants.

Only 80 km of the 856 km-long international border with Bangladesh remains unfenced in the Gandacherra subdivision of Dhalai district, and this is the principal point of ingress for militants from Bangladesh. Following the Agartala serial blasts, in which the perpetrators are known to have used the unfenced border to bring in

[23] 'UCM Petitions Governor for Proper Implementation of SoO', *Imphal Free Press*, 4 June 2008, http://ifp.co.in/FullStory.asp?NewsID=2424 (accessed on 5 July 2008).

men and explosives into Tripura, there has been a renewed emphasis on completing the tasks of fencing, enhancing force presence and patrolling, introducing modern electronic sensors and flood lighting the border. The entire process is scheduled to be completed by 2011–12.

Nagaland

Continuous engagement with the NSCN-IM and the NSCN-K remains central to the government's conflict management policy in Nagaland. Representatives of the NSCN-IM and the government continue to meet periodically to carry the negotiations forward. Two rounds of peace talks with the NSCN-IM were held on 16 April and 28 May 2008. The NSCN-K is yet to negotiate; the ceasefire with it has been extended till 28 April 2009.

Little success has been achieved in breaking the deadlock over the NSCN-IM's demand for integrating the 'Naga-inhabited' areas of Assam, Manipur and Arunachal Pradesh into Nagaland. Given the strong resentment that the proposal is bound to elicit from states like Manipur, no attempt has been made to involve these state governments in the peace process. Notwithstanding its public posturing, the NSCN-IM is gradually veering towards accepting a solution within the Indian Constitution and abandoning its demand for an independent Nagaland. Confirming this, the Union Labour and Employment Minister Oscar Fernandes said on 13 July that the NSCN-IM has met senior government functionaries in the Prime Minister's Office (PMO) and is 'inching towards accepting the Indian Constitution'. The outfit, on its part, issued a statement reaffirming its faith in an independent Nagaland.

The overriding dominance of the Naga insurgents has not been challenged by any effective security force action. The insurgents, especially the NSCN-IM, exercise immense influence over the political regime in the state, and the latter remains support the designs of the outfit. Interestingly, the ruling Democratic Alliance (DAN) government pursues a policy of 'equi-closeness' with both the insurgent formations. Chief Minister Neiphiu Rio on 23 April said: 'The state government will support the cause of the Eastern Nagas in Myanmar to help them get due political recognition and rights from the government there... They have been neglected by Yangon. The Nagas in Nagaland should unanimously support them to facilitate their development along with other Naga communities'.[24] Rio has asked the military regime in Myanmar to declare a truce with the NSCN-K.

Several initiatives for the de-escalation of violence have been taken up by concerned citizens of the state. Peace rallies consisting of thousands of people were organised by the *gaon buras* (village chiefs) and *dubashis* (chiefs of Naga customary courts) in all 11 district headquarter towns on 20 May, asking the warring Naga factions to stop violence in the state. Spontaneous protests by harried citizens have also occurred in the wake of escalating tensions between the warring NSCN factions in various parts of the state.

The Naga Reconciliation Forum, headed by Baptist clergyman Wati Aier, Baptist World Alliance and a UK-based Quaker group, organised a reconciliation meeting of the Naga factions, community-based Naga organisations and tribal Hohos at Chiang Mai in Thailand in June. The unification move received a jolt when the NSCN-K rejected the offer made by the rival NSCN-IM for a dialogue outside the country.

CONCLUSIONS

Apart from Tripura, where police-led counter-insurgency operations continue to consolidate the gains made by the state against the insurgents, three states of the region — Assam, Manipur and Nagaland — continue to witness large-scale violence. Assam, where the insurgency situation appeared to have improved in the first three-quarters of the year, suddenly dipped to record the worst ever serial bomb blasts and there has been little respite since then. The surrender of 70 cadres of ULFA's 28th battalion did generate hopes of an early solution to the conflict. But the outfit managed to get over its losses by reactivating its 709th battalion. ULFA's violence continues to dominate the discourse on insurgency in Assam. At the same time, fringe insurgent formations like the KLNLF and the BW continued targeting the migrant population in the hill districts of Assam. They also carried out several attacks on the train services passing through these districts. Intermittent intertribal clashes continue between the Bodo tribals and the non-Bodo population in the western Assam districts.

---

[24] 'NSCN Inching Towards Accepting Indian Constitution: Fernandes', 13 July 2008, http://www.theindian.com/newsportal/world-news/nscn-inching-towards-accepting-Indian-constitution-fernandes_10070978.html (accessed on 30 July 2008).

In Manipur the suspension of operations with the Kuki outfits since 2005 remains the only achievement of the state's counter-insurgency efforts. This has brought some respite from violence in the hill districts. However, the civilian population continues to be affected by persistent violence in the valley areas where the Meitei outfits dominate. Militant diktats rule supreme in the state. The government's efforts are further constrained by the historical divide between the valley and hill areas. The spilling over of insurgency from neighbouring Nagaland continues to aggravate Manipur's woes.

Ceasefire agreements between the government and the insurgent factions have little meaning for the people of Nagaland. Their daily lives continue to be seriously affected by factional clashes between the insurgents. The lack of progress in the dialogue between the NSCN-IM and the Indian government generates no hopes for an early solution. It appears almost certain that the tryst of the civilian population with internecine clashes, abduction and extortion activities by the insurgents will be prolonged. Despite the efforts of civil society organisations, the ethnically divided insurgents continue to target each other.

The remnants of insurgency in Tripura have the potential of erupting into violence. Much will depend on the management of the open border with Bangladesh, which is being exploited by the insurgents for egress and ingress. The support of the Bangladeshi regime would also be crucial if insurgency movements are to be completely neutralised in Tripura.

The continuing ceasefire agreements with insurgent outfits remain problematic. Without end goals in sight, they resemble instruments for delaying peace. In the north-east, nearly 30 outfits have negotiated ceasefire agreements with the government. But in every case, the ground rules of ceasefire are violated with impunity. No effort has been made by the government to enforce these ground rules in letter and spirit. Insurgents often leave the designated camps to extort, abduct and, in the case of NDFB in Assam, participate in terrorist strikes. As a result, the exercise of entering these ceasefire pacts loses its credibility.

The surrender and rehabilitation schemes of the government no longer attract insurgents wishing to join the mainstream. Formulated more than a decade back, the scheme has not been revised in terms of increasing the financial incentives or providing vocational training to the surrendered insurgents. The surrendered insurgents complain of non-implementation or inadequacy of the schemel hence their participation in the counter-insurgency operations of the security forces remain lukewarm.

The continuing insurgencies and the failure of counter-measures focusing on security forces operations create a feeling of despondency in the civilian population about the possibility of bringing these conflicts to an end. As a result, popular support to back up these measures continues to wane, making the counter-insurgency operations largely ineffective. The lack of support from the state police is also making the task of the army and paramilitary forces difficult in terms of holding and establishing control over the liberated territories.

Following the 26 November multiple terrorist attacks in Mumbai, Union Home Minister P. Chidambaram spoke about the need to address the Bangladesh factor behind the continuing insurgency in the north-east. For years, successive regimes in that country, especially those led by the Bangladesh Nationalist Party (BNP) have remained apathetic to Indian concerns. The Awami League's (AL) victory in Bangladesh in the 29 December parliamentary elections has stirred a measure of optimism over the possibility of concerted action against the insurgent havens in that country.[25] Sheikh Hasina, after her elections promised that the territory of Bangladesh will not be allowed to be used for anti-Indian activities. If these announcements are operationalised, Assam and Tripura would greatly benefit. While Tripura can hope to rid itself of this problem, Bangladesh's co-operation would sound the death knell for ULFA. But it remains to be seen whether the Sheikh Hasina government will have the capacity — or the will — to act forcefully against the various insurgent groups. Following the electoral victory of the AL, speculation was rife about the extradition of arrested ULFA general secretary, Anup Chetia, to India. While that is yet to occur, the arrest of other active insurgent leaders based in Bangladesh, and their extradition to India looks very unlikely. Intelligence sources indicate that ULFA chief, Paresh Baruah,

---

[25] Sheikh Hasina, whose grand alliance bagged 262 seats in the 300-member parliament, said in her first post-victory press meet on 31 December, 'The Bangladeshi soil will never be used to carry out any terrorist act against our neighbours'. She added, 'When we were in power we took a strong position on this (terrorism) and we will do that in the future. I have always maintained that we want peaceful relations with our neighbours'. See 'Bangla Soil Will Not be Allowed for Terror Acts', *Assam Tribune*, 1 January 2009.

and others have left the country for a South-East Asian destination anticipating trouble from the AL government.

India, over the years, has paid scant attention to the ungoverned spaces in the Indo-Myanmar border region, which has been home to a number of Manipuri outfits, the NSCN-K and the ULFA. Neutralisation of these facilities has been sought by intermittent operations of the Myanmarese army, which remains unable to permanently cleanse the area of insurgents The presence of the insurgents in Myanmar has only facilitated the smuggling of drugs and contraband into India. Fencing the Indo-Myanmar border has not been a priority for the Indian government, allowing the insurgents several points of entry and exit. There is a need to revisit this policy. The Myanmarese authorities must be engaged on a permanent basis to deny the insurgents safe havens in that country.

8

Bangladesh: The Clampdown

Sandeep Bhardwaj

A BRIEF HISTORY

In its short history, Bangladesh has remained one of the most unstable and underdeveloped nations in the world. As a nation which has had just as many years under military rule as under a democracy, security dynamics in Bangladesh have coupled themselves with larger sociopolitical landscape of the nation.

Since 1991, when democracy was restored in Bangladesh, government has been a game of musical chairs between two political parties — Awami League (AL) and the Bangladesh Nationalist Party (BNP). The resulting politics was petty and violent. Rampant corruption and poverty led to the further deterioration of conditions. By 2006, 15 years of democracy had failed to create strong institutions and people had lost faith. As the 2007 General Elections approached, huge discrepancies in voter lists and violations of electoral laws in the nation led to violent polarisation. On 11 January 2007, in light of excessive political violence and general chaos in the country, the Bangladesh Military took over the de facto power through the proxy of a Caretaker Government (CTG).

The CTG promised the public better governance and the restoration of democracy by the end of 2008. While some of the CTG's reform agenda was implemented, it failed to achieve several of its high-priority goals. In addition, the emergency brought in government-led rigid military control and flagrant human rights violations. It was under such a state of governance that Bangladesh entered year 2008.

Bangladesh is a predominantly Muslim nation, enjoying an attribute unique in South Asia — it is largely ethnically uniform. Also, the version of Islam prevalent in Bangladesh is tolerant, preached by *sufis* and saints. As a result, it did not face religion-based or ethnic violence for a long time after its liberation from Pakistan. However, since the early 1990s, Bangladesh has seen politicisation of Islam as well as the emergence of extremist groups. Some of the Bangladeshis believed to have taken part in Soviet–Afghanistan War returned to Bangladesh to set up militant groups within the country. In the early part of this decade (2001–05) these groups rose suddenly and shockingly, capturing the nation's attention with their strength and brutality. The BNP-led government continued to stay in denial, ignoring the growth of radical Islam in the country. In some of the cases even complicity on the part of government was suggested. Under CTG rule, a strict clampdown was imposed on these activities leading a few to believe that such right-wing organisations had been effectively dismantled.

Unlike right-wing terrorism, the left-wing militancy has been a part of Bangladesh since its beginning. However, there is much disorganisation and fragmentation in the left-wing organisations. Activities of left-wing organisations have largely been local. Further, the criminalisation of these organisations has led to their de-legitimisation as a credible fighting force for the people. Weak performances of left-wing political parties in elections have proved as much. Effectively, the government has been successful in transforming left-wing militancy into a law and order problem in people's perception.

Another source of conflict in Bangladesh are the international border disputes. Over the past decades relations of Bangladesh with its neighbours — India and Myanmar — have become one of suspicion and intolerance. This has led to several minor incidents of border violence between these nations.

THE PRINCIPAL ACTORS

State Actors

Armed Forces

The skewed civil–military relations in Bangladesh have left the nation with a disproportionately strong military. Inheriting from its parent organisation — the Pakistan Army — the Bangladesh Army has a long of history of interfering and dominating in civil matters. In the past, Bangladesh military has even been accused of supporting right-wing fundamentalists.

In recent years, however, the Bangladesh Military has shown a shift in its behaviour. With its vast corporate interests and a stake in UN Peacekeeping missions,[1] the Bangladesh military has become very conscious of its international image as a neutral and responsible armed force.[2]

Counter-Terrorism Agencies

In recent years the Rapid Action Battalion (RAB) has emerged as the most prominent law enforcement agency and principal state instrument used to respond to terrorism. Created from a pool of deputed officers from the police and armed forces, the RAB is predominantly comprises military officers and relies heavily on military tactics. Despite its spectacular record, the RAB has been heavily criticised for its human rights violations.

Directorate General of Forces Intelligence (DGFI) is the military intelligence wing, acting as primary intelligence gathering agency in the country. Years of military rule has resulted in a strong DGFI, often accused of using underhand tactics against its own fellow citizens.

Years of political patronisation, corruption and undemocratic practices has resulted in a weak police.

Non-State Actors

Right-Wing Groups

While there are several Islamist extremist groups operational in Bangladesh, these organisations have shown remarkable co-operation with each other. Indeed, some of these organisations are simply aliases for each other.

Jamaat-Ul-Mujahideen Bangladesh (JMB) came into the limelight in the early part of this decade with several terrorist acts, including murders, abductions and bomb blasts. However, the government remained lenient towards the group until the 2005 attack.[3]

---

[1] The Bangladesh Military is one of the top three contributors to UN Peacekeeping Missions, earning vast sums of money in compensation.

[2] It is believed that the Bangladesh Military sought unofficial clearance from the United Nations before taking over power in Bangladesh.

[3] On 17 August 2005, JMB exploded 458 locally-made bombs within the space of one hour in 63 of the 64 districts in Bangladesh.

The subsequent crackdown and execution of the group's leadership has left the outfit largely inactive. However, analysts believe a regrouping of the organisation is taking place.[4]

Harkat-ul-Jihad-al-Islami (HuJI) is an organisation affiliated with Al Qaeda and some other international terrorist organisations. Like Al Qaeda, HuJI is believed to provide support and training to other terror groups, in addition to carrying out its own terrorist acts. While it was believed for a long time that HuJI did not operate inside Bangladesh; recent findings, however, have proved the contrary. HuJI has also been known to have political ambitions.[5]

Other terror groups include the Jagrata Muslim Janata Bangladesh (JMJB,) Hizbut Tauhid, Allahr Dal and Hizb-ut-Tahrir. While these organisations have not yet carried out a substantial terrorist attack, they have been involved in activities and propaganda subversive to the state. The financing network for the right-wing terrorist groups in Bangladesh has been extensive and elaborate. In 2005, Bangladesh security agencies identified 10 foreign aid agencies suspected of funneling money into Bangladesh for terror financing.[6] However, several of these agencies are still functional in the country or have been allowed to transfer funds and staff to other agencies.

Left-Wing Groups

Unlike their right-wing counterparts, left-wing organisations in Bangladesh are extremely divided. Splintering, in-fighting and splitting have become the norm with these organisations, resulting in a chaotic movement with no singular ideology or objective. The left-wing organisations that have recently been active include the Purba Banglar Communist Party (PBCP), Red Flag, Gono Mukti Fouz (GMF), Biplobi Communist Party, Sarbahara Party, Janajuddho, Gono Bahini and Mukti Bahini. In recent times, the PBCP and its multiple factions have emerged as the most active left-wing group. Left-wing extremist

---

[4] 'Militants Regrouping for Attacks, Says Study', *Daily Star*, 12 June 2008, http://www.thedailystar.net/story.php?nid=40819 (accessed on 8 December 2008).

[5] For the parliamentary elections of 2008, HuJI floated a political party called the Islamic Democratic Party. The Election Commission, however, rejected the application for party registration on technical grounds.

[6] Chris Blackburn, 'Terrorism in Bangladesh: The Region and Beyond', paper presented at the Policy Exchange conference on 'The Rise of Political Islam in Bangladesh: What's at Stake in the 2007 Elections?', London, 14 November 2006.

activities have largely confined themselves to the mid-western and south-western parts of the country, including Satkhira, Khulna, Jessore, Jhenaidah, Magura, Chuadanga, Meherpur, Kushtia, Pabna and Rajshahi.

POLITICAL ACTORS

In Bangladesh, political violence and militant activities are far too embroiled with each other to be able to make a clear distinction. Politics invariably has a role to play in all the internal security problems in the country. Accordingly, in such matters political parties become a significant actor. Hardline Islamist parties, like the Jamaat-e-Islami Bangladesh, have often been accused of providing patronage to Islamist terrorist organisations. Similarly, several of the left-wing extremist groups are the military wings of political parties in the country.

The two big political parties in the country — BNP and AL — continue to play the game of petty politics in what can be called a 'winner takes all' democracy. In addition, these parties have not remained above patronising criminal elements or political violence. Over the past decade, both parties have become involved with extremism or terrorism, not as governments but political entities. The BNP has been repeatedly accused of patronising right-wing extremists during their rule in 2001–06. The AL, on the other hand, has been targeted by Islamist groups like HuJI in terrorist attacks including an attempt on Sheikh Hasina's life.

International Actors

India-Bangladesh have been subject to mood swings ever since the latter's liberation. While there is no apparent irresolvable source of contention between the two nations, they have failed to develop a mutually beneficial and trustworthy relationship. Bangladesh, plagued with its deep-seated insecurity, remains skeptical of its bigger neighbour, while India continues to seek a *quid pro quo* relationship with Bangladesh which is not possible. The resultant deterioration in relations between the two countries has led to a situation where their borders have become witness to constant low-intensity violence.

Myanmar-Bangladesh relations remain a subject of suspicion. The Bangladesh–Myanmar border faces the same problems as the India–Bangladesh border with a converse situation. Bangladesh faces a huge immigration of Rohingya Muslims into the country from Myanmar. While these immigrants identify themselves as refugees, Bangladesh continues to refuse entry claiming they are economic migrants. On the other hand, Bangladesh and Myanmar fail to tackle with their maritime border dispute. Given the possibility of huge natural gas and oil reserves in the region, this issue has become complicated.

CONFLICT IN 2008

Under military rule, 2008 in Bangladesh saw almost no violent extremist activity from either the left or right-wing. Throughout the year, the government kept up the pressure on militant groups as the security forces led a massive crackdown on them. Prevention became the motto of the security agencies (RAB and police) which went on a proactive offensive as opposed to the reactive tendencies they exhibited during the BNP term during 2001–06. Armed with emergency powers, the security agencies pursued its suspects with greater independence and authority, sometimes even extra-legally. During the year, the security forces arrested at least 100 right-wing extremists, and 74 left-wing extremists, and 47 left-wing extremists were killed in the 'crossfire'.[7]

There were four separate incidents of bombings in the year, but none of them caused any deaths.[8] The bombs were homemade and of low intensity. In the given circumstances it is difficult to ascertain whether the bombings even had a political reason or were simply a criminal act. Meanwhile, the government strengthened the security forces through the use of new legal instruments. In May, the government approved the new Anti-Terrorism Ordinance which allowed for more rigorous punishment. It also gave Bangladesh Bank the power to monitor financial transactions to track down the channels of terror financing. The government also introduced the Right to Information Ordinance, making it more accountable to the public and civil society.

As the year drew to an end, all national attention swung to the political drama that was unfolding. In the beginning of the year it seemed

---

[7] South Asia Terrorism Portal, www.satp.org.
[8] *Ibid*.

that the CTG had been successful in removing the two most prominent politicians — the battling begums — from the political scene. However, it soon became apparent that the two ladies were inseparable from the Bangladesh politics. The subsequent negotiations between the government and political parties dragged on as everyone braced for the political violence that inevitably precedes Bangladesh elections. However, the CTG managed to achieve an almost incident-free run-up to the elections.

The December 2008 parliamentary elections in Bangladesh were truly historic. Not only did its transparency make it fairest elections ever held in the country, the result was also unprecedented. The AL and its allies swept into power with more than two-thirds majority in the Parliament in an unparalleled victory.

Trends in Right-Wing Violence

The spectacular rise of Bangladeshi Islamist extremist groups in the early part of this decade had garnered a lot of attention across the world. Analysts believed that like rest of the world, the problem of right-wing terror will only worsen in Bangladesh, leading some to even dub it as 'the next Afghanistan'.[9] However, Bangladesh still keeps at bay from such an unfortunate fate. In 2008, Islamist terror groups in Bangladesh remained largely ineffective, limiting their activities to propaganda and regrouping. While there were a few threats of violence issued by these groups, they were either not carried out or were foiled by the law enforcement agencies. The only significant case of violence brought to light was the murder of the wife of the lone witness to the 17 August 2005 serial bomb blasts by JMB men. Such an incident, though unfortunate, is a far cry from the level of sophistication and impunity with which JMB was operating only few years earlier in Bangladesh. In the early 2000s, JMB and other Islamist organisations were carrying out public executions[10] and large-scale bomb blasts. The trends have changed substantially since then.

---

[9] In 2005, Hiranmay Karlekar's book, *Bangladesh: The Next Afghanistan?*, became one of the most cited resources on Bangladeshi terrorism.
[10] 'Bangla Bhai Men Slaughter 2 Today', *Daily Star*, 20 May 2004, http://www.thedailystar.net/2004/05/20/d4052001055.htm (accessed on 15 March 2009).

By and large, the Bangladeshi population has restrained itself from taking up on the idea of jihad. The Islamist right-wing parties do enjoy a steady support base, but this number is small and shows an insignificant growth rate.[11] The ideology of right-wing fundamentalists has failed to relate itself with the socio-economic issues facing Bangladesh. A significant amount of Islamist terrorists in Bangladesh are, in fact, educated middle-class people, indicating a lack of popular mass support.[12]

It is believed by some that the right-wing extremism in Bangladesh is viewed an answer to the left-wing violence that drags on in parts of the country.[13] According to uncorroborated sources, right-wing extremism was in fact used as an instrument by factions of the government to counter the left-wing threat in the early 2000s. However, since then, right-wing extremism has become a substantial threat on its own, surpassing the threat posted by the left wing.

Nevertheless, Islamist terror groups of Bangladesh do threaten to return. All through 2008, there have been several reports of JMB and other terror groups regrouping. Militant organisations like Allahar Dal are recruiting and collecting tolls from the south-western part of Bangladesh. Analysts fear a likely possibility of the return of these organisations in the future. It has been reported that Hizbut Touhid organised a 4-day training course held on board a launch under the guise of a boat journey from Dhaka to Kuakata from 4–7 April 2007, where over 1,500 people, including 700 women activists, took part. One of the participants in the course informed us that 'male participants took training in bomb making and other weapons operation separately while women participants took training in recruiting techniques. Party leaders prefer women members as they can easily motivate the local people, especially the local women.'[14]

---

[11] In the 2008 elections Islamist parties only received 7–8 per cent votes.
[12] Farooq Sobhan et al., 'Countering Terrorism in Bangladesh: A Strategy Paper', Bangladesh Enterprise Institute, July 2007.
[13] Zohra Akhter, 'Trends in Militancy in Bangladesh: August 2007–May 2008', Bangladesh Enterprise Institute, 11 June 2008.
[14] *The Daily Star*, 19 January 2008, as quoted in Zohra, 'Trends in Militancy in Bangladesh'.

Since the open declaration of JMB's existence in 2005, law enforcement agencies have steadily cracked down on terrorist activities throughout the country. There have been dozens of arrests and the execution of the top leadership of JMB, which has left these organisations handicapped. However, the government is yet to effectively act against the support infrastructure of these organisations. The foreign NGOs that had been identified as terrorism sponsors in 2005 are still operational or were allowed to transfer their resources and staff to other agencies. Bangladesh still hosts a large number of unregulated private madrasas in the country, many of which go unregistered. It should be noted that several of the arrested terrorists have been known to have links with such madrasas. In August 2008, Asadullah Al Galib, the chief of Islamist militancy sponsor Ahle Hadith Andolan Bangladesh (AHAB) was released on bail from the prison.[15] While such a support infrastructure remains unmolested in Bangladesh, there will always loom a threat of Islamist militancy's return.

In addition, there is a strong political lobby emerging in Bangladesh that is causing cultural changes in society, leading towards an intolerant version of Islam. The case of Baul sculptures would be a perfect example to elucidate this line of argument. In October of 2008, five Baul (folksinger) sculptures, under construction in front of the Zia International Airport at Dhaka, were removed by the employees of the Roads and Highways Department and the Civil Aviation Authority of Bangladesh. This step, taken under pressure from religious groups (such as Khatme Nabooat, Zia International Roundabout Resistance Committee and Islami Oikya Jote, specifically), sparked off nationwide protests among secularists and cultural groups. Several reports mention police reluctance in quelling the violence perpetrated by religious factions against the subsequent secularist protests.[16] Such unsecular actions by the government lead only to the strengthening of intolerant lines of thought in the country.

---

[15] 'Bangladesh Assessment 2008', South Asia Terrorism Portal, http://www.satp.org/satporgtp/countries/bangladesh/index.htm (accessed on 10 March 2009).

[16] 'Removal of Sculptures Sparks Protests', *Daily Star*, 17 October 2008, http://www.thedailystar.net/story.php?nid=59085 (accessed on 6 December 2008).

Weapons captured from right-wing terrorist groups often include sophisticated arms and explosives, including the infamous Arges Grenades.[17] This indicates a supply route of arms and ammunitions to the terrorists from outside the country.

Trends in Left-Wing Violence

In 2008, left-wing extremist groups in Bangladesh were involved in a variety of activities ranging from bomb blasts, murder to extortion and kidnapping. However, these activities largely had local implications and most of them were criminal in nature. Most of the murders or bomb blasts carried out by these organisations were political in nature, targeting a member of a rival political party or a member of their own organisation. For example, in February, Farman Ali, a member of PBCP-Janajuddha was murdered by party rivals. Similarly in March, two members of PBCP-ML (Janajuddha) and the PBCP Janajuddha were slaughtered for allegedly betraying the party. Other reasons for murders include dispute over money, unpaid extortions or even personal quarrels. For example, in November, a businessman was killed by GMF cadres in Ratulpara village for not paying the extortion money. It is significant to note that in May 2008, suspected left-wing extremists attacked a police patrol team, killing one officer, and also looted firearms.[18]

Left-wing organisations in Bangladesh have become too criminal and factionalised to pose a threat to national security.[19] The infighting that has followed, resulted in a chaos of ideologies, none strong enough to actually mount a national or regional struggle. Moreover, the government has been very severe in dealing with these organisations, keeping the pressure high. In 2008, law enforcement agencies killed 47 left-wing extremists in 'crossfire' (a government euphemism for extra-judicial killing). Meanwhile though, dozens of

---

[17] Arges grenades have been a popular weapon used throughout South Asia by Islamic terrorists. They have been used in many major terrorist attacks in Pakistan and India. It is believed that Arges grenades originate from Pakistan.
[18] 'Bangladesh Assessment 2008, South Asia Terrorism Portal, http://www.satp.org/satporgtp/countries/bangladesh/index.htm (accessed on 10 March 2009).
[19] Zohra, 'Trends in Militancy in Bangladesh'.

Islamist extremists were arrested in 2008, none of them was killed in 'crossfire'.

The weapons used by left-wing extremists are largely home-made, produced in underground factories, or looted from the police; indicating a lack of support from international actors.

The Success of Elections

In December 2008, Bangladesh held general elections across the country, witnessing a record-high turnout and no significant incidents, despite the warnings from almost every extremist group. This can be considered substantial proof of the inability or the handicap that the extremist groups are currently experiencing in Bangladesh.

State-Sponsored Violence

Military rule in Bangladesh has had a significant impact on every internal security problem in the country. With the withdrawal of political patronage, many of the extremist groups became inactive. It is believed by some analysts that this inactivity is a tactical retreat. The general clampdown by security agencies armed with emergency powers has indeed made a difference to the law and order situation in Bangladesh.

However, the emergency also brought with it gross violations of human rights, extra-judicial killings and corruption. According to Human Rights Watch, the government imprisoned more than 500,000 people, including politicians, journalists, lawyers, activists and government officials in its two-year regime.[20] The larger political reform movement envisaged by the military included the imprisonment of a majority of the current political leadership to clear way for an alternative.

Since its establishment in 2004, the RAB has been regularly criticised by international and national organisations, and by civil society. Due to such criticism and to project a credible image of military rule, extra-judicial killings by the RAB dropped significantly in 2007 and in early 2008. However, in late 2008 this number surged dramatically.

---

[20] 'Human Rights Watch Letter in Response to Bangladesh Home Ministry', *Human Rights Watch*, 6 October 2008, http://www.hrw.org/en/news/2008/10/06/human-rights-watch-letter-response-bangladesh-home-ministry (10 March 2009).

According to HRW, in a period of only three months since June 2008, RAB killed at least 50 individuals.[21] In addition, the corruption that inevitably follows such power resulted in further illicit activities. There were reports of the DGFI abducting businessmen and extorting money or property from them in exchange for not framing trumped up charges against them. DGFI has often been accused of torture, abduction and killings. Such incidents helped in discrediting the CTG, several of whose well-intentioned reform programmes were failing during 2008. Despite its best efforts, the CTG failed to create an alternative political landscape in Bangladesh. Coupled with the worsening economic situation in the country, the CTG lost popular support.

Border Conflicts

Relations between India and Bangladesh have been subject to mood swings for many years. Relations between the two countries on an institutional level have worsened much more than on a political level, leading to a deep-seated mistrust on both sides at the ground level. Porous borders between the two nations has resulted in problems like illegal immigration into India and the illicit trafficking of man and material. Coupled with border disputes (land and maritime) between the two nations, these issues often result in violence. The two nation's paramilitaries — Bangladesh Rifles and the Border Security Force — often exchange fire with each other across the border leading to military as well as civilian causalities.

In 2008 the BSF killed 59 Bangladeshi citizens including two BDR soldiers in July.[22] Similar problems exist on the Bangladesh–Myanmar border. In November, two Burmese naval ships entered the disputed maritime boundary escorting South Korean vessels exploring natural gas in the region. The situation escalated to a potential conflict when the Bangladesh Navy dispatched vessels of its own to fend off the perceived infiltration. As a result, for three days the ships of the two navies held their ground, facing each other, fingers on the trigger. It was only

---

[21] 'Bangladesh: End Wave of Killings by Elite Forces', Human Rights Watch, 10 August 2008, http://www.hrw.org/en/news/2008/08/10/bangladesh-end-wave-killings-elite-forces (12 March 2009).

[22] '2008 Human Rights Report: Bangladesh', Bureau of Democracy, Human Rights, and Labor, US State Department, 25 February 2008, http://www.state.gov/g/drl/rls/hrrpt/2008/sca/119132.htm (12 March 2009).

after the Chinese intervention that the situation was resolved and the Burmese ships turned back.[23]

CONFLICT MANAGEMENT

Tackling Militancy

A crackdown on terrorism has been a high-priority agenda for the government. Through co-ordinated efforts of the RAB and the police, the government was able to arrest a large number of militants, both left and right-wing. In addition, security forces also recovered a large number of explosives and arms during the year. Such massive drives have resulted in the most peaceful year in Bangladesh since 2002. However, the crackdown methods used by the security forces have been heavily criticised by human rights organisations and civil society. The extrajudicial killings which surged during later part of the year have especially attracted attention from around the world. Observers have also questioned the credibility of the security forces in some cases.

Security sector reforms are an essential requirement for Bangladesh. Due to corruption, political patronage and disregard for human rights, law enforcement in the country is a difficult task. Institutions like the police are often found to be incompetent or complicit with the criminals. The CTG has tried several measures to counter this problem. In the first 10 months of the CTG rule, action was taken against 10,000 officers for involvement in crimes and corruption and the breach of internal discipline.[24] The caretaker government took strong and comprehensive measures to reform the Bangladeshi police. A new ordinance entitled the 'Bangladesh Police Ordinance 2007 (Draft)' was proposed to change the existing Police Act of 1861. The key objective of this amended ordinance is to promote the improvement of police service. The reforms include creating a national police commission, removing the political patronisation of police, improving police behaviour, and making the police more responsible, transparent and

---

[23] Anand Kumar, 'Bangladesh disputes Myanmar explorations in Bay of Bengal', South Asia Analysis Group, Paper No. 2931, 21 November 2008.

[24] Nazrul Islam, 'About 10,000 Lawmen Punished in less than 10 months', *The New Age*, 12 November 2007.

accountable to the people.[25] However, the ordinance draft is yet to become a law. With the return of democracy, political patronising has also returned, undoing many of the steps taken by the CTG. Demilitarization of the internal security architecture is also an essential requirement for Bangladesh. Skewed civil–military relations in the country have resulted in the Bangladesh military getting involved in internal security issues. The response to terrorism in Bangladesh has often been militaristic or quasi-militaristic (in form of RAB and DGFI). While such responses may bring down terrorist activity for some time in the area, they almost never provide a permanent solution.[26] Further, the military procedures employed by law and order agencies like the RAB result in gross violations of human rights. Hopefully, recent reforms like the Right to Information Ordinance and separating the judiciary from the executive branch will bring in some of the desired changes. However, it is unlikely that Bangladesh military will willingly give up its influence over civil matters which it directly exercises under the gambit of national security.

Dismantling of all terrorism support infrastructure is a critical issue demanding urgent attention. Time and again it has been pointed out that a substantial part of Islamist terror activities in Bangladesh and from Bangladesh (to India) have been sponsored by international actors. It is apparent that a complex network for channeling money has been set up in Bangladesh that is yet to be dismantled. While this may have been due to the inability of the government to keep up with international terror financing crafts (a problem that several nations including the US are finding hard to tackle), there is a marked laxity on part of the Bangladesh government on this front. Moreover, the vast number of unregistered madrasas (a figure quoted as high as 64,000)[27] does allow terror groups to recruit from a large pool of semi-educated, brainwashed students. For as long as such an infrastructure exists within Bangladesh, the possibility of completely eradicating the threat of Islamist terrorism is impossible.

New laws like the Anti-Terrorism Ordinance and the updated Anti-Money Laundering Ordinance have no doubt increased the capabilities of security forces to go after terrorism financiers and patrons. Moreover, the government has time and again sought help from

[25] 'Promulgate Police Order to Remove Cop-People Caps', *The Daily Star*, 3 August 2008.
[26] Sobhan et al., 'Countering Terrorism in Bangladesh'.
[27] Tony Birtley, 'Bangladesh's War with Extremism', *Al Jazeera English*, 2 April 2007.

foreign agencies with much larger resources and more expertise like FBI and Scotland Yard. However, without strong political will these instruments are unlikely to make a significant impact.

Democratisation was on top of the CTG's agenda during its two-year rule. The mammoth task of electoral reforms carried out by the Election Commission under deadline pressures is no doubt commendable. The general elections held in December were the fairest elections the country has ever seen. However, the government crash landed on other aspects of its reform agenda — namely political reforms. Through various methods, including intimidation, bribery and political arrests, the CTG attempted to create an alternative political landscape in the country over the period of two years. However, it failed in its attempts, resulting in the same old matriarchal politics that Bangladesh has seen in the past two decades. It must be noted that Bangladesh requires much more than just a fair election to ensure a stable, progressive democracy. Given the history of the nation it is apparent that democracy in Bangladesh has been regularly abused by petty street politics. A return to such a situation threatens to undo a lot of what the government has achieved.

Corruption is one of the core causes of all Bangladesh's problems. With rampant corruption permeating every aspect of governance, any significant reform agenda is bound to be ineffective. In 2007, the CTG initiated a massive anti-corruption drive, aimed at the grass-roots level. However, after two years of the campaign, it has now become apparent that corruption in Bangladesh has not really declined. In 2008, Transparency International issued a statement to that effect.[28]

Bangladesh needs, moreover, to initiate fruitful bilateral relations with both its neighbours. Considering the low-intensity violence that plagues the Bangladesh borders, this step is urgent. With proper dialogue on boundary disputes, immigration, etc., Bangladesh can ensure that its borders are violence free. Moreover, unresolved issues can always lead to major border conflicts like the one that could have happened during the naval standoff in November. In addition, Bangladesh also needs co-operation from both its neighbours to combat terrorism. With porous borders in the region, terrorists and militants in Bangladesh cannot be tackled by the nation's security forces alone. The country does require international co-operation, especially from its neighbours, to effectively counter the terrorist threat.

---

[28] Annual Report 2007, Transparency International Bangladesh, available at http://www.ti-bangladesh.org/Annual Report 2007.pdf

While the CTG did make some attempts at achieving bilateral convergence with India, these attempts remained largely half-hearted. Moreover, the institutional mistrust between the two countries makes the permeation of political goodwill down to the ground level all the more difficult. While at a political level the two governments have agreed to tackle terrorism in co-operation, on the ground level this was not the case. In a conference between the directors of the BSF and BDR, Bangladesh was handed over a list of 140 terrorist camps operational in the country. However, no action was taken. The same conference saw the signing of memorandums of understanding promising joint patrols and intelligence-sharing. These decisions are yet to be implemented. Hopefully, with the arrival of the AL-led government, the pace of bilateral dialogue will pick up.

CONCLUSIONS

It is fortunate for Bangladesh that while the rest of the South Asia saw terrible violence in 2008, the nation faced almost no terrorism. However, this period of peace cannot be considered a measure for all time to come. There are several concerns about the future that Bangladesh must prepare for.

It has to be emphasised that while the government has claimed that the 'back of Islamist terrorism' has been broken, there is still a threat of resurgence that looms over the nation. As discussed earlier, the support infrastructure for jihadis in Bangladesh is still intact. Moreover, it is apparent that there is a vested interest of foreign actors in the proliferation of Islamist extremism in Bangladesh. There are several political and economic actors inside the country dedicated to the cause of jihad. Until and unless this infrastructure is dismantled, religious violence will continue to threaten the country.

Luckily, Islamic extremism has failed to become popular among large segments of population. Thus there is an opportunity for the government to criminalise and delegitimise this phenomenon before it becomes stronger. However, to achieve this the new democratically elected government will have to tackle the strong political lobbies operating in Bangladesh's landscape.

Transitioning into democracy is the most immediate challenge Bangladesh has to face. The vacuum that the military rule has left will not be easy to fill. The two-year emergency has transformed several aspects of the government which will have to be reconfigured. The efficiency of governance, which could have been achieved during the CTG rule, may not be possible anymore. The first victim of this void will no doubt be law and order. Already there have been reports of a rise in crime in several parts of the country.

The two-year CTG rule was, with all said, autocratic and capable of taking strict and unpopular decisions. A democratically elected government, no matter how popular, will always be weaker than its successors in certain aspects. Under such circumstances a democratic government may not be able to follow the CTG's policies of law and order and counter-terrorism. While the formula may have been very effective under CTG rule, the newly elected government will have to rethink the entire security architecture for the country.

In fact, this transition has been an unusual one for South Asia. Military rule that has been voluntarily given up and not forced out will have a legacy of its own. Civil–military relations have always been a precarious balance in Bangladesh. With the restoration of democracy these relations face the danger of becoming more complicated during the transition phase. Hopefully, both civil as well as military wings of the government will demonstrate maturity in dealing with each other.

It has to be considered that in almost none of the cases of insurgency or militancy in Bangladesh did the government seek a political solution. As has been seen earlier, a militaristic approach to the problem may suspend extremist activities for some time, but it can not resolve the conflict permanently. What must be rethought by the Bangladesh government is which of the conflicts are a result of genuine socio-economic grievances of the people. These conflicts must be identified and dealt with politically, instead of being lumped together as law and order problems. Otherwise, the problem will simply drag on.

What remains a serious concern for Bangladesh is the possibility of a spillover. Entire South Asia is embroiled in terrible violence. The year 2008 has brought winds of change for all countries, for better or for worse. Nepal saw the establishment of a Maoist government, while the Naxal movement in India is gaining momentum. On the other hand, the Taliban virus has infested entire Pakistan and has penetrated India. Year 2008 saw terrible and bloody attacks from Islamic extremists in both countries. All these developments pose a threat to the peace of Bangladesh. These are the threats that Bangladesh cannot tackle alone. It must seek co-operation from its neighbours as has been promised by the new Sheikh Hasina government. However, the feasibility of such co-operation, given the mistrust everyone, harbours is the question that needs to be addressed.

The most important challenge that remains for the nation is to not let the system slide back to its old ways. Political patronage, corruption, political violence and the lack of political will have been an intricate part of the Bangladeshi brand of democracy. These problems are likely to return if not kept under strict check. Fortunately, the new democratic government of the AL coalition has come to power with unprecedented popular support. Under a dynamic leadership, this support can provide the necessary strength to continue on the way forward.

In 2006 Bangladesh was a country on the brink of collapse. This interlude of two years has provided Bangladesh with a golden opportunity of beginning nation-building in earnest. With the restoration of democracy, a new chapter has begun in the history of Bangladesh. Despite its shortcomings, the two-year military rule in Bangladesh has laid the groundwork for democracy in Bangladesh to move forward in a new direction. It must be noted that the landmark elections held in December 2008 were not the final step, but first steps towards restoring democracy in the country.

9

Nepal: Out with the Old, In with the New

Oliver Housden

A BRIEF HISTORY

Historically, Nepal is one of the poorest and most underdeveloped countries in the world. Under the autocratic rule of the Shah monarchy, between 1962 and 1990, the country struggled to tackle savage inequality, build a suitable infrastructure and emancipate numerous ethnic and caste minorities, especially in the far to mid-western and eastern regions of the country, that had struggled for their survival for decades. So when Nepal made its initial transition to a multi-party democracy in 1990, triggered by the first *Jan Andolan* (people's movement) in light of the fall of the Berlin Wall and collapse of communism, Nepalis sensed a radical transformation in politics that would bring economic prosperity and social change.[1] However, this hope quickly dissipated into disillusionment with the new political system which failed to deliver what many Nepalis had been promised: power remained locked in elitist power structures in Kathmandu, economic opportunities continued to be scarce and those previously alienated minorities continued to be marginalised from state development. It was within this context the Maoist insurgency ultimately flourished.[2]

---

[1] John Whelpton, *The History of Nepal* (Cambridge: Cambridge University Press, 2005), p. 13.
[2] For more on the history and environmental factors that shaped the civil war, see Deepak Thapa, *Understand the Maoist Movement of Nepal* (Kathmandu: Martin Chautari, 2003).

Having endured a 10-year civil war, a Comprehensive Peace Agreement (CPA) was signed on 21 November 2006 that brought an end to the conflict.[3] The agreement was precipitated by a second *Jan Andolan* in April 2006, backed by major international players such as India, the US and the UN. The then Community Party of Nepal-Maoist (CPN-M) agreed to join the people's coalition, comprising a host of political actors including the Seven Party Alliance (SPA), Madhesis, communists, democrats, united by their odium of the despotic King Gyanendra, who had imposed Emergency Rule and abandoned a democratically elected government on 1 February 2005.[4]

Jan Andolan II, sparked by violent protests in the Tarai, has subsequently led to the proliferation of armed political groups operating in Nepal. These have tended to be Madhesi movements fighting for an autonomous or independent Tarai region but also included Hindu and Royalist movements advocating a unified Nepal under a Hindu monarch. Throughout 2006 and early 2007, these groups were responsible for numerous killings, bombings and abductions that terrorised ordinary Nepalis. While several key players, such as the Madhesi Janadhikar Forum (MJF) have officially renounced the use of the violence and entered multi-party democracy, law and order in the Tarai, like many parts of the country, is at best limited as numerous illegal political and criminal activities continue to flourish.

On 11 January 2008, Nepal announced it would hold a general election in April. In a result that bamboozled political analysts, the Nepali political establishment and themselves, the Maoists scored a stunning win and now head the ruling coalition government. However, problems seemingly synonymous with Nepali politics such as intra-party bickering and corruption have prevented the coalition's ability to form a consensus and enact reforms demanded by the electorate, threatening the stability of the peace process.

---

[3] Comprehensive Peace Agreement, Kathmandu, 21 November 2006 (unofficial translation), http://www.satp.org/satporgtp/countries/nepal/document/papers/peaceagreement.htm (accessed 4 March 2009).
[4] International Crisis Group, 'Nepal's Royal Coup: Making a Bad Situation Worse', Asia Report No. 91, February 2005, p. 2.

THE PRINCIPAL ACTORS

State Actors

The Maoist's participation and victory in the April elections has not only marked the party's remarkable transformation from a guerrilla fighting force to a democratic player, it has also dramatically changed the shape of the Nepali political establishment.[5] Consistent with their rhetoric throughout the civil war and in the election manifesto, the Maoist's first move in government was to unite the Constituent Assembly (CA) and dissolve Nepal's 240-year-old monarchy.[6] The CPN-M now leads the ruling government coalition that includes the United Marxist-Leninists (UML), the MJF and Nepal Sadbhavana Party (NSP), headed by the charismatic and controversial leader Pushpa Kamal Dahal 'Prachanda'. Although the performances of the NSP and the Chure Bhawar Rastriya Ekta Party (CBREP) were notable features of the election, it was the impressive performance of the MJF that was so striking.[7] The MJF now occupies a strategically crucial position in the ruling coalition and has firmly planted Madhesi issues at the heart of political discourse in Kathmandu.

Quasi-State Actors

While the Maoists have entered the democratic system, the party still relies on its paramilitary wing the Youth Communist League (YCL) to act as a parallel policing unit. After *Jan Andolan II*, the CPN-M revived the YCL in order to re-energise grass-roots political support as the leadership recognised that the Nepali youth were a vital vote bank in the democratic system. Although the number of incidents involving the YCL has decreased since 2007, the Maoist's continue to utilise them for illicit purposes. However, having seen the success

---

[5] International Crisis Group, 'Nepal's New Political Landscape', Asia Report No. 156, 3 July 2008, p. 3.

[6] 'Nepal Becomes a Federal Democratic Republic', 28 May 2008, http://www.nepalnews.com/archive/2008/may/may 28/news 18.php (accessed on 6 February 2009).

[7] See summary of the 10 April 2008 Nepalese Constituent Assembly Election Results, http://www.election.gov.np/reports/CA Results/report Body.php (accessed on 4 March 2009).

and fear generated by the YCL, opposition and coalition parties have created their own paramilitary youth groups — such as the UML's Youth Force (YF) and the MJF-Youth Forum (MJF-YF) — in order to counter the influence of the YCL at grass-roots level.

Non-State Actors

The Tarai–Madhesi Groups

Janatantrik Tarai Mukti Morcha (JTMM): The most prominent armed Madhesi group, JTMM was formed in 2004 by Jai Krishna Goit, a former Maoist dissatisfied by the leadership's failure to deliver promises made about supporting the Madhesi cause. In 2006, a faction led by another ex-Maoist Jawala Singh broke away to form JTMM-Jawala Singh (JS), who claims to be active in 12 districts across the Tarai. The JTMM-G, renamed Akhil Tarai Mukti Morcha (ATMM) in 2008, is the only (known) Tarai group that demands complete secession and an independent Tarai state.[8] Currently there are eight factions of the JTMM now operating in the Tarai, the most important of which (other than ATMM-G and JTMM-JS) are the Samyukta Janatantrik Mukti Morcha (SJMM), headed by Prahlad Giri 'Pawan', and JTMM-Rajan (R).[9] On 13 January 2009, ATMM, STMM and JTMM-JS united to form the Tarai Janatantrik Party launched in light of the disintegrating Tarai movement.[10]

Tarai Madhesi Mukti Tigers (TMMT): Although the TMMT begun in 2004, they came to the fore after a series of bombings and killings in 2007. Led by Praful Yadav, they demand the release of detained leaders involved with terrorist activities and the withdrawal of criminal charges against them.[11]

Tarai Cobra: Another one of the many groups responsible for the escalating violence throughout 2007 when conflict in the Tarai was

---

[8] Goit sees issue as one to with colonialism – other JTMM factions use Tarai independence as a bargaining chip. International Crisis Group, 'Nepal's Troubled Tarai Region', Asia Report No. 136, 9 July 2007, p. 5.

[9] 'Ethnic identity crisis gathers momentum', *IRIN News*, 20 March 2009.

[10] 'Three Tarai rebel organisations unite', http://www.nepalnews.com/archive/2009/jan/jan14/news02.php, 14 January 2009 (accessed on 21 March 2009).

[11] Prasanta Kumar Pradhan, 'Nepal: Turmoil in the Tarai', *South Asian Intelligence Review: Weekly Assessments & Briefings*, 6(4), 6 August 2007.

at its most intense.[12] While the Tarai Cobra initially supported an independent Madhesi state, they have engaged in dialogue with the government for peace talks and will most likely agree to regional autonomy.

The Tarai–Hindu and Royalist Movements

The Nepal Defence Army (NDA), led by ex-Maoist Parivartan, wants to restore Nepal as a Hindu kingdom and protect the country from the perceived threats of Christianity and Islam. However, despite the historic presence of the Rashtriya Swayamsevak Sangh (RSS) and the Bharatiya Janata Party (BJP) in the region, it is unlikely that NDA has strong links to Hindutva or to Hindu fundamentalist groups in north India.[13]

Beyond the Tarai

Tharus: The Tharu movement is divided into two — camps, the Tharuhat Liberation Army (TLA), led by Laxman Tharu, and the Tharuwan Welfare Assembly, of which Raj Kumar Lekhi is General-Secretary. Both groups demand an autonomous ethnic-Tharu zone in far-western Nepal.[14]

The Limbuwans: The Federal Limbuwan State Council (FLSC) demands that nine districts lying east of the river Arun should be declared an autonomous Limbuwan State.[15] The Limbuwans have resorted to sporadic violence and organised *bandhs* which have caused considerable disruption to everyday life.[16]

---

[12] 'Tarai Cobra Strikes, One Person Killed', 3 March 2007, http://www.nepalnews.com/archive/2007/mar/mar03/news08.php (accessed on 21 March 2009).

[13] International Crisis Group, 'Nepal's Troubled Tarai Region', Asia Report, No. 136, 9 July 2007, pp. 10–11.

[14] 'Tharuhat Liberation Army is Formed', 4 November 2008, http://www.nepalnews.com/archive/2008/nov/nov04/news06.php (accessed on 14 February 2009).

[15] Nepal Assessment 2009, http://satp.org/satporgtp/countries/nepal/index.html (accessed on 27 February 2009).

[16] 'Nine Eastern Districts Reel under Limbuwan Bandh', 30 November 2008, http://www.nepalnews.com/archive/2008/nov/nov30/news08.php (accessed on 25 February 2009); 'FLSC Strike Cripples Eastern Nepal for 2nd Day', 1 December 2008, http://www.nepalnews.com/archive/2008/dec/dec01/news08.php (accessed on 25 February 2009).

Muslims: Although the Muslim community has become deeply involved with civil society in their attempt to pressurise the government over formalising their rights in a new constitution, Muslim activists have also been part of illegal civil disobedience activities such as mass strikes across the Tarai.[17]

International Actors

The United Nations Mission in Nepal (UNMIN): Although the UNMIN's mandate has been drastically reduced since June 2008 it is still an important player in Nepal's ongoing peace process. The Mission not only monitored the April elections, it also oversees seven core military cantonments housing the former PLA and the Maoist's weapons from the civil war; mine-clearing operations; and coordinates UN agencies operating in Nepal such as the Office of the High Commissioner of Human Rights (OHCHR)-Nepal, the Office for the Coordination of Humanitarian Affairs (OCHA) and the UN Development Programme (UNDP).[18]

CONFLICT IN 2008

Although 2008 witnessed some hugely symbolic moments for Nepal, which could provide the foundation for peace, lawlessness and low-intensity violence remained an acute problem. According to OCHA, a total of 312 people were abducted and 440 killed in security related incidents during 2008.[19] *Bandhs* continue to severely disrupt production worth billions of rupees every year.[20] Yet, while many incidents at the beginning of 2008 followed a similar pattern to those in

---

[17] Many Tarai-based Muslims have expressed a desire to become more involved with grass-roots political activity but fear they will become tarnished as zealots or fundamentalists if they express their grievances. 'Ethnic Identity Crisis Gathers Momentum', *IRIN News,* 20 March 2009.

[18] See UNMIN website for more details on history and function of the Mission, http://www.unmin.org.np

[19] OCHA, 'Nepal: Total Reported Security Incidents in 2008', http://www.un.org.np/reports/maps/OCHA/2009/2009-01-15-Security-Incidents-2008.pdf (accessed on 23 March 2009).

[20] OCHA, 'Nepal: Report of Bandhs/Blockades, 2008', http://www.un.org.np/reports/maps/OCHA/2009/2009-1-15-Bandhs-Blockades-Jan-Dec-2008.pdf (accessed on 23 March 2009).

the previous year the announcement of the April elections in January provoked a spate of violent episodes. For example, in the first four months of the year there were a total of 220 explosions involving IEDs. Armed political groups attempted to disrupt the elections until polling day; the JTMM-JS detonated six IEDs in Bhuriya Municipality on 3 April.[21] As for political parties, the YCL received considerable criticism for their use of violence during the election campaign. Not only were they accused of intimidating rival political party candidates, the YCL were also charged with deploying children armed with sticks to intimidate voters on polling day.[22] However, other political parties such as the UML and the Nepali Congress were also cited by election watchdogs for electorate intimidation and, in some cases, the misuse of children for political activities.[23] Nevertheless, episodes of violence and corruption were far less prevalent than many analysts anticipated. Political parties tended to observe the electoral code of conduct and engaged in legitimate campaigning that was by and large exceptionally monitored by the UNMIN.[24]

The election result dealt a severe blow to Nepal's established political parties such as the Nepali Congress and the CPN-UML. Initially, the Nepali Congress and UML attempted to rubbish the result as 'illegitimate', accusing the Maoists of intimidation and coercion, and highlighting the YCL's political activities.[25] Forming a ruling coalition, therefore, took several months after the results were announced in May, and it was not until 25 June that an agreement was reached between all coalition partners and on 13 July finally an Interim Constitution was formed. After months of squabbling, in particular due to the Maoist's insistence on keeping both the Prime Minister's and

[21] OCHA, 'Nepal: Total Reported Security Incident', 1–29 February 2009, http://www.un.org.np/reportsmaps/OCHA/2009/2009-03-09-Security-Incidents-2009.pdf (accessed on 28 March 2009).

[22] UNMIN Election Report: No. 2, http://www.unmin.org.np/?d=peaceprocess&p=election (accessed on 28 March 2009).

[23] See UNMIN Election Reports: Nos 1, 2 and 3 for more on violent incidents during election campaign. http://www.unmin.org.np/?d=peaceprocess&p=election (accessed on 28 March 2009).

[24] Carter Center, 'Nepal Constituent Assembly Election: Preliminary Statement', Kathmandu, 12 April 2008, http://www.carter center.org/news/pr/nepal-prelim-041208.htm

[25] International Crisis Group, 'Nepal's New Political Landscape', pp. 7–9.

the President's positions as well as spoiling efforts from the UML and the Nepali Congress, a compromise was reached with Ram Baran Yadav being named President and Prachanda the Prime Minister of Nepal.[26]

2008 failed to see any improvement in law and order in the Tarai as incidents of political violence and criminal activity continued to take place. In the second half of the year alone, 140 people were killed and over 100 were abducted in security related incidents in the region.[27] The region remains prone to violent and oppressive *bandhs* which, if not observed, can lead to vicious reprisals. In one especially brutal incident, a passenger on a bus was burnt to death by 12 armed activists from the Madhes Rastriya Janatantrik Party for defying a general strike in Saptari district.[28] The most high-profile criminal activity discovered in the period was a counterfeit Indian currency racket based in Birgunj, believed to be the largest of its kind in the subcontinent.[29]

With Nepali security and the peace process caught in a precarious situation, UN Secretary-General Ban Ki-Moon stated on 2 January 2009 that the UN Mission in Nepal should be extended for a further six months, although the report advocated a greatly reduced UN presence.[30] The extension followed two similar moves made in 2008 after its initial mandate had expired, first in January, so that the UNMIN could assist in monitoring the elections, and then July at the request of the new coalition government.[31]

---

[26] Robert Fenner and Anoop Agrawal, 'Former Nepal Rebel Prachanda Chosen as PM', 16 August 2008, http://www.bloomberg.com/apps/news?pid=20601110&sid=a TuQvD.38eRc (accessed on 16 February 2009).

[27] OCHA, 'Nepal: Total Reported Security Incidents in 2008'.

[28] 'One Burnt to Death When a Bus Torched in Saptari', *Kantipur Report*, 2 December 2008 .

[29] 'Real or Fake', *Nepali Times*, 31 October–6 November 2008.

[30] UN Security Council, Report of the Secretary-General on the Request of Nepal for United Nations Assistance in Support of its Peace Process, 2 January 2009, p. 14.

[31] UNMIN Spokesperson Kieran Dwyer, 'Press Briefing on the Extension of UNMIN's Mandate', 24 January 2008, Kathmandu, http://www.unmin.org.np/downloads/pressreleases/2008-01-24-UNMIN.Spokesperson.Media.update.ENG.pdf (accessed on 19 March 2009).

Major Trends in the Conflict

Although Nepal did not exhibit any radically different patterns of conflict during 2008, many existing trends continued into the new year. Violence remains sporadic, committed by a host of culprits who are largely unknown, rendering analysis extremely difficult. Much to the alarm of international observers, the period of study also witnessed the re-emergence of trends akin to the civil war, especially in terms of how and why many combatants were recruited to illegal armed groups.

Violence in Tarai–Madhesi Groups

Beyond major cities such as Kathmandu, Biratnagar and Pokhara and other district capitals, state presence is minimal. The Tarai region is the most pertinent illustration of this dynamic, host to numerous illegal, armed political and criminal groups, whose numbers have risen sharply from 14 to an estimated 40. Although the military capacity of these armed groups is hard to gauge, they tend to be poorly armed with low-calibre weapons, smuggled by criminal gangs over the open border from Bihar, and rudimentary IEDs. Funding for their weapons is primarily sourced through land seizures and forced donations, particularly from wealthy businessmen and landowners who have become increasingly targeted throughout 2008.[32] The relationship between armed groups and Tarai-based parties, such as the MJF or NSP for Madhesi groups or the CBREP for Hindu or *pahari* movements, is unclear but it is likely they maintain regular contact with each other if not funding or supply chains.

There are several reasons why the number of these groups, the majority of whom are fighting for Madhesi autonomy or independence, has increased so rapidly. At its core, the Madhes movement it is not a class-based or socio-economic struggle.[33] Rather, Madhesis object to being lumped together with Nepali culture which is alien to many in the Tarai and demand recognition of the Madhesis in the constitution. This important feature of the Madhesi movement explains why the decision of the MJF to enter multi-party politics in Kathmandu has

---

[32] 'Businessmen Face Donation Terror', *Kantipur Report*, 29 October 2008.
[33] Prashant Jha, 'Recent Events in the Tarai', lecture at British–Nepal Academic Study Day, University of Edinburgh, 30 March 2009.

led to widespread criticism from so many Madhesi activists who accuse the party of submitting itself to the ruling *pahari*[34] establishment who they see — quite legitimately — as having dominated all aspects of Nepali life for centuries with the deliberate exclusion of Madhesis.[35]

Consequently, the MJF's inclusion into the coalition government not only hardened the position of existing groups it has lead to the formation of new ones. However, many new groups have splintered from active organisations, illustrated by the fragmentation of the JTMM into eight factions since 2004. The speed at which they are formed means they have little time to consolidate their structures, causing them to be vulnerable to internal discord and to constant splitting. As with the Madhesi movement in general, these splits are often caused by leadership struggles and caste politics.[36]

Although the names of criminal gangs and protection rackets are largely unknown, their role in the current unrest in the Tarai region is palpable. Like armed political movements, they attract the alienated and poorer sections of society, especially Muslims in the Tarai, into their activities which range from petty bootlegging of soap or detergents to smuggling of building materials, timber and involvement in the drug economy. Larger criminal gangs are also in cahoots with armed political groups, offering them shelter and supplying them with weapons that come through Bihar.[37] As stated above, the most high-profile criminal activity recently exposed was a counterfeit Indian currency racket. According to the Indian government the ring was co-ordinated by Pakistan's ISI, a claim which once again heightened fears over the presence of radical Islam in the Tarai region. As with arms smuggling, this discovery indicates that political and criminal groups are inextricably linked to one another and drawing a distinction between them is almost impossible. Most significantly, it illustrates the conceptual difficulty of analysing unrest in the region which makes finding a solution that much more taxing.

---

[34] People from the hill regions of Nepal.

[35] For more on the history and politics of the Madhesis, see International Crisis Group, 'Nepal's Troubled Tarai Region', Asia Report No. 136, 9 July 2007, pp. 4–6.

[36] Prashant Jha, 'Madhesi Movement Splintered by Caste and Militancy', *Nepali Times*, 21–27 November 2008.

[37] Author's interview with Sunsari District Commander of ATMM, Sunsari District, 13 November 2008.

More than the Madhesi — Competing Religious and Ethnic Grievances

However, illegal political activity in the Tarai, as well as in the far-east and far-west regions of Nepal, cannot be attributed solely to Madhesi activists. On the contrary, other groups operate in these regions who advocate competing ethnic, religious and regional objectives in conflict with the Madhesis. Although royalist movements have subsided after the dissolution of the monarchy, Hindu and *pahari* groups are active players in regional unrest. On 29 March, the NDA detonated an IED bomb inside a mosque in Biratnagar, killing two and injuring four.[38] The attack indicates that Muslim–Hindu tensions are still tangible and have the potential to escalate and terrorise local populations.[39]

Most significantly, Nepal has also witnessed the growth of new or invigorated ethnic or identity politics,[40] as demonstrated by the Limbuwan and the Tharu ethnic agitations — the latest manifestation of the 'ethnicisation of Nepali politics' that has grown since the second *Jan Andolan*.[41] What is especially striking about these groups is that their demands for autonomous States include districts in Tarai and are therefore in direct conflict with Madhes movement. Indeed, the Tharu movement fundamentally objects to being referred to as Madhesi, demanding the delisting of Tharu people from this category and replacing it with 'Tarai Tharuhat' in the Interim Constitution.[42]

---

[38] 'Nepal: Reports of Security Incidents — 1–31 March 2009', map prepared by OCHA.

[39] The source of antipathy between Hindus and Muslims, however, tends not to be religious sectarianism but regional, i.e., *pahari* versus Madhesi. Muslims are a key target for *paharis*, as the latter feel the growing importance of Muslims represents the increasing prominence of Madhesis at their expense in Tarai politics. Author's interview with Prashant Jha, Lalitpur, 11 November 2009.

[40] Although fresh identity movements appear to pop up on a regular basis, ethnic or religious associations are not a new phenomenon in Nepal. The Tharus, for example, have had councils or organisations representing their interests since the 1950s that were suppressed during the partyless panchayat period. See Gisele Krauskopff, 'An Indigenous Minority in a Border Area: Tharu Ethnic Associations, NGOs and the Nepalese State', in David Gellner (ed.), *Resistance and the State: Nepalese Experiences* (UK: Berghahn Books, 2007).

[41] Krishna Hatchethu, 'The Second Transformation of Nepali Political Parties', in L.R. Baral (ed.), *Nepal: New Frontiers of Restructuring of State* (New Delhi: Adroit, 2008), p. 135.

[42] 'Tharus unveil plans for second round of protests', http://www.nepalnews.com/archive/2008/apr/apr17/news17.php, 17 April 2008 (accessed on 25 February 2009).

Having seen the success of the Maoists and then the MJF it was difficult for the government to prevent ethnic agitations from becoming militant. Given the sheer number of competing agendas voiced by the various movements, the government could not — and should not — bow to every new demand made of it. However, their paltry and disingenuous efforts at dialogue so far have only made the situation worse. In particular, their unwillingness to either talk or keep promises made with moderate or semi-moderate ethnic movements, such as the Tharu movement before the TLA was formed, has angered their leadership and made them more inclined to pursue violent strategies to achieve their goals.[43]

State-Sponsored Violence

The establishment of a new government after the elections has not precluded the use of violence by all political parties looking to seize control at a grass-roots level. The Maoists continue to be indicted for unlawful and violent land seizures against landowners as part of their continuing 'revolution'.[44] Furthermore, the brutal murder of former Maoist confidant Ram Hari Shrestha, who was beaten to death over missing money in May 2008, illustrates that although the party has undergone remarkable change, their transformation into a peaceful and democratic actor is far from complete.[45]

Yet it is the Maoist's repeated use of the YCL in their political activities which has attracted the most consternation from human rights observers.[46] There is a widespread belief amongst analysts that former PLA members were transferred to the YCL instead of the seven military cantonments to be verified UNMIN in late 2006 so as to utilise their military expertise and bolster party support,[47] a fact that would help explain the sophisticated and militarised structure

[43] Manjushree Thapa, 'Nepal's Misty Season', *Open Democracy*, 7 April 2009, http://www.opendemocracy.net/article/nepal-s-misty-season (accessed on 28 April 2009).
[44] 'Nepal Assessment 2009', South Asia Terrorism Portal, http://www.satp.org/satporgtp/countries/nepal/index.html (accessed on 20 April 2000).
[45] 'Nepal Maoists Hit by Murder Scandal', *AFP*, 20 May 2008, http://afp.google.com/article/ALeqM5ghSAZ8I4zwrYZtU1xDZcGn4jgAdA (accessed on 19 March 2009).
[46] See OHCHR pamphlet, 'Allegations of Human Rights Abuses by the Youth Communist League (YCL)', Kathmandu, June 2007.
[47] Sudeshna Sarkar, 'Nepal: Maoists face UN criticism', *ISN Security Watch*, 12 January 2009, http://www.isn.ethz.ch/isn/Current-Affairs/Security-Watch/Detail/?lng=en&id=95232 (accessed on 2 April 2009).

of the organisation. One of the most high-profile cases involving the YCL occurred after the bodies of two youths abducted by the group who had been missing for several weeks were found dead, a discovery which sparked furious protests against the YCL across Kathmandu.[48]

The YCL continues to refute these allegations. Their leadership argues that they are the victims of media smear campaigns, insisting that the YCL only assists with development projects and will resort to violence only in 'self-defence'.[49] Certainly, to focus on the YCL as the source of post-peace anarchy in Nepal is misplaced analysis.[50] In many parts of Nepal, and not just in isolated rural areas but major power centres such as Kathmandu, the YCL are seen as being more legitimate and offer Nepalis more effective security than the state.[51] Nevertheless, the number of allegations made against the YCL suggests that they are culpable of committing brutal attacks on civilians.

Furthermore, a new feature of localised violence in Nepal during the year was the increasing number of clashes between the YCL and youth wings from rival political parties. Although the UML's Youth Force and MJF's Youth Forum are not as sophisticated as the YCL, they have adopted the same structure as their predecessor and offer similar crude self-defence and military training to new recruits.[52] All these groups have instigated and been involved with numerous clashes with each other that escalated throughout 2008 and into early 2009.[53]

[48] 'Two Youths Abducted by YCL Found Killed; Protests in Kathmandu', 19 November 2008, http://www.nepalnews.com/archive/2008/nov/nov19/news01.php (accessed on 15 December 2008).

[49] Author's interview with the Head of YCL Biratnagar, Biratnagar, 11 November 2008; author's interview with Deputy-Head of YCL Banke District Chairman, Nepalgunj, 14 November 2008.

[50] Jason Miklian, 'Nepal – The (Flawed) View from the United States', *Strategic Analysis*, 32(3), May 2008, p. 350.

[51] Author's interview with Manish Thapa, Asian Study Centre for Political and Conflict Transformation, Kathmandu, 7 November 2008.

[52] Author's interview with Local Leader of MJF-YF, Rangali, Morang District, 11 November 2008.

[53] 'Youth Cadre Killed in Dhading', 2 October 2008; 'Dozens Injured in YCL-YF Clash', http://www.nepalnews.com/archive/2008/oct/oct27/news01.php (27 October 2008); 'Youth Organisations Accuse Each Other of Promoting Impunity, Unruly Acts', 2 November 2008, http://www.nepalnews.com/archive/2008/nov/nov20/news 04.php (accessed on 16 November 2009).

Copying the Maoists?

The replicated model of the YCL is not the only imitation of the Maoist's military organisation undertaken by rival political parties and advocacy movements. Given the success of the Maoists in securing minority power in the government and that many armed political actors in ethnic insurgencies are former Maoists, it is unsurprising how Madhesi, Tharu and Limbuwan armed groups that are organised, funded and recruit combatants follow tactics that are similar or identical to those utilised by Maoist insurgents during the civil war. All factions of the JTMM, for example, have adopted an organisational structure and hierarchy which mirrors the Maoists. Illegally exporting arms over the open border with India, seeking shelter in Bihar and funding their movement through forced donations are other characteristics that were familiar to the Maoist insurgency.[54] For instance, shortly before the TLA was formed, reports emerged that Tharu activists — lead by Laxman Tharu, an ex-Maoist — were demanding money and shelter from villagers in Dang for their planned insurgency.[55]

One particularly alarming trend that has reappeared is the increasing misuse of children in political activities. Although senior members of youth wings tend to be young male adults, persons under 18 are a vital constituent of the YCL, YF and MJF-YF's membership. They target schools, youth groups and associations for recruitment and subsequently press-gang children into enforcing blockades, strikes and voter intimidation during elections.[56] However, the most pressing challenge concerning the potential recruitment of children is presented by armed groups operating in the Tarai. In an interview conducted with a senior military commander of the ATMM, the commander stated that he was ready to begin large-scale enlistment of children wherein ATMM activists would convince families to donate one of the cause of their children to the cause of their insurgency.[57]

---

[54] For more on Maoist tactics and human rights abuses during civil war, see Amnesty International Report, 'Nepal: A Spiralling Human Rights Crisis', 2002, pp. 37–43.

[55] Author's interview with (anonymous) civil society leader, Nepalgunj, 15 November 2008.

[56] Author's interview with villagers from Rangali, Morang District, 11 November 2008.

[57] Author's interview with Sunsari District Commander of ATMM, Sunsari, 13 November 2008.

This strategy is reminiscent of the Maoist's 'one family, one child' recruitment policy adopted during the civil war.[58]

CONFLICT MANAGEMENT

Implementing the Peace Process

Army Integration

The primary political project during 2008 was the implementation and consolidation of the peace process set out in the CPA and the Interim Constitution. The most critical aspect of the process yet to be completed is the amalgamation of the Nepali Army (NA) and the Maoist's People's Liberation Army (PLA), and subsequent rehabilitation of those members of the PLA who do not make the new integrated armed forces.[59] In spite of persistent squabbling and the unwillingness of both sides, especially the NA, to shift from their dogmatic line, an Army Integration Special Committee (AISC) consisting of representatives from Unified Communist Party of Nepal-Maoist (UCPN-N), MJF and UML was finally announced in March 2009 with an agreement expected by July 2009.[60]

Drafting a New Constitution

Although a Constitution Committee (CC) was formed on 16 December 2008, it will struggle to complete drafting a constitution by its proposed deadline of May 2010.[61] The process has generated a rich debate over the future of Nepal, a discussion focused around the question of Nepali federalism. By decentralising power, peace-brokers hope to foster local democracy, as groups that were previously marginalised

---

[58] Human Rights Watch (HRW), 'Children in the Ranks: The Maoist's Use of Children in Nepal', New York, January 2007, pp. 26–31.

[59] Article 146 of the Comprehensive Peace Agreement. See *The Interim Constitution of Nepal 2063 [2007]*, (Nepal: United Nations, 2008), http://www.undp.org.np/constitutionbuilding/constitutionnepal/contitutionfile/Interim_Constitution_bilingual.pdf (accessed on 19 December 2008).

[60] 'Army Integration by mid-July', *Kantipur Report*, 11 April 2009.

[61] Keshpa Poudel, 'Meeting Schedule', *Spotlight*, 28(21), February 2009, http://www.nepalnews.com/contents/2009/englishweekly/spotlight/feb/feb05/coverstory.php (accessed on 18 March 2009).

from the political establishment will be given greater stake in the future of the country.[62] However, if Nepali federal states were to be based on ethnicity, then which ethnic boundaries does one use to demarcate the country? The competing agendas of the Madhesis, Tharus and Limbuwans highlight the number of difficulties in implementing ethnic federalism in practice. Conversely, if Nepal was to be split along geographical lines, then who controls physical geographical features such as rivers which transcend these boundaries?[63]

While intra-party politicking is a major roadblock to building consensus, internal divisions within the Maoists are perhaps more important when considering the destiny of the current coalition government. The party is split into a dogmatic faction, led by (amongst others) Mohan Vaiyda, who demand the instant inauguration of a people's republic, and a smaller, pragmatic faction including Prachanda and Baburam Bhattarai, who are willing to reach a compromise with other political parties and accept multi-party democracy. The Maoist's internal dissent is bound to affect every policy decision the party makes.[64] The process has been made even more complicated in light of the party's unification with Masal to become the Unified Communist Party of Nepal-Maoist (UPCN-M) on 4 January 2009.[65]

Dismantling Paramilitary Youth Structures

The violent activities of the YCL, YF and MJF-YF prompted the UN Secretary-General in October 2008 to exasperate over the difficulties of 'implementing Nepal's peace process at the local level'.[66] Although dissolving the military structures of these youth wings is enshrined

---

[62] L.R. Baral, 'Nepal: The Restructuring of a Neo-Patrimonial State', in L. R. Baral (ed.), *Nepal: New Frontiers of Restructuring of State* (New Delhi: Adroit, 2008), p. 21.

[63] For a cross-section of opinion on the federal structure of Nepal, see 'Facets of Federalism: A Nepal News Discussion', http://www.nepalnews.com/archive/2008/jul/federal_interviews.php (accessed on 12 February 2009).

[64] A Maoist cadre's leadership conference was postponed for several days after disagreements between rival factions within the party over the future direction of the party. See 'Differences Within Maoists Force Postponement of Cadres' Conference', http://www.nepalnews .com/archive/2008/nov/nov20/news02.php, 20 November 2008 (accessed on 2 December 2008).

[65] 'Jana Morcha, Masal merge', *Kantipur Report,* 4 January 2009.

[66] UN Security Council, 'Report of the Secretary-General on the request of Nepal for United Nations assistance in support of its peace process', [S/2008/670], New York, 24 October 2008, p. 5.

in the CPA and the Interim Constitution, there appears to be little evidence that political parties are ready to do so. Fundamentally, the YCL is a military organisation that was formed to smash pro-royalist forces during the elections and stoke revolutionary sentiments at the local level.[67] Its members, who have enjoyed considerable autonomy for several years, are also scattered amongst towns and villages across the country.[68] Therefore, not only would reining in the activities of the YCL be problematic at a practical level, demilitarising the organisation would erode its core. The emergence of rival youth wings since the CPA was written has made the issue more complicated as no political party is inclined to cease its youth wing's activities if they secure support for their cause. Local state security forces are powerless to take any legal action against them, as the police are susceptible to rampant corruption and bribery by these militant youth wings.

Ending the Culture of Impunity towards Human Rights

The levels of state-sponsored violent activity and the unwillingness of all political parties to bring those who committed atrocities during the civil war to justice has led human rights groups to suggest that a 'culture of impunity' towards basic human rights is endemic in Nepal.[69] Any government efforts that have been made so far have been castigated by national and international observers, in particular over the liberal provision for amnesties outlined in the first Truth and Reconciliation Commission (TRC) bill formed in 2007.[70] In spite of such criticism, the government has continued to stall sending a revised TRC and 'Disappearances' bill to parliament, much to the frustration of human rights campaigners.[71]

---

[67] OHCHR Pamphlet, 'Allegations of Human Rights Abuses by the Youth Communist League (YCL)', Kathmandu, June 2007, p. 28.

[68] According to the YCL, they have 1 million members, 50,000 active members and 7,000 'whole-timers' who are predominantly responsible for their political activism. Of these 7,000 whole-timers, 1,200 live and operate in Kathmandu. Thus, whilst they are scattered across the country, they maintain an effective power base in the centre as well. D. Kumar, 'Nepal's Future: Order in Paradox', *AAKROSH*, 11(40), July 2008, p. 31.

[69] Charles Haviland, 'Nepal's Post-War Culture of Impunity', *BBC News*, 1 March 2009, http://news.bbc.co.uk/1/hi/world/south_asia/7917191.stm (accessed on 4 March 2009).

[70] Amnesty International Report, 'Nepal: Reconciliation Doesn't Mean Impunity', London, 13 August 2008, pp. 8–9.

[71] HRW, 'Nepal: Send Human Rights Bills to Parliament', 29 January 2009, http://www.hrw.org/en/news/2009/01/29/nepal-send-human-rights-bills-parliament (accessed on 23 February 2009).

Peace Talks — Dealing with the Tarai and Beyond

As stated above, the government's efforts at peace talks have received stark criticism. Moreover, their effectiveness depends on several factors, some of which are beyond their control. Given that armed groups exploit the open border with India for shelter and smuggling in weapons through Bihar, implementing security in the Tarai also depends on New Delhi implementing the rule of law in northern India. However, the success of peace talks, in the short-term at least, will ultimately depend on which group the government is speaking to. For instance, the Tharu and Limbuwan leaderships have held talks with the government.[72] Currently, the Limbuwans have suspended their ethnic agitation but the Tharus, incensed by the government's failure to delist Tharu from Madhesi in the Interim Constitution, have begun fresh rounds of protests.[73] Furthermore, any Madhesi group that flirts with power in Kathmandu risks charges of hypocrisy and selling-out to the *pahari* establishment. As explained above, it is for this reason that numerous tiny new groups have mushroomed since the MJF entered the government coalition. There are so many groups now with similar demands that identifying major groups and key actors has become a logistical nightmare. In light of this, peace negotiations with armed Madhesi groups often disintegrate as soon as they have begun.

International Linkages

Appeasing Big Brother — Improving Relations with India

The Maoists have striven to improve bilateral relations with India. After relations between New Delhi and Kathmandu soured through the summer of 2008, Prachanda made a 'goodwill' visit to India in September 2008 to allay Indian fears about Nepal's relationship with China.[74] At the end of his visit, India and Nepal made a commitment to

---

[72] 'Nepal: Ethnic Identity Crisis Gathers Momentum', *IRIN News*, 20 March 2009.
[73] 'Tharus Warn of Indefinite Protests', *Himalayan Times*, 17 April 2009.
[74] Prachanda's decision to make his first foreign visit as Nepali PM to China – rather than India – for the Olympics worried New Delhi that Kathmandu was growing close to Beijing and exacerbated tensions which had existed since the civil war. 'PREVIEW: Nepal's Maoist PM to Reassure India over China Fears', *Reuters*, 13 September 2008, http://www.reuters.com/article/latestCrisis/idUSDEL231834 (accessed on 10 September 2008).

a new era of 'strategic partnership' rooted in fair, mutually beneficial political and economic agreements.[75]

UNMIN

The total electoral turnout of 61.7 per cent, which included a surprisingly high number female voters, was an astonishing result for the UNMIN who helped co-ordinate the Nepali Electoral Commission and publicise the elections with tremendous efficiency.[76] Without doubt, the elections were a huge success that received international commendation from many quarters and could not have been achieved without the UNMIN.[77] Furthermore, the UNMIN are the only actor that political parties, especially the Maoists, genuinely respect and, as a result, provide essential checks and balances against outrageous violations of the peace process.

Having said this, the role of the UNMIN in the Nepali peace process remains extremely controversial. Given that the mandate of the UNMIN is so narrow, many Nepalis question why it is still there. A failure to adequately explain its reformed role to the electorate has left them open to criticism from rival political parties. They have also failed to woo the Indian, and to a lesser extent the Chinese governments, who are suspicious of a long-term UN presence in their backyard.[78] Therefore, while criticism of the UNMIN is often unjustified and the mission is still an essential conduit for Nepal's peaceful transition, the organisation's poorly managed public relations have severely damaged its sphere of influence in Kathmandu and its reputation with the Nepali people.

---

[75] Bibhudatta Pradhan, 'Nepal Government to Change Industrial Policies, Prachanda Says', http://www.livemint.com/articles/2008/09/15220019/Nepal-to-change-industrial-pol.html 15 September 2008.

[76] UNMIN, 'NEPAL: Electoral Expert Monitoring Team: Fifth Assessment Report', Kathmandu, May 2008, http://www.unmin.org.np/?d=peaceprocess&p= election (accessed on 19 October 2008).

[77] Carter Center, 'Nepal Constituent Assembly Election: Preliminary Statement', 12 April 2008, http://www.cartercentre.org/news/pr/Nepal_prelim_041208.htm (accessed on 5 February 2009).

[78] Author's interview with former Indian Ambassador to Nepal, K.V. Rajan, Institute for Integrated Learning in Management, New Delhi, 30 October 2008.

Nepal: Out with the Old, In with the New ▲ 187

CONCLUSIONS

In 2008, Nepal took many positive steps along the uneasy path to peace and democracy. The CA elections, heralded as a huge success by the international community, saw an unprecedented victory for the Maoists and a strong performance of the MJF, which has irrevocably changed the face of the Nepali political establishment. The ruling coalition is the most representative governing apparatus ever constructed in Nepal and includes more women than any other government in South Asian politics.[79]

However, inter-party squabbling is wrecking a golden opportunity for change. Progress on many key aspects of the peace agreement, such as army integration, drafting a new constitution and dismantling the paramilitary youth wings of not only the YCL, but the UML's Youth Force and the MJF-Youth Forum as well, are worryingly behind schedule. Political parties continue to engage in illegal practices and systematically violate the basic human rights of ordinary Nepalis in order to consolidate power. Local police forces, poorly equipped, under-funded and vulnerable to corruption, are incapable of providing effective security.

Moreover, the unwillingness to bring anyone from either the UCPN-M or the NA to justice over crimes committed during the civil war has further damaged the legitimacy of the state and the judiciary. A failure to tackle law and order issues has facilitated conditions for the rapidly expanding number of armed political and criminal groups. While many new groups operating in the Tarai continue fight for either Madhesi independence or, to a lesser extent, Hindu or *pahari* demands, Nepal has witnessed a burgeoning of other ethnic and caste agitations that have attracted the attention of the government and the media. Given that the leaders of these agitations are often ex-Maoists, the structural organisation and military tactics they use are strikingly similar to those adopted during the civil war.

The Future

The possibility of the Maoists abandoning the ballot for the bullet once more is unlikely, but not implausible. Whilst in power, the

---

[79] International Crisis Group, 'Nepal's New Political Landscape', pp. 4–5.

UPCN-M's patience has been severely tested because the party has not been able to implement the far-reaching reform it had hoped for and promised to nepalis. This is both a problem of its own making, by failing to comply with democratic rules and procedures, whilst also a failure of other political parties, in particular the Nepali Congress, to come on board and help build a consensus. Several analysts have argued that any sign of a political party violating the political process will prompt some kind of military coup; yet evidence so far suggests this is unlikely given that all political parties have flagrantly tried to illegitimately undermine the political process since the April elections. Therefore, it will only be in such extreme circumstances as the Maoists abandoning democracy and returning to the jungle, that the army may intervene and assume control of the government.

The fragmentation of the key actors involved in Jan Andolan II has also reduced the possibility of a second civil war or large-scale insurrection. The Madhesi movement is afflicted by leadership struggles and caste disputes. Dalit activists, for example, have refused to participate in any future Jan Andolan or armed movement with Madhesis because of the overwhelming presence of higher and Yadav castes. The Tharus and Limbuwans have competing agendas and will also not be the last ethnic movements to use quasi-militancy in pursuit of their goals, independent of the Madhesis. Therefore, while it is possible for armed Madhesi groups to occasionally join forces for one-off strikes and short-term goals (such as the unification of ATMM, JTMM and STMM into the TJP), the possibility of sustaining a united armed Madhesi movement, or conglomerating the disparate number of other groups with competing ethnic grievances and objectives under one umbrella, is again highly unlikely. It is for similar reasons that the future of the democratic Madhesi movement is also unclear. The nuanced and historical peculiarity of the Madhesi problem — rooted in its hatred of the *pahari* establishment — means that the MJF's apparent collusion with Kathmandu has damaged their legitimacy, which has left a space to challenge their authority in the Tarai. As Prashant Jha notes, 'the big question now is which political force will capitalise on this growing disillusionment with the Madhesi outfits and the resultant political vacuum'.[80]

As for implementing other aspects of the peace process, forging a consensus and arriving at a resolution to the current conflict in Nepal is a far trickier and complex process for peace brokers than it was say in 1990 or 2006. Barring any massive schisms within the Maoists or arguments with the NA, a solution to army amalgamation should be reached within six months. This is not to ignore the significant political problems the AISC faces, such as who will run the army and what will happen to the PLA and NA[81] who are removed from the armed forces, which are potential pitfalls to the process. Nevertheless, a lasting solution is feasible.

However, with respect to a new constitution, the government faces a massive challenge in that it has to include a number of different voices into the new constitution. Change cannot be implemented in a political vacuum and unless there is a radical transformation of political culture in Kathmandu — with an end to human rights violations and the guilty being brought to justice — the peace process will continue to struggle.[82] A change is also required vis-à-vis the liberal us of *bandhs* in Nepal. Even though they are disruptive and can be enforced aggressively, the government is reluctant to clamp down on the parties that use them. *Bandhs* are one of the few relatively by nonviolent methods of dissent available to protest against the state, so to outlaw them completely risks pushing agitators towards greater violence. Therefore, even if a constitution is drafted on time, continued violence and disruption is seemingly inevitable.

Having said this, the medium to longer term prospects do not have to be so bleak. While a new constitution may not preclude violence in the short term, an imaginative and radical redistribution of power through federalism could pave the way for progressive change and peace in Nepal. If the current government engages in dialogue and offers tangible rewards with moderate voices, such as Muslim or Dalit civil society activists that are starting to thrive, then militancy will

---

[80] Prashant Jha, 'Madhesi Movement Splintered by Caste and Militancy'.

[81] The current size of the army, roughly 90,000, is beyond the means and requirements of Nepal. A variety of suggestions have been drafted so far for either those members of the PLA who do not make the grade or soldiers cut from the NA, including a border police, armed police force and social development project guards.

[82] Kim Soo A., 'New Constitution Alone Cannot Reform Nepal', UPI Asia, Hong Kong, 15 October 2008, http://us.oneworld.net/issues/corruptiontransparency/-/article/358025-new-constitutionneeds-extra-thought-before-enacted (accessed on 18 December 2008).

become a less desirable strategy for political movements to achieve their goals. Furthermore, strengthening collaborative governance with the Bihari government on the Indian border could stem the flow of illegal actors and weapons, and is one example of how bilateral relations could improve security in the Tarai. Indeed, with international support and realistic expectations, Nepal does stand a chance of securing peace. However, unless economic and political pressure is levied on (both) governments, the status quo appears unlikely to change and Nepal will remain in the grip of lawlessness and violence for many — and unnecessary — years to come.

10

Sri Lanka: Unprecedented Violence, Unclear Future

N. Manoharan

A BRIEF HISTORY

The history of the ethnic conflict in Sri Lanka is the history of radicalised Sri Lankan Tamil youth resorting to arms due to the failure of moderate politics. At the height of the Tamil insurgency in the mid-1980s there were five major and nearly 30 splinter militant groups, prominent among them being the Liberation Tigers of Tamil Eelam (LTTE).[1] Belief in militancy and sympathy for the militants gradually rose among the Tamils after the ethnic riots of 1983. With the massive migration of Sri Lankan Tamil refugees after the 1983 riots, India could not 'remain unaffected by the events'.[2] New Delhi, to protect its national security interests and ensure stability in the region, offered its good offices to resolve the conflict. At the same time, Indian intelligence agencies provided military training to prominent Tamil militant groups. This strengthened the militants to take on the Sri Lankan forces with more confidence in what is known as the 'Eelam War'.[3] In response, the

---

[1] Other prominent organisations were the Tamil Eelam Liberation Organisation (TELO), People's Liberation Organisation of Tamil Eelam (PLOTE), Eelam Revolutionary Organisation of Students (EROS), and Eelam People's Revolutionary Liberation Front (EPRLF).

[2] Prime Minister Indira Gandhi, while rejecting a Bangladesh-type intervention in Sri Lanka on behalf of the Tamils, said in the Indian Parliament: 'India stands for the independence, unity and integrity of Sri Lanka.... However, because of the historical, cultural and other close ties between the peoples of the two countries, especially between the Tamil community of Sri Lanka and us, India cannot remain unaffected by the events there'. See A. J. Wilson, *The Break-up of Sri Lanka: The Sinhalese-Tamil Conflict* (London: Christopher Hurst, 1988), p. 203.

[3] This continued for four years (1983–87) till the Indian Peace Keeping Force (IPKF) landed in Sri Lanka in July 1987.

Sri Lankan armed forces used excessive force in the North to 'restore law and order'. The failure of various peace missions prompted India to enter into an accord with Sri Lanka in July 1987 'to establish peace and normalcy' in the Island.[4]

As part of the Indo-Sri Lanka Peace Accord, India sent its troops, the IPKF, to Sri Lanka. Unable to implement the Accord, the IPKF got embroiled in the conflict, fighting the same Tamil guerrillas whom the Indian establishment had trained. In a surprising turn of events the Sri Lankan state turned against India and secretly helped the LTTE against the IPKF.[5] However, a short time after the IPKF's departure from Sri Lanka, 'Eelam War–II' broke out between the LTTE and the Sri Lankan security forces in June 1990. In its determination to establish peace by annihilating the LTTE, the Sri Lankan government undertook aerial bombing of civilian areas and economic blockade of the Jaffna peninsula. The 'Eelam War – II' ended in a stalemate.

In 1994, the new government under Chandrika Kumaratunga initiated talks with the LTTE based on a comprehensive devolution package. The talks, however, broke down due to the LTTE's obduracy resulting in 'Eelam War–III'. Gradually, Chandrika became convinced of the rightness of the 'war-for-peace' programme after the security forces achieved some spectacular victories in 1995 and early 1996, including the wresting of Jaffna from the LTTE. But the government forces started facing reverses after July 1996. The major blow to Colombo came with the fall of Elephant Pass in April 2000. However, the LTTE were unable to recapture Jaffna. Thereafter, a stalemate ensued on the military front, with the LTTE ensconced in the Wanni region.

On 22 February 2002, following Norwegian mediation, a ceasefire agreement (CFA) was signed between the Sri Lankan government headed by Ranil Wickremasinghe and the LTTE. In due course,

---

[4] The Indo-Sri Lankan Accord was signed by Indian Prime Minister Rajiv Gandhi and Sri Lankan President J.R. Jeyewardena on 29 July 1987 in Colombo. For a detailed discussion on the provisions of the Accord, see S.D. Muni, *Pangs of Proximity: India and Sri Lanka's Ethnic Crisis* (New Delhi: Sage Publications, 1993); V. Suryanarayan (ed.), *Sri Lankan Crisis and India's Response* (New Delhi: Patriot Publishers, 1991); N. Seevaratnam (ed.), *The Tamil National Question and the Indo-Sri Lanka Accord* (Delhi: Konark Publishers, 1989).

[5] Ranasinghe Premadasa, the then Prime Minister, took out an anti-Accord procession when the Accord was signed, and pursued this policy even after he became President in 1988, asking the IPKF to quit the island.

however, the CFA was relegated to oblivion. The LTTE's suicide and air attacks triggered an 'open confrontation' between the two antagonists in August 2006. The Sri Lankan government under Mahinda Rajapakse unilaterally abrogated the CFA in January 2008 and vowed to 'finish the LTTE',[6] and thus began 'Eelam War–IV'. By January 2009, the government forces had captured Killinochchi, the administrative capital of the Tigers, and Elephant Pass. By mid-May 2009, the remaining LTTE-controlled areas also came under the government. And the possibility of a regroup by the LTTE looked impossible.

THE PRINCIPAL ACTORS

The principal internal and external actors in the Sri Lankan armed conflict include the Sri Lankan security forces, the LTTE, non-LTTE Tamil groups, India, Norway, United States, Japan, and the European Union.

Internal Actors

Sri Lankan Security Forces

The security forces of Sri Lanka include its army, navy, air force, police and paramilitary forces. The Sri Lankan Army was initially created to assist the police in maintaining law and order. However, the Janatha Vimukthi Peramuna (JVP) uprising in 1971 and Tamil militancy later underlined the need for professional armed forces. Since 1983 the modernisation of weaponry has taken place rapidly. The birth of the LTTE's naval wing drew the Sri Lankan Navy (SLN) into counter-insurgency operations. The Sri Lankan Air Force (SLAF) has also been used extensively for bombing missions as part of their counter-insurgency operations and to neutralise the striking power of the 'Air Tigers'. The Ministry of Internal Security was created in March 1984 to handle the rising Tamil militancy. A Joint Operations Command (JOC) was created in 1985 to co-ordinate overall anti-insurgency operations. On independence, the Sri Lanka Police was transferred

---

[6] Sri Lanka Army Commander Lt. Gen. Sarath Fonseka's interview, *Sunday Observer*, 7 December 2008.

from the Ministry of Internal Affairs to the Ministry of Defence. The Police Special Task Force (STF) was formed in 1983[7] to guard police stations, repulse rebel attacks, and penetrate deep into territory held by the LTTE.[8] These apart, there are Home Guards drawn from local communities to provide security for the Muslim and Sinhalese communities living in the north-east.

The problems in the security forces were aggravated in the mid-1950s due to the politicisation and ethnicisation of recruitment and promotions, and the use of the armed forces to assist the police during civil disturbances.[9] Politicisation increased in the 1970s with the appointment of influential political persons to the security forces and those who toed the government line. The rise of Tamil militancy in the north-east transformed the security forces into a more professional but ethnically-based force. More Sinhalese personnel were sent to Tamil-dominated areas as the government felt that Tamil security personnel were either unreliable or inefficient.[10] Consequently, the Tamil minority saw the security forces as 'oppressive', having the sole aim of fulfilling the state's majoritarian agenda.[11]

LTTE

Founded by Vellupillai Prabhakaran on 5 March 1976, the main aim of the LTTE was to establish a separate Tamil nation (*Eelam*) via armed struggle. The 'cult of martyrdom' and the ideology of vengeance in the LTTE were based on appeals to a heroic Tamil past. The Central Committee was the highest decision-making body with Prabhakaran as its Chairman. It had both a political and a military wing. Area commanders with many years of fighting experience were responsible for tactical decision-making. At the macro level the Tigers' strategy had four key components:

---

[7] See Sri Lanka Police Online, http://www.police.lk/index.html (accessed on 25 March 2009).

[8] S.P. Dharmadasa Silva, 'Law Enforcement and Human Rights Training: Experiences of Sri Lanka', paper presented at the Commonwealth Workshop on Human Rights Training for Senior Law Enforcement Officers, 27 November–1 December 1995, Nicosia, Cyprus.

[9] K.M. de Silva, 'Sri Lanka: Political–Military Relations', Working Paper Series No. 3, Conflict Research Unit, Netherlands Institute of International Relations 'Clingendael', November 2001.

[10] *Ibid.*

[11] Daya Somasundaram, *Scarred Minds: The Psychological Impact of War on Sri Lankan Tamils* (New Delhi: Sage Publications, 1990), p. 14.

(*i*) Use of peace to prepare for war, in line with the Maoist doctrine of retreat and recuperate.
(*ii*) Attain total control over the Tamil struggle to gain legitimacy as the 'sole representative' of the Sri Lankan Tamils.
(*iii*) Subordination of the political struggle to the military one.
(*iv*) Use of conventional and guerrilla mode of resistance.

In addition, the LTTE made use of suicide bombers; it was one of the few militant organisations to adopt them as an article of faith. A separate unit called 'Black Tigers' existed for this purpose.

The Tigers' international network extended from Canada and the United States in the West to Australia in the East. Its links were forged by the presence of Tamil refugees who had fled Sri Lanka due to the ethnic conflict.[12] Crackdowns on the Tigers by the United States, Canada, European Union, India, Australia and South Africa diminished their support base. The LTTE has now been neutralised as its cadres and leaders are either killed, surrender or scattered.

Non-LTTE Tamil Groups

The non-LTTE Tamil groups consist of the Tamil United Liberation Front (TULF), Tamil National Alliance (TNA), Eelam People's Revolutionary Liberation Front (EPRLF), People's Liberation Organisation of Tamil Eelam (PLOTE), Eelam People's Democratic Party (EPDP) and Tamil Makkal Viduthali Puligal (TMVP). Except for the TULF and TNA all other Tamil groups are former militant groups, but are now functioning as political parties.[13] Besides these there are also some Muslim armed groups operating in the east.

External Actors

India

Due to geopolitical, sociocultural and economic linkages India is an important external actor in the Sri Lankan ethnic question. In the early 1980s, New Delhi used its diplomatic skills to find a mutually

---

[12] Anthony Davis, 'Tamil Tiger International', *Jane's Intelligence Review*, 8(10), 1996, pp. 472–73.

[13] These groups, however, possess limited weapons for self-defence. 'Suicidal for Us to Disarm Right Now: TMVP', *Daily Mirror*, 8 April 2008.

acceptable solution, but in vain. Later, it had to get directly involved in the conflict through the Indo-Sri Lankan Accord of July 1987. Though the Accord was hastily signed, it had provisions that sought to be fair to all the parties in the conflict.[14] But, the Agreement faced difficulties from the first day because of opposition from even within the Sri Lankan government and, most importantly, the LTTE. The Accord committed India to send a peacekeeping force (the IPKF), which could not make much difference to the overall situation and ultimately had to leave the island unceremoniously in March 1990. India's 'hands-off policy' towards the ethnic conflict got further strenthened after the assassination of Rajiv Gandhi, former Indian Prime Minister, by a LTTE suicide bomber in May 1991. However, India did not sever its military and economic ties with Sri Lanka. India also provided humanitarian assistance to the war-affected areas from time to time. Government to government relations are also good, especially in the economic sphere.[15]

Other Actors

Other important actors include Norway, the United States, Japan, and the European Union. Norway's involvement in the conflict resolution process goes back to 1997, although the formal process only commenced with the signing of the CFA on 22 February 2002. Oslo facilitated six rounds of talks between the Sri Lankan government and the LTTE. In due course, unfortunately, both antagonists disregarded Norway's role. With the abrogation of the CFA in January 2008, Oslo's facilitation role in the ethnic issue ended.[16]

The US did not support a separate Tamil nation in Sri Lanka, but, wanted the rights of all the communities to be respected. It encouraged efforts by countries like India and Norway to help settle the ethnic issue through political means. It also committed substantial financial and human resources, in concert with the EU, Japan, and Norway (collectively called Donor Conference countries) to boost

---

[14] For a detailed discussion on the provisions of the Accord, see n. 4, *infra*.
[15] See text of statement released by Sri Lankan Ministry of Foreign Affairs on the eve of Indian Foreign Secretary Shiv Shankar Menon's visit to Colombo, 16 January 2009.
[16] 'Recapture: Norway's Facilitation', *Daily Mirror*, 10 September 2008.

the peace process. Washington designated the LTTE as a 'Foreign Terrorist Organization' in 1997, but maintained that it will consider its delisting if the group was 'committed to a political solution and to peace'.[17]

Japan strongly backed the Norwegian facilitation and went on to host a round of peace talks between the LTTE and the Government of Sri Lanka (GoSL) in March 2003. Rehabilitation and reconstruction of the war-ravaged north-east has been Japan's concern. Its policy is 'to help consolidate the peace process and help rehabilitation and reconstruction work even before a final settlement'.[18] It appointed Yasushi Akashi as its special envoy to oversee and give advise on this policy objective.

European countries have been playing a major role in the ethnic issue. A sympathy wave after the 1983 ethnic riots, the consequent refugee exodus, and the Tamil diaspora lobby are the main factors that influenced Europe's outlook till the mid-1990s. But the patience of the EU ran out when the LTTE began indulging in indiscriminate killings. Britain banned the Tigers, and the EU followed by blacklisting the LTTE as a terrorist organisation. The ban came after several warnings, which the LTTE chose to ignore.[19]

CONFLICT IN 2008

Violence in Sri Lanka, that was gradually building since 2006, reached a new high in 2008–09 as the government under President Mahinda Rajapakse determinedly pursued its 'war for peace' programme: of resolving the ethnic issue by defeating the LTTE. By mid-May 2009, the government had defeated the LTTE and brought the whole of Sri Lanka under one flag after virtually three decades.

---

[17] Richard Armitage said this during his inaugural address at the Washington Donor's Conference on 17 April 2003.
[18] Statement of Tetsuro Yano, Senior Vice-Minister of Ministry of Foreign Affairs of Japan, on the occasion of his visit to Jaffna, 3 August 2003.
[19] For the full text of the Declaration see http://www.eu2006.gv.at/en/News/CFSP_Statements/May/3105LTTE.html?month=3&day=1 (accessed on 15 March 2009).

End of Ceasefire and Beginning of Ceaseless Fire

With the momentum gained in the east, the GoSL wished to launch full-scale operations in the north. It therefore abrogated the CFA in January 2008 stating that 'the agreement has become a dead letter' in the wake of 'senseless violence by the LTTE'.[20] In reality, however, the government felt the CFA stood as an obstacle for its military thrust against the Tigers. President Rajapakse was also under tremendous pressure from hardline parties like the JVP and Jathika Hela Urumaya (JHU) ever since he signed MoUs with them during his bid for presidentship in 2005.[21] One of the conditions laid down by the two parties for supporting Rajapakse was abrogating the CFA. Rajapakse evaded this issue for two years, but could not hold out any longer.

'Declared war' commenced with the government forces launching a four-pronged attack on the LTTE-controlled areas (comprising the districts of Mullaitivu and Kilinochchi and parts of Mannar, Vavuniya and Jaffna). Task Force 1 and 58 Division were entrusted with the Mannar front; Task Force 2 and 57 Division advanced from Vavuniya; the newly raised 59 Division was put in charge of Weli Oya area; 53 and 55 Divisions guarded the forward defence lines along Muhamaalai on the northern front. The plan was to gradually encircle Kilinochchi, the LTTE's administrative capital, from all sides.[22]

The advance of the government forces on the Mannar front was relatively rapid. In April 2008, Madhu was captured. In July, Viduthalaitivu, one of the key bases of the 'Sea Tigers', fell. By August, the military took control of Vellankulam, Kalekuda jetty, Thunkkai, Uyilankulam, Palamoddai and Thannimuruppukulam. During the year the army captured several other strategic positions from the LTTE, like Adamban, Viduthalaithivu, Illuppaikaduvai, Nachikuda, Akkarayankulam, Devil's Point, Pooneryn, Nedunkerni, Maankulam and Paranthan. Kilinochchi, the administrative capital of the LTTE, fell on 2 January 2009 and the strategic Elephant Pass a week later. This was a major blow to the LTTE and a clear indication of the end. The re-establishment of control of Elephant Pass by the Sri Lankan

---

[20] B. Muralidhar Reddy, 'Ceasefire with LTTE Invalid, says Sri Lanka government', *The Hindu*, 3 January 2008.

[21] 'JVP and JHU Sign Agreements with Premier', *Daily News*, 8 September 2005.

[22] For more details of military operations from the government's perspective see 'Situation Report', http://www.defence.lk (accessed on 16 March 2009).

forces enabled them to proceed full-throttle on all fronts to clear the Tigers from the remaining part of Mullaitivu district.

The SLAF and SLN ably aided the army in the advance. The SLAF — that gained the means to overcome the air defence systems of the LTTE — played a vital role in supporting the ground troops and destroying the Tigers' military installations and conventional defences. Precision bombings to kill LTTE leaders (based on specific intelligence), has been the SLAF's priority tasks. One of the strategies, is 'not just go for terrains, but [to] go for the kill'.[23] The SLAF has also been mandated to neutralise the airpower capability of the LTTE. Since the LTTE's first air attack on the Kattunayake air base in March 2007, the air dimension of the Tigers' threat has been one of the major concerns of the Sri Lankan security forces. The SLN has been used to interdict maritime supply lines of the LTTE and weaken the 'Sea Tigers'. Co-operation with the Indian Navy was crucial in this regard.[24] With the addition of a Rapid Action Boat Squadron that uses Rigid Hull Inflatable Boats, the SLN was able to operate even in shallow waters.

It should be pointed out that the overall professionalism of the Sri Lankan armed forces has greatly improved in the recent past. New training modules, coupled with increased training tenure, attractive monetary compensation, sophisticated weapons system, and new fighting strategies and tactics have increased the confidence of the Sri Lankan security forces. The employment of 'Deep Penetration Units' (under Long Range Reconnaissance Patrol) by the army, for instance, was a novel and unconventional tactic to proceed against select LTTE targets.[25] This paid rich dividends by neutralising some important LTTE commanders, but also by penetrating the impregnable LTTE-controlled territories. Significantly, this was ably backed by a strong and determined politico-military leadership in Colombo. The government skillfully exploited the international environment against 'terrorism' to proceed against the Tigers. In addition, the Sri Lankan military has benefited from military assistance received from various countries like China, Pakistan, Israel, India, United States,

---

[23] 'LTTE's Days Numbered — Fonseka', *The Hindu*, 1 July 2008.
[24] 'India–Sri Lanka Naval Co-operation "Extremely Successful"', *Colombo Post*, 15 January 2008.
[25] D.B.S. Jeyaraj, 'Deep Penetration Squads Notch Up Success Against the LTTE', http://transcurrents.com/tamiliana/archives/489 (accessed on 20 March 2009).

Ukraine and Iran.[26] The GoSL has been fairly successful in obtaining the diplomatic support of important countries like India and the United States to disrupt the LTTE's supplies — monetary and material — from outside.

On its part, during the 'Eelam War–IV', the Tigers have been following three broad military strategies against the government forces. First, at the conventional level, the main aim of the Tigers has been to resist the rapidly advancing Sri Lankan army with the help of aerial bombardment. The LTTE, however, failed miserably in this strategy, which has resulted in the shrinking of its territory from 15,000 sq km in 2006 to nil in May 2009. The Tigers were overwhelmed both by the superior fire power and the numbers of the government forces. The LTTE has lost and it is unlikely to regain its conventional capabilities. Second, the LTTE has been using 'hit and run' tactics in the east and in Jaffna to make its presence felt, but also to keep the security forces occupied. As its conventional capability dwindled the Tigers started falling back on guerilla tactics as their dominant mode of resistance. The idea is also to kill 'informers' and 'traitors' especially those belonging to non-LTTE Tamil groups like TMVP, EPDP, PLOTE and EPRLF. Third, the Tigers used suicide tactics to attack VIPs and vital military and economic targets across the island. The LTTE also used its air wing to launch sporadic attacks on important targets, and this helped them maintain an element of surprise. With the aid of the air wing, the LTTE was in a position to strike any part of the island at anytime, despite the numerous security measures in place. Their objective was not only to create a sense of fear among the people, but also to further dent the Sri Lankan economy.

Despite these three strategies, the LTTE had to face a severe military setback because of a few important factors. First, Karuna, one of the more able LTTE commanders from the East, deserted with a group of LTTE cadres in March 2004 to co-operate with the government forces. Karuna's men knew the terrain well, and also provided timely intelligence to the government forces. They also helped reduce local support for the Tigers in the east, one of the largest recruiting grounds for the LTTE. Second, during this period, the LTTE also started facing international isolation for various reasons. The international community was irritated over the LTTE's obduracy

---

[26] 'Pakistan, China Role Limits Indian Influence in Sri Lanka', *Daily Times*, 30 January 2009.

for not being willing to negotiate, except on its own terms. Also, the way the Tigers violated the ceasefire agreement further annoyed the international community, which, especially after 9/11, equates any use of illegal violence by non-state actors to 'terrorism'. Meanwhile, the 'international safety net' woven by the previous Ranil Wickremasinghe regime has worked. As a result, as of early 2009, the LTTE was banned by as many as 31 countries, the latest being Sri Lanka itself.[27] Its proscription by important countries like the United States, EU, Canada and India, where most of the Sri Lankan Tamil diaspora are concentrated, severely affected arms and funds flows to the Tigers. The LTTE's network with various Indian militant groups indirectly pushed New Delhi to co-operate with the Sri Lankan state to dent the Tigers' military capability.[28] Third, the LTTE had lost some of its best leaders in the recent past. The list includes, apart from Karuna, Shankar, the founding chief of the LTTE's air wing, who also possessed many technical skills crucial for the LTTE; Anton Balasingham, the political advisor and ideologue of the LTTE, who acted as the international face of the militant group for over 25 years; Tamilselvan, chief of the LTTE's political wing, known for his clear articulation of the Tigers' ideas on various aspects of the ethnic issue; Balraj, considered one of the chief military strategists of the LTTE, who led the Tigers in many successful military missions, including the capture of the Wanni region and the Elephant Pass military base in 2000; Charles, head of the LTTE's military intelligence and considered an able fighter. The loss of these 'important pillars' obviously weakened the LTTE tremendously.

In order to effect a turnaround, the LTTE has been desperately looking for a lifeline. During his 'Hero's Day' speech, delivered on 27 November 2008, the Tiger chief Prabhakaran appealed to the international community 'to understand the deep aspirations and friendly overtures of our people, to remove their ban on us and to recognise our just struggle'. He especially requested the leaders and people of Tamil Nadu 'to raise their voice firmly in favour of our struggle for a Tamil Eelam state, and to take appropriate and positive measures to remove the ban which remains an impediment to an amicable relationship between India and our movement'.[29] Prabhakaran knew

---

[27] 'Sri Lanka Reimposes Ban on the LTTE', *The Hindu*, 8 January 2009.
[28] 'Maoists Approaching LTTE, ULFA for Arms Procurement', *Indian Express*, 9 September 2008.

that, apart from India, nobody can throw a lifeline to the LTTE. However, the LTTE chief was not sure of a positive response from the Indian regime. The appeal, therefore, was made through Tamil Nadu. Recent protests in Tamil Nadu urging New Delhi to force Colombo to announce a ceasefire made Prabhakaran feel there was strong support for a Tamil Eelam in the southern Indian state. In reality the support for the LTTE is not very great in Tamil Nadu. The protests were mainly directed at the humanitarian aspects of the war.[30]

However, the LTTE has been adept in renewing supply lines from India as resource flow from other sources dwindled. India is not only geographically close, but also easier for building networks due to the ethnic factor and the presence of a large number of Sri Lankan Tamils in Tamil Nadu. The list of smuggled materials include the wherewithal for making bombs, steel or aluminium ingots for improvised explosive devices, detonators, chemicals, batteries, rations, fuel, medicine, motors used to operate speed boats, resin, boat parts, chopped coir mats for building boats, clothes, adhesives, walkie-talkies, GPS devices, mobile SIM cards, multitester meters, pistol covers, battery rechargers, torchlights, satellite receiver phones, combat uniforms, compact discs and life jackets.[31]

The procurement modules were controlled directly by LTTE agents operating in the southern states of India. The *modus operandi* was for LTTE men to come as refugees and develop a smuggling network with the help of LTTE sympathisers and other refugees who had knowledge of local conditions. Requisite materials were procured from all over India and smuggled via fishing villages along the coasts of Tamil Nadu, Andhra Pradesh and Kerala. In Tamil Nadu the network operated mostly along the Rameswaram–Tuticorin–Cuddalore stretch. Both Indians and Sri Lankans were part of the network. Some were there to help the cause of a separate Tamil Eelam, but for large numbers it was simply a quick way of making money. Fishermen who were to be used as couriers were identified carefully; the LTTE agents lived amongst the fishermen for some time and, after establishing confidence, commissioned the task of carrying goods. There was no

---

[29] For full text of the speech, see http://www.sangam.org/2008/11/Prabakaran_2008.php?uid=3169 (accessed on 19 February 2009).

[30] 'Protests in Tamil Nadu even as DMK Slams LTTE, India', *The Times of India*, 30 January 2009.

[31] 'India Breaks Another LTTE Smuggling Ring', *Hindustan Times*, 5 April 2009.

pattern regarding the frequency and timing of the movement of supplies. However, the smuggling took place by night under the cover of darkness. Supplies of a lethal nature were camouflaged by food materials taken for personal use. Goods were delivered in mid-seas or near the shore. The LTTE used smaller vessels to receive these goods from the Indian couriers.[32]

The Cost of Conflict

The ongoing conflict has caused severe human and material losses that can only be approximately calculated at this time. The contours of the humanitarian crisis include civilians caught in the conflict zone, the plight of those internally displaced in the north-east and those who flee the country as refugees. Even by conservative estimates, at least 100,000 civilians were trapped in the crossfire in Mullaithivu district till the government forces captured the remaining LTTE-controlled areas in May 2009. They were extremely vulnerable to indiscriminate shelling, firing and bombing from both sides. The government did suspend aerial raids, which would have caused enormous casualties, but the situation remained threatening because of the continued shelling and firing. There was a severe shortage of food, life-saving drugs and other essentials, including water. People were surviving on the food supplied by the World Food Programme and International Committee of the Red Cross (ICRC). It had become difficult to evacuate the sick and wounded from the 'safe zones' to hospitals located in the government-controlled areas.[33]

The government had designated 'safe zones' in the contiguous areas for the trapped civilians to cross over. But, the 'safe zones' were not really that safe. While the GoSL wanted to use these zones to filter out the LTTE cadres from the non-combatants, the Tigers wished to infiltrate government-controlled areas through these 'safe zones'. Fearing a further loss of territory and attrition, the Tigers did not want the civilians to move to 'safe zones' or 'cleared areas' and expose their fighting cadres to the advancing government forces. The standard refrain from the LTTE was: 'we are fighting your war, then why should you desert us?' The Sri Lankan government was unwilling to

---

[32] 'Politics of Tamil Eelam in TN-II', *News Today*, 10 September 2008.
[33] '"Clock Ticking" for Sri Lanka's Civilians, Warns UN Humanitarian Chief', UN News Center, New York, 8 April 2009.

allow aid agencies and the media into the 'safe zones' citing safety concerns. In truth the government thought that the presence of media personnel and aid agencies would hinder their military operations to capture the remaining territory. The government was not willing to assure the safety of aid workers, as a result it was difficult for them to conduct humanitarian operations.[34]

The civilians who have crossed over into government-controlled areas remain displaced, taking shelter in camps and welfare centres. Overall, about 600,000 people are displaced internally, including 265,000 in the past few months; over 30,000 have fled to India as refugees during the 'Eelam War IV' braving arrests by the Sri Lankan and Indian navies.[35]

Unexplained disappearances have become routine in Sri Lanka. After the unilateral abrogation of the CFA by the GoSL in January 2008, nearly 150 persons have disappeared from Colombo. The figures may be higher in the Tamil-dominated north-east. Sri Lanka ranks second only to Iraq in terms of the number of killings, displacement and disappearances. Threats to civil society organisations and media functionaries were grave under an island-wide Emergency declared in August 2005. Since 2006, as many as 50 journalists have been killed. In a democracy, maintaining basic human rights is imperatives which becomes all the more important in a post-conflict society looking to prevent the situation from sliding back into conflict.

The Sri Lankan economy has been severely affected by this three-decade-old ethnic conflict. The island is suffering from expensive short-term foreign debts, declining foreign exchange reserves and a high budgetary deficit. The present foreign exchange reserves of about $1.5 billion are enough only to finance two months of imports. Although oil prices are down, fluctuations may result in the current reserves being used up sooner. The ongoing global economic crisis has only added to these woes by affecting key export sectors like tea and garments. The garment industry, especially, is in peril due to a threat of permanent suspension of lucrative trade concession by the EU if the Sri Lankan government continues to ignore human rights concerns. Called 'the GSP+ scheme', these concessions helped Sri Lanka net a record $2.9 billion from EU markets in 2007, or 37.5 per cent of

---

[34] 'Trading Danger for Captivity', *The Economist*, 5 March 2009.
[35] 'More Lankan Refugees Arrive in Tamil Nadu', *Daily Mirror*, 22 April 2008.

its total export income.[36] In addition, travel advisories from important countries like the United States, Australia, Germany, Canada, Russia, Britain and New Zealand have constrained the flow of tourists. This is noteworthy because tourism is one of Sri Lanka's main sources of foreign exchange, along with garments, remittances and tea. The eastern parts of the island, one of its best tourist attractions, have not yet been made safe for visitors.

Foreign remittances, yet another major foreign exchange earner, have been able to meet the balance of payments crisis thus far. However, there are concerns that these inflows will decline if there is a sudden change in the economic fortunes of oil-producing countries with the decline in oil prices. This apart, in the context of global recession, there is a significant fall in foreign direct and portfolio investments.[37]

The rate of inflation has come down but remains a cause of concern to the common man whose real income has not kept pace with inflation. Rural areas, President Rajapakse's main power base, have largely been shielded from economic woes through populist budgets and development projects. How long this can be sustained is the big question.[38] The government is counting on aid-flows meant for post-war reconstruction to bail it out of the crisis. But, too much reliance on post-dated cheques is unwise. At the same time, a durable peace can bring about a turnaround in the ailing economy. Agriculture and fisheries are promising sectors in a peaceful north-east. And Sri Lanka can also emerge as one of the key backyards of the services sector, especially for business and knowledge outsourcing.

CONFLICT MANAGEMENT/RESOLUTION

During this period, efforts aimed at conflict management/resolution were totally absent. Whatever few initiatives were taken by the antagonists were designed to further their own politico-military interests rather than address short- or long-term conflict mitigation.

Interim All Party Representative

---

[36] 'Stripping Garments of GSP plus', *The Sunday Times*, 31 August 2008.
[37] K.R. Pushparajan, 'How the Global Economic Crisis Affects Sri Lanka', *Mawbima Lanka News*, 28 March 2009.
[38] 'Lanka's Inflation will Slide Below 18% after 2010 — ADB Country Director', *Sunday Observer*, 21 September 2008.

Committee Report (APRC)

The APRC, appointed in 2006 to 'fashion creative options that satisfy minimum expectations as well as provide a comprehensive approach to the resolution of the national question', submitted an interim report in January 2008. In the Report, the Committee advised the President to implement the 13th amendment to the Constitution, which outlined devolution to the provinces after the Indo-Sri Lankan Accord of 1987. Even after 63 meetings and deliberations for over 18 months the Committee could produce nothing 'creative'. It only did what President Rajapakse wanted in order to be able to show to the international community that 'good progress' was being made on developing a devolution package.[39] In reality, the problem with the APRC is its unrepresentative character. Important parties like the opposition United National Party (UNP), JVP, the Sri Lanka Muslim Congress (SLMC), and TNA are not part of the Committee. Thus, the principal objective of 'generating a consensual political document' on the ethnic issue has been lost. Unless these shortcomings are overcome, the efforts of the APRC will be in vain.

It is significant that President Rajapakse conducted elections first to the local councils in Batticaloa district in March and then to the de-merged Eastern Province in May 2008. Contesting under the United People's Freedom Alliance (UPFA) banner, the TMVP returned 11 out of the 19 members to the Batticaloa Municipal Council, while the main opposition party, the UNP, and the main Tamil party, the TNA, boycotted the polls.[40] This laid the foundations for the conduct of Provincial Council polls in the de-merged Eastern Province on 10 May 2008, ushering in a 'new dawn in the East'.

A total of 1,342 candidates, belonging to 18 parties and 56 independent groups, contested the 37 seats in the three districts of Trincomalee, Batticaloa and Amparai. Of the 982,721-strong electorate 60 per cent voted. Not surprisingly, the ruling UPFA, in alliance with the TMVP and dissident SLMC, won 20 seats gaining a slim majority

---

[39] Kumar David, 'APRC Report is a Sham', *Island*, 3 February 2008.
[40] 'Who Really were the Victors of the East?', *Daily Mirror*, 13 March 2008.

to form the government. Except for the pro-LTTE TNA, all the opposition parties joined the elections, that were being held after 20 years. This gave greater legitimacy to the polls. However, poll rigging negated this credibility. Rigging took place in two stages. In the pre-election stage, opposition candidates could not campaign freely, whereas the UPFA contestants liberally used state resources and the media for personal electoral gains. Electors were also threatened to vote for a particular party or 'face consequences'. On the day of the elections there were reports of ballot stuffing and impersonation. For instance, the independent Centre for Monitoring Election Violence (CMEV) recorded '64 incidents of violence and among them 48 were classified as major offences and 16 as minor. Of the Major Offences, systematic impersonation was the most widespread. The majority of the major offences (28) were committed in the Batticaloa district followed by Amparai (12) and Trincomalee (8)'.[41] Condemning the results as 'irreparably flawed' the opposition announced a mass agitation. Brushing aside opposition allegations, the government interpreted the results as a green signal for its war against the LTTE in the north. President Rajapakse said, 'I note that the people of the east have given a clear mandate for peace through the defeat of terrorism, the strengthening of democracy and the development of the country'.[42] However, post-election governance in the east under the 13th amendment does not appear promising. Unfortunately, the Rajapakse regime is planning to emulate this model in the north as well.

This is an opportunity for the government to demonstrate its earnestness over sharing power with the minorities. The opportunity, however, has been misused, to show the international community that 'democracy has been restored in the former fascist areas'. Unless the strategy on the political side is strengthened, no military strategy can result in a comprehensive victory. The future does not so seem robust, and a lasting peace is nowhere in sight. The current eastern situation could be converted into an opportunity to begin the long journey towards peace.

---

[41] For detailed report see, http://cmev.wordpress.com/?s=eastern+province (accessed on 1 April 2009).
[42] 'Eastern Victory Shows People's Endorsement of Govt's Policy – President', *The Island*, 12 May 2008.

Truce Offer

The LTTE's call for a ceasefire in February 2008 was not surprising given that they were cornered in a small geographical area in Mullaithivu district. The LTTE needed a breather — a ceasefire or a truce — and also an opportunity to demonstrate to the international community that it was a 'liberation group' and was ready for a negotiated settlement. As expected, the Sri Lankan government rejected the offer and asked the LTTE to 'lay down arms and surrender unconditionally'. From Colombo's point of view, it was winning and any ceasefire at that juncture would have demoralised its forces. Second, the GoSL thought the LTTE was desperate and was therefore requesting a halt to the ongoing military operations so as to be able to regroup. The GoSL did not want to provide any such respite to the Tigers and wished to 'finish them off'. Also, the Tigers do not have a good track record in abiding by ceasefires. Third, President Mahinda Rajapakse needed a convincing military victory over the LTTE to face parliamentary elections next year. Riding on this military victory he might advance presidential elections to make a bid for a second term. Considering these factors, the GoSL continued to disregard demands for a humanitarian ceasefire being made by the international community.

However, a truce, if not a ceasefire, could have been considered between the two antagonists on humanitarian and political grounds. If there was genuine concern for rescuing the civilians trapped in the crossfire, a truce would have facilitated their crossing over to the 'cleared' areas. This could, in fact, have been made one for the conditions for the truce and many lives could have been saved. Such a shift in the civilian base would have denied the LTTE the possibility of any new recruits being hired and being used as a 'human shield'. Also, any truce at that juncture would not have been militarily disadvantageous to the GoSL. So far, ceasefires had come about either due to a military stalemate or to the advantage of the Tigers. As a result, it was the LTTE that dictated the terms during negotiations. This time there was an opportunity for the GoSL to have the upper hand. This gesture would have been greeted positively not only by the international community, but also by the Tamil community, which was apprehensive of a solution being imposed on them in the aftermath of a military triumph. It was also a chance for the Rajapakse government to gain the moral high ground and negate the LTTE's criticism that 'the Sri Lankan state had always been genocidal'.

CONCLUSIONS

During 2008–09, Sri Lanka witnessed unprecedented violence, resulting in large casualties, human suffering and economic loss. Despite severe military setbacks, the LTTE was obdurate in its resistance to Colombo's repeated calls for surrender. For the militants it was their 'final war'. For its part, the GoSL pursued its 'war for peace' progamme and went on to 'tame the Tigers'. Military victories in the east during 2006–07 boosted its confidence. The ultimate victims of this war, however, are innocent civilians, who are trapped, killed, wounded, constantly displaced, starved, and suffer all kinds of abuses. Both the antagonists, however, disregarding the humanitarian dimension, stuck to their 'maximalist' positions. Efforts towards conflict management or resolution have been minimal, and movement towards a lasting political settlement has been lethargic.

It is, therefore, the responsibility of the international community to exercise maximum leverage on the Sri Lankan government to deliver a meaningful devolution package to the minorities. India can take the lead role here. Any meaningful devolution should go beyond the present 13th Amendment. However, for the Sinhala hardliners even the 13th amendment is unacceptable. In reality though, devolution under 13th Amendment is not only 'too little and too late', but also unsustainable in the longer run.

Devolution of powers based on a federal model is durable and viable for accommodating plurality and ending the cycle of violence. The fear of the majority Sinhalas that 'federalism is the first step towards separation' is exaggerated, particularly in the present context when the pro-separatist LTTE has been defeated. Interestingly, the federal idea had come from the Sinhalas originally, when they made representations before the Donoughmore Commission in the late 1920s to divide Sri Lanka into three units — north-east, Kandyan and Coastal. This idea, however, was rejected.

The international community should make sure that the present military victory over the LTTE should not result in the triumphalism of the Sinhala-dominated regime over the Tamil minorities. A suitable reconciliation policy should be adopted to construct bridges between all the communities on the island. This is where a good interim arrangement aimed at ameliorating the sufferings of the affected populace and, at the same time, building confidence between the majority and the minority communities is vital. The affected communities need not wait for a lasting political settlement which lies in the distant future. Relief, rehabilitation, resettlement and reconstruction is what needs urgent attention otherwise there remains a 'clear and present danger' of militancy regaining strength.

It is important that both the interim and the lasting political settlements are consensual and agreed to by all parties, otherwise they will not be sustainable. All Sinhala parties and, at the same time, non-LTTE parties and Muslims should be part of this process. One of the main drawbacks of the earlier peace process was that it had failed to address the Muslim factor, which continues to be a 'weak link' in the entire peace chain. The two main Sinhala parties — the UNP and SLFP — should moderate their confrontational politics in the interest of the country. Bipartisanship oZn the ethnic issue is a must for its settlement. This is yet another challenge which requires more energy and greater maturity. One hopes that 'plebiscitary politics' does not return once again to haunt the ethnic question. The international community must strive to help in this regard. Track 2 and 3 levels should be explored to make the process more broadbased and increase the number of stakeholders involved.

Any peace process will not be credible as long as human rights abuses do not cease and the humanitarian crisis continues. These issues require immediate and serious attention. It will be difficult for the government to win over the Tamil population as long as the state security forces are the major cause for human rights abuse. For this, the current regime has to shed its present authoritarian character and switch to a more democratic mode. Shattered democratic institutions require rebuilding, else, Sri Lanka may be forced join the list of failed states.

11

Failed and Failing States and Armed Conflict in South Asia

Sonali Huria

There is growing apprehension that India is precariously positioned in a geographical region marked by a contiguous cluster of 'failed or failing' states. With weakened democratic institutions and the emergence of severe challenges to state authority in South Asia, including a radicalisation of politics, the political instability that surrounds India has sounded alarm bells within academic, journalistic and political circles. India's Home Minister, P. Chidambaram recently expressed fears that Pakistan had become 'pretty dysfunctional' and was 'perilously close' to becoming a failed state[1] — a reference to the disconcerting developments within Pakistan presaging the rapid spread of the Taliban in its tribal areas.

These so-called failed states have become a matter of concern because it is believed that disturbances within their territories may produce similar destabilising tendencies across borders within India through conflict spillovers, refugee flows and weapons proliferation. From concerns about the takeover of Pakistan's nuclear assets by extremists to a faltering war in Afghanistan which has led to the resurgence of the Taliban; the growing unrest and instability in the South Asian region has become a major cause for worry for India and the rest of the world.

Eight years since the launch of the 'War on Terror', Afghanistan continues to teeter on the brink of collapse. Mounting civilian casualties, rampant corruption within the government and judiciary, record levels of poppy production (which funds the resurgent Taliban) and the lack of any significant improvement in livelihood opportunities

---

[1] 'Pak Close to Becoming a Failed State: Chidambaram', *Rediffnews,* 22 March 2009, http://www.rediff.com/news/2009/mar/22pak-close-to-becoming-a-failed-state-chidambaram.htm (accessed on 7 April 2009). Also see, Shobhan Saxena', 'Amid Failing States', *The Times of India,* 1 March 2009.

for the people, have compounded the country's problems, leading the incumbent US administration to re-think America's Afghan–Pakistan policy.

The Afghan–Pakistan border has also become the site of much turmoil with Afghan guerilla fighters having established bases in FATA to fight against the US/NATO forces in Afghanistan, from where they wage a growing insurgency struggle in southern Afghanistan. Pakistan, on the other hand, seems to be staggering from one crisis to another, with the state itself having become the target of the Taliban's attacks, as demonstrated recently in the assault on a police training centre in Lahore in March 2009. This has led many to argue that Pakistan is well on its way to collapse.

The repressive military junta in Burma with an abysmal human rights record, the recent challenge posed to the newly-elected government in Bangladesh by the soldiers of the Bangladesh Rifles (BDR), the humanitarian emergency caused in the wake of the Sri Lankan state's offensive against the LTTE — are all indicative of the growing unrest within the subcontinent. Bhutan and Maldives appear to be the only two exceptions to this rule, being relatively more stable than their neighbours in South Asia. The worsening poverty, hunger, conflict and chaos in these fragile countries, the World Bank believes, places them at considerable risk from terrorist networks, increases the likelihood of internal armed conflict, and the possibility of the outbreak and spread of disease and epidemics.

UNDERSTANDING STATE FAILURE

It is commonly argued now that the greatest threats to world order and security come, not from strong and well-organised sovereign states, but the world's most fragile states, alternatively called 'failing', 'quasi', 'faltering' or 'weak' states, which are steeped in poverty and are often mired in violent conflict. At the heart of the discourse on failed states lies the notion of the modern Weberian state and the basic functions that it is expected to perform. Max Weber defined the state as an institution which exercises authority over a defined territorial area and, to this end, is vested with a monopoly over the means of physical violence, seen as being legitimate by its citizens. However, when a state is unable or unwilling to carry out one or a combination of its assigned state functions, it is said to have 'failed', or at least started its descent into failure. The idea of what a state is or ought to be and an assessment of how effectively or ineffectively it conforms to its designated role, helps determine whether it is 'successful' or 'failing'.

In a Weberian sense, therefore, state failure can be narrowly defined as a 'process of gradual loss of *de facto* sovereignty [or] an inability of state institutions to enforce a monopoly on the legitimate use of force vis-à-vis an existing population and across the entire territory within the internationally recognized boundaries of a state'.[2] However, with attempts to broaden the scope of security by including a wide array of potential threats to it and moving the security debate to both the 'level of the individual or human security and up, to the level of global security, with regional and societal security as possible intermediate points';[3] the parameters to judge state weakness have also broadened.

While there is no single definition of failed states, an assessment of the current literature reveals certain commonalities in all the available definitions. These are states whose governments are believed to have weakened to such an extent that they are unable to provide basic public goods like territorial control, security, education and healthcare, basic socio-economic and political rights to their citizens, and legitimate institutions to the people. Most accounts of failed states centre on the 'erosion' of state capacity or their inability to perform the basic functions of state responsibility like ensuring peace and stability, effective governance, territorial control and economic sustainability.[4] Additionally, 'failed' states are seen as those that are mired in or are at a risk of conflict and instability; where the persistence of violence causes state structures to become ineffectual.

US-AID, OECD, the US Commission on Weak States and the National Security Council of the US, for instance, broadly define these states as those that are unable to assert effective control over their territory or legitimacy over the means of coercion; unable or unwilling to provide basic public services to their citizens; and are characterised by ongoing violent conflict, or the likelihood of its occurrence. Additionally, these states are faced with a legitimacy crisis, that is,

---

[2] Stefan Wolff, 'State Failure in a Regional Context', Working Paper, http://www.stefanwolff.com/working-papers/state-failure.pdf (accessed on 12 April 2009).

[3] Navnita Chadha Behera, *State, People and Security: The South Asian Context* (Har-anand: New Delhi, 2002), p. 11.

[4] Liana Sun Wyler, 'Weak and Failing States: Evolving Security Threats and US Policy', Congressional Research Service Report RL 34253, 15 November 2007, p. 3.

according to the citizens' perception, these governments lack the legitimate authority to rule.[5]

The World Bank uses an additional criterion to judge the fragility of states — economic stability. It labels such countries as 'Low-Income Countries Under Stress' (LICUS) — those with a 2006 gross national income (GNI) per capita of $905 or less with 'dismal social indicators and poor prospects for achieving Millennium Development Goals (MDGs)'.[6]

THE 'STATE FAILURE' PROBLEMATIQUE

The growing concern with failed states is based on the idea that states today face threats not only from other state actors (that is, traditional security threats), but, more importantly, from a multitude of transnational threats, rooted in state failure, which emanate from both state and non-state actors. The threats that are believed to stem from failed states are broadly — terrorism, transnational crime, weapons proliferation, regional instability, the spread of disease and epidemics, and armed conflict.

The US initiated its Global War on Terror (GWOT) after 11 September 2001, when it invaded Afghanistan. 'Terrorism', now at the centre stage of world politics, has become the primary international concern, especially for the developed world, which believes it is increasingly being targeted by international terrorist networks operating out of the world's weakest states. In the immediate aftermath of the WTC attacks, the US identified Afghanistan (and other such 'failed states') as safe havens that provide fertile breeding grounds for terror networks, with easy access to weapons, finance and recruits. It is commonly argued that weak and failing states are the primary base of operations for most 'US-designated foreign terrorist organizations', including the Al Qaeda, since states that are not in control of their own territories and people, are seen as suffering from a 'vacuum' that terrorists, criminal groups or insurgents can fill up.[7]

[5] *Ibid.*, pp.19–21.
[6] World Bank, 'Engaging with Fragile States: An IEG Review of World Bank Support to Low-Income Countries Under Stress', Washington DC, 2006, http://lnweb90.worldbank.org/oed/oeddoclib.nsf/24cc3bb1f94ae11c85256808006a0046/a4d6461b0067e049852571f500551e1b/$FILE/licus.pdf (accessed on 14 March 2009).
[7] Wyler, 'Weak and Failing States', p. 5.

As with terrorist groups, transnational organised crime, involving the production and/or trafficking of drugs, weapons, people, and other illicit goods, is also believed to thrive in failed states. A report of the US Interagency Working Group, titled 'International Crime Threat Assessment' argues that 'weak states can be useful sites through which criminals can move illicit contraband and launder their proceeds, due to un-enforced laws and high levels of official corruption'.[8] The White House released its annual 'Presidential Determination on Major Drug Transit or Major Illicit Drug Producing Countries for Fiscal Year 2008', which identified about 20 countries as 'major' actors in the illicit global drug network. The list includes, among others, Afghanistan, Brazil, Burma, Colombia, Haiti, India, Mexico and Pakistan.[9] Countries with poor economic and political institutions and structures are considered most vulnerable for the development of illicit trade. 'Nearly 90 per cent of global heroin comes from Afghanistan and is trafficked to Europe via poorly governed states in Central Asia or along the "Balkan route"'.[10]

In addition to the threats of terrorism and transnational crime, there is growing concern with regard to the proliferation of Weapons of Mass Destruction (WMDs). According to the International Atomic Energy Agency (IAEA), between 1993 and 2006, member states reported 1,080 confirmed cases of nuclear and radiological material being trafficked across porous international borders due to weak international controls.[11] The developments in Pakistan over the last few years, beginning with the confession by A. Q. Khan in 2004 of having been part of a clandestine international network indulging in nuclear weapons technology proliferation from Pakistan to Libya, Iran and North Korea,[12] and the rapid spread of extremist elements within the country, have led to fears that in the event of state collapse, Pakistan's nuclear arsenal may find its way into the hands of jihadi groups.[13] Additionally, there is concern about the spread of con-

---

[8] *Ibid.*, p. 7.

[9] 'Presidential Determination on Major Drug Transit or Major Illicit Drug Producing Countries for Fiscal Year 2008', 17 September 2007, http://www.whitehouse.gov/news/releases/2007/09/20070917-1.html (accessed on 7 June 2008).

[10] Stewart Patrick, 'Weak States and Global Threats: Fact or Fiction?', *The Washington Quarterly*, Spring 2006, p. 39.

[11] Wyler, 'Weak and Failing States', p. 7.

[12] 'Dr AQ Khan Provided Centrifuges to N. Korea', *The Dawn*, 24 August 2005.

[13] See David E. Sanger, 'Obama's Worst Pakistan Nightmare', *The New York Times*, 8 January 2009.

ventional weapons that also pose a grave threat to human security. It is argued that weak states or states in crisis are important actors in the global proliferation of small arms and light weapons. According to a Geneva-based survey on small arms (2003) over '640 million such weapons circulate globally, many among private hands and for illicit purposes'.[14]

Countries ravaged by violent conflict also engender regional instability. This is because in weak states with porous borders it becomes difficult to contain humanitarian emergencies and violence within the state's territorial limits. A spillover of instability is in fact a natural corollary of conflict in failed states, and ends up destabilising neighbouring countries and the region at large. As governance and political structures weaken and decay in these states, their territorial borders become more permeable; thereby allowing a huge outflow of refugees into neighbouring areas, in addition to the spread of violence and instability.

Weak states, it is believed, are also vulnerable to the outbreak of diseases and epidemics, since their governments invest very little in public sanitation and primary healthcare. Such states, argues Patrick, 'may serve as important breeding grounds for new pandemics and, lacking adequate capacity to respond to these diseases, endanger global health'.[15]

STATE FAILURE AND ARMED CONFLICT: EXPLORING THE LINKAGES

In addition to the reasons outlined above, another reason why state weakness elicits concern is that such states are recognised as being vulnerable to violent conflict. South Asia is home to a myriad ethnic, linguistic, religious and other identity groups and is a region where public spaces are deeply contested.

The region's insecurity, manifest in a host of intra-state conflicts is 'attributable to the exacerbation of latent tensions and instabilities; [with] their historical roots...embedded in persisting ethnic, communal and linguistic asymmetries'.[16] The nature of armed conflicts in South

---

[14] Patrick, 'Weak States and Global Threats', p. 37.
[15] *Ibid.*
[16] P.R. Chari 'Security and Governance in South Asia: Their Linkages', in P.R. Chari (ed.) *Security and Governance in South Asia* (New Delhi: Manohar, 2001), pp. 9–10.

Asia varies both between states and even within them — the region has been marked by conflicts for 'independence or autonomy, ethnic/tribal assertions, violent socio-economic movements, and insurgency and terrorism'.[17] India itself is the site of several conflicts of varied character — while the Naxalite movement was chiefly driven by socio-economic grievances, deprivation and oppression of peasants in a feudal economic structure; those in India's north-east are violent movements demanding, among other things, greater autonomy and the assertion of ethnic identities.

It would be pertinent to offer an explanation of what causes armed conflicts, particularly in the South Asian context. The security problematique of South Asia, argues Behera, is rooted in the processes of state formation in the sub-continent which attempted to replicate the Westphalian model of the nation-state, whose key characteristics included 'more or less homogeneous populations; [their] unquestioned loyalty…; the consolidation and legitimacy of state institutions and, fixed and legitimized territorial boundaries'.[18] The application of this monolithic nation-state model on the diverse and 'deeply multicultural societies of the Third World [however] was structurally flawed',[19] as the entire process sought to impose a uniformity 'on the [diverse] sub-nationalities in the interest of the nation-state'.[20]

Behera identifies this as the motivating force behind most separatist and secessionist movements in the region — Assamese, Tamil, Baloch, Kashmiri, which though diverse, converge on an 'uncompromising opposition to centralized political authority'. The 'state's identification with only *one* [dominant] identity' which is often also in control of the 'levers of state power', has been deeply problematical as it denied to other sub-nationalities the space to assert their own identities, thereby alienating and marginalising them. Subsequently, what often followed in the region was an attempt by these identities to create their own political spaces, often employing violence in the pursuit of their objectives, 'especially [so] if political and constitutional means to achieve [their] objectives [were] either exhausted or perceived to be ineffective'.[21]

---

[17] See Dipankar Banerjee, 'Promoting Peace in South Asia', in D. Suba Chandran (ed.), *Armed Conflicts and Peace Processes in South Asia 2006* (New Delhi: Samskriti, 2007).

[18] Behera, *State, People and Security*, p. 14.

[19] *Ibid.*, p. 21.

[20] *Ibid.*

[21] Navnita Chadha Behera, 'The Argument', in *State, Identity and Violence: Jammu, Kashmir and Ladakh* (New Delhi: Manohar, 2000), pp. 24–30.

Mohammed Ayoob, in an attempt to explain the security dilemma of the Third World, focuses attention on the evolution of the modern nation-state. While European states developed into nation states over a period of four to seven centuries; countries in the global South, he argues, are expected to complete this 'nation-building' process in the course of a few decades, 'that too, by simultaneously undertaking all the stages of nation-building…with all its inherently contradictory pulls and pressures. As a result, many Third World states with highly plural and diverse societies, are not yet politically and socially cohesive units'.[22]

In South Asia what drove these wedges further was the drawing up of arbitrary national boundaries by the colonial powers who disregarded the 'demographic spread and distribution of ethnic groups',[23] creating artificial divisions between members of the same ethnic community, and consequently denying 'their aspirations for a separate nation-statehood'.[24] Borders in South Asia did not evolve over a period of time, but were arbitrarily carved out, leaving in their wake both unsettled border disputes between neighbouring states, and forcibly divided ethnic groups as in the case of the Afghan–Pakistan border which divided the Pashtun tribes, leading to demands for a separate 'Pashtunistan'. The 'non-coincidence of demographic and political boundaries' and strong cross-boundary cultural linkages, therefore, led to a significant degree of violent ethnic mobilisation in the pursuit of demands made by these groups. Chatterjee identifies the movements in India's north-east for a 'greater Nagaland', 'greater Mizoram', and 'Kukiland' as examples of such 'irredentist ethnic claims'[25] that extend beyond state boundaries and involve the territories of other neighbouring states.

Conflicts in the region, in addition to the complexities and pressures of nation-building, have been exacerbated by poor governance or ineffectual state structures. Poor economic conditions, repressive political systems, relative deprivation, and corruption, compounded by ethnic and other identity faultlines have all served to contribute to the rise and continuation of conflict. Most accounts of armed conflicts

[22] Behera, *State, People and Security*, p. 19.
[23] Shibashis Chatterjee, 'Ethnic Conflicts In South Asia: A Constructivist Reading', *South Asian Survey*, 12(1), 2005, p. 82.
[24] P. Sahadevan, 'Ethnic Conflicts and Militarism in South Asia', *International Studies*, 39 (2), 2002, p. 105.
[25] Chatterjee, 'Ethnic Conflicts in South Asia'.

proceed along the explanatory axis of 'greed versus grievance' — both of which are believed to characterise states that are institutionally weak.

While ethnicity in itself is not a cause for conflict, a sense of deprivation among various ethnic communities vis-à-vis each other or the dominant ethnic group, and uneven regional and ethnic development, enhance the likelihood of resistance and conflict. Says Gurr, 'the primary causal sequence in political violence is first, the development of discontent; second, the politicization of discontent; and finally, its actualization in violent action against political objects and actors. Discontent arising from the perception of relative deprivation is the basic, instigating condition for participants in collective violence'.[26] The sense of deprivation among the minority Tamil community vis-à-vis the dominant Sinhalese community for instance, was accentuated by the discriminatory policies of the Sri Lankan state in deliberately reducing for instance, resource allocation to the Tamil-dominated provinces, which became an important cause for economic disparity.[27]

Says Rubinoff, internal colonialism or state action which is perceived as exploitation of a province within the state has also played an important role in the heightening of resentment and conflict. He cites the example of Assam, which produced 60 per cent of the country's crude oil, but was given a measly 3 per cent of the returns from its sale, leading to the 'belief that local wealth was being siphoned off by the centre without corresponding reinvestment'.[28]

It is these sentiments of relative deprivation, discriminatory treatment, internal colonisation, lack of provincial autonomy and the violent suppression of the Baloch identity by the Pakistani state that shaped Baloch resentment against the state, particularly the Punjabis, who dominate practically every aspect of political, economic and social life in Pakistan. Their resentment also stems from the belief that the province is being treated as a colony of the federal government, with the dominant Punjabi ethnic group exploiting the resources of Balochistan (which supplies more than 40 per cent of Pakistan's primary energy needs — natural gas, coal and electricity) for their

[26] Ted Gurr, *Why Men Rebel* (Princeton, NJ: Princeton University Press, 1970), p. 13.

[27] Sahadevan, 'Ethinic Conflicts in South Asia', p. 110.

[28] Arthur G. Rubinoff, 'The Multilateral Implications of Ethno-Nationalist Violence in South Asia', *South Asian Survey*, 7(2), 2000, p. 282.

own development, with little benefit to the Baloch.[29] Additionally, the province is among the least developed in Pakistan. In terms of human development indicators like literacy, the province is much worse off than the other provinces of Pakistan — the literacy level in Balochistan stands at a dismal 24.8 per cent compared to 46.6 per cent in Punjab and 45.3 per cent in Sindh.[30]

Poor governance, grievances on account of poverty, lack of employment opportunities and development, and general neglect by the state have accrued over long periods and resulted in greater support for those agitating against the state. The FATA in Pakistan also suffer from high levels of illiteracy and unemployment. 'There are no universities in FATA, and political parties are absent due to colonial-era tribal laws, robbing youth of an outlet for talent and expression'.[31] Add to this the inability of the tribal system to provide the youth with viable life and livelihood opportunities, and the destruction wrought upon the region by war and the military operations of the Pakistani army, that entered the tribal areas for the first time in 2003, and there is little wonder that an increasing number of youth are turning to the Taliban in the hope that they will usher in peace and 'normalcy' in the area.

Inter-group inequality, with both caste and ethnic dimensions, was also a primary driving factor of the Nepalese civil war. Ethnic groups in Nepal's mid- and far western regions of Nepal are economically the most marginalised and 'most disadvantaged in terms of human development indicators and asset (land) holdings'.[32] It is the degree of inequality, both real and perceived, that best explains the intensity of conflict across the different districts of the country. Argue Murshed and Gates, abject poverty, lack of employment avenues and other forms of 'horizontal inequality', helped the Maoists recruit and retain guerilla fighters, since 'life in Maoist cadres [seemed] a relatively attractive option'.

---

[29] Alizeh Haider, 'The Baloch and the State: Conflict of Perceptions', *The News*, 10 June 2008.

[30] Fazal Hussain and Muhammad Ali Qasim, 'Inequality in the Literacy Levels in Pakistan: Existence and Changes Overtime', *South Asia Economic Journal*, 6(2), 2005, p. 254.

[31] David Montero, 'Why the Taliban Appeal to Pakistani Youth', *The Christian Science Monitor*, 16 June 2006.

[32] S. Mansoob Murshad and Scott Gates, 'Spatial-Horizontal Inequality and the Maoist Insurgency in Nepal', 28 February 2003, http://www.sas.upenn.edu/~dludden/inequalityMAOISMnepal.pdf (accessed on 12 April 2009).

Governance in the South Asian region is also marked by high levels of corruption, which Chabal and Daloz define as the 'reprehensible deviation from a politically legitimate state of affairs, most notably the violation of public duties by private interests when rules or norms objectively define these two realms'.[33] The literature on armed conflict and governance establishes clear links between corruption and political violence. According to Mauro, there is a positive correlation between corruption and political instability, with regions described as the most corrupt also being the most affected by political violence and vice-versa.[34]

Rulers engaged in illicit trade with criminal networks portend a 'criminalisation' of the state, which undermines state institutions and results in 'greater competition over state rents and corrupt proceeds that can degenerate into large-scale violence if competitive groups can challenge the ruler's monopoly of violence'.[35] This criminalisation and competitiveness of corruption, argues Billon, were characteristic of Yugoslavia in the 1990s, and in present times, Afghanistan.

Afghanistan is regarded by many as among the quintessential examples of a failed state. Endemic corruption, roving militias, and a growing nexus between narco-warlords, the Taliban, and officials within the Karzai government, have made a huge dent in the credibility of the current political arrangement. 'Many governors and chiefs of police, rather than confronting the Taliban and neutralizing drug lords, are increasingly intertwined with them, either for political or monetary gain'.[36] According to an Integrity Watch Afghanistan survey, Afghans consider the justice sector, security sector, customs and municipalities among the most corrupt public institutions in Afghanistan. Its ranking on the Transparency International Corruption Perceptions Index slipped from 172 in 2007 to 176 in 2008.

The unconcealed corruption that plagues Afghanistan's judicial system is well documented, and is among the many reasons why, increasingly, people are being forced to look to the Taliban for 'justice' that may be brutal but is certain to come about. Corruption, coupled

---

[33] Philippe Le Billon, 'Buying Peace or Fuelling War: The Role of Corruption in Armed Conflicts', *Journal of International Development*, 15, 2003, p. 414.

[34] P. Mauro, 'Corruption and Growth', *Quarterly Journal of Economics*, 60(3), 1995, pp. 681–712.

[35] Philippe Le Billon, 'Buying Peace or Fuelling War', p. 418.

[36] David Montero, 'Corruption Eroding Afghan Security', *The Christian Science Monitor*, 28 April 2006.

with forced poppy eradication drives, mounting civilian casualties, the lack of any significant improvement in the development of basic infrastructure or livelihood opportunities despite billions of dollars of aid flowing into the country, have all led to an increase in public grievances, helped the insurgency gain sympathy and the Taliban a reasonable degree of political legitimacy among the people.

It is clear from the above discussion that an unfortunate mix of the state's failure and [often] deliberate attempts to ineffectively and inequitably distribute resources and provide life opportunities, coupled with deeply corrupt state institutions, in addition to historical factors, have resulted in and perpetuated armed conflicts in South Asia.

IS SOUTH ASIA FAILING?

According to the annual Failed States Index (FSI) 2008[37] brought out jointly by the *Fund for Peace* and *Foreign Policy* magazine, sub-Saharan Africa, Central Asia, parts of Latin America, and almost the whole of South Asia are becoming severely unstable due to these so-called 'failed' or 'failing' states. Of the 177 countries ranked in order of the most to the least vulnerable/failing states; six from the South Asian region, namely, Afghanistan (7th), Pakistan (9th), Bangladesh and Myanmar (12th), Nepal (23rd), and Sri Lanka (20th) have been placed in the top 25. The index ranks Bhutan, Maldives, and India as being relatively more stable than their regional neighbours, awarding them the 50th, 67th and 98th positions respectively; although India's position has worsened since 2007, when it ranked 110th.

The Global Peace Index 2008,[38] which ranks countries on the basis of the 'ongoing civil and trans-national wars' among other parameters, does not paint a pretty picture of the region either. Afghanistan, Pakistan, Myanmar and Sri Lanka have been ranked as being among the most dangerous and unsafe places in the world. Additionally, South Asian countries are also perceived as being among the most corrupt. Out of a total of 180 countries ranked, the Global Corruption

---

[37] 'Failed States Index 2008', *The Fund for Peace and Foreign Policy Magazine*, July/August 2008, http://www.foreignpolicy.com/story/cms.php?story_id=4350 (accessed on 8 December 2008).

[38] 'Global Peace Index 2008', Economist Intelligence Unit, http://www.visionofhumanity.org/gpi/results/rankings.php (accessed on 12 March 2009).

Perception Index 2007[39] ranks Myanmar (179), Afghanistan (172), Bangladesh (162), Pakistan (138), and Nepal (131) as among the most corrupt. In most of the literature on failed states, corruption has been identified as a major contributing factor to state weakness since it is believed to have a 'corrosive effect on economies and rule-based institutions'.[40]

In terms of human development indicators, South Asia has a dismal record. The Millennium Development Goals Report 2008 has estimated that mounting food prices are likely to push as many as 100 million people into 'absolute poverty', mostly in 'sub-Saharan Africa and Southern Asia, already regions with the largest numbers of people living in extreme poverty'.[41] The Global Hunger Index (GHI) 2008 spells more discouraging news for the region. According to the report, Sub-Saharan Africa and South Asia share the highest regional GHI scores (23.3 and 23.0 respectively), making poverty and hunger levels in these regions 'alarming'.[42]

With raging armed conflicts, loss of effective state territorial control and dismal human development and human rights indicators, South Asia seems to be trudging on perilous terrain. Further, if the indices reflecting the state of human development and state weakness are to be believed, it is easy to conclude that South Asia is, in fact, on a downward spiral into chaos and instability. However, even though the failed states discourse is valuable, in that it reflects the democracy deficit and institutional weaknesses that developing countries face; it fails to capture the complex and multi-faceted ground realities of these states, and consequently, provides a skewed understanding of the challenges that countries of the South are beset with.

To begin with, the FSI is itself riddled with glaring inconsistencies and defects. There is little plausible explanation as to why the

---

[39] Johann Graf Lambsdorff, 'Corruption Perceptions Index 2007, in *Global Corruption Report 2008* (New York: Transparency International, Cambridge University Press), pp. 296–320, http://www.transparency.org/publications/gcr/gcr_2008#7.3 (accessed on 12 April 2009).

[40] Philippe Le Billon, 'Buying Peace or Fuelling War: The Role of Corruption in Armed Conflicts', p. 414.

[41] United Nations, 'Millennium Development Goals Report 2008', http://www.un.org/millenniumgoals/pdf/The%20Millennium%20Development%20Goals%20Report%202008.pdf (accessed on 4 April 2009).

[42] International Food Policy Research Institute (IFPRI), 'Global Hunger Index: The Challenges of Hunger 2008', October 2008, http://www.ifpri.org/pubs/cp/ghi08.pdf (accessed on 10 April 2009).

12 particular indicators employed by the index were chosen to judge state failure — the basis for the selection of these criteria (and not others) remains a mystery. Pritchett, in his study of the challenges facing the Indian state in effectively governing its territory and delivering public goods, exposes the most fundamental flaw of the FSI. He uses a set of criteria vastly different from those employed by the index, including infant mortality and immunisation, availability of doctors in Delhi and nurses in Rajasthan, and acquisition of drivers' licences, among others, and concludes that on the basis of these criteria, not only does India dramatically lag behind most of its neighbours, but has in fact, shown retrogression.[43] The implications of his study are that a change in the criteria for judging state failure can completely alter the ranking of countries. Hence, depending on which criteria are chosen, one can arrive at a wide range of rankings of 'failed' states, each of which may be at complete variance with the others.

Further, if one were to shift attention from the mere presence of democratic institutions to democratic practice, the index would look very different — India, in particular, might rank several notches lower in terms of state failure/weakness. The effectiveness of a state does not depend solely on or cannot be judged on the basis of the presence of democratic institutions alone. Achieving democracy in a 'fuller sense' requires both democratic institutions and democratic practice.[44] The existence of institutions can be undermined or rendered useless if they become dysfunctional on account of corruption or inefficiency. Dreze and Sen use the example of India's judicial system to emphasize this point. While the legal system is institutionally strong, its practical functioning is 'virtually paralyzed by a backlog of millions of pending cases', thereby making legal protection — vital for a functioning democracy — unavailable for the poor and marginalised.

The index also seems to suffer from a 'chicken or egg' causal dilemma — the indicators of state failure seem at once, the causes and consequences of state failure. For instance, the twelfth indicator employed by the FSI for ranking countries is 'intervention of other states or external political actors', which the index explains thus:

[43] Lant Pritchett, 'Is India a Flailing State? Detours on the Four Lane Highway to Modernization', Harvard Kennedy School, 19 September 2008, http://ksghome.harvard.edu/~lpritch/Papers/Is%20India%20a%20Flailing%20State_v1.pdf (accessed on 21 March 2009).

[44] Jean Dreze and Amartya Sen, 'Democratic Practice and Social Inequality in India', *Journal of Asian and African Studies*, 37(6), 2002, p. 6.

'military or para-military engagement in the internal affairs of the state at risk by outside armies, states, identity groups or entities that affect the internal balance of power or resolution of the conflict'. The argument suggests that if a state 'requires' foreign military intervention, then this is reflective of the state's weakness. The implicit argument here is that not only does state failure call for outside intervention, but that external intervention is an effective way to address the problem.

The case of Afghanistan, however, can be used to turn this argument on its head. One can argue that foreign intervention was not undertaken because Afghanistan's failure 'required' it, but that foreign intervention was itself a cause for Afghanistan's failure. It is a state with a history of foreign interventions, which are also responsible for its gradual descent into fragility, compounded by the various ethnic, sectarian and tribal faultlines within the country. These interventions, consequently, prevented or at least decelerated the organic growth of effective public institutions within Afghanistan.

What this reveals is yet another obvious failing of the dominant discourse on failed states, which is that it offers an *ahistorical* account of the weakening of states. By focusing exclusively on the 'failure' of states, the discourse conveniently glosses over the historical processes that might have led to their weakening, such as their colonial legacy and great power intervention during the Cold War. It places the responsibility for state failure squarely on the shoulders of the state itself and ignores any external responsibility. In addition, it is incorrect to treat states as isolated entities that alone are responsible for what goes on within their boundaries. In today's globalised world, states increasingly find themselves enmeshed in transnational structures that include among others, foreign economic actors and the aid system, to which they become accountable. Decisions in these states are not made by the state governments, but a host of other transnational actors as well.[45]

Additionally, threats to human security also have their roots in the present global political economy. The global food crisis which engulfed the world in a wave of rioting and protests last year against the spike in the price of essential foods — from Egypt, Senegal, Cambodia, Mexico, Indonesia, the Philippines, Uzbekistan, and most of sub-

---

[45] See David Sogge, 'Something Out There: State Weakness as Imperial Pretext', in Achin Vanaik (ed.) *Selling US Wars* (Northampton, MA: Olive Branch Press, 2007), pp. 241–67.

Saharan Africa, to India, Pakistan, Sri Lanka, and Bangladesh in South Asia — was transnational in character. Last year, in April, the Director General of the UN's Food and Agriculture Organisation, Jacques Diouf, warned of civil war in countries in sub-Saharan Africa, Asia, and Latin America owing to shortage in food stocks and crippling price rise; a fear reiterated by Diouf in January 2009.[46]

In fact, this was a factor which caused most Third World countries to slip lower on the FSI from 2007 to 2008. The food crisis, however, was not the result of domestic factors but the cumulative result of several factors, including climate change, owing to global warming, trading in food by speculators, and the diversion of crops to manufacturing biofuels, predominantly in the US and Brazil, which the index fails to acknowledge.

Additionally, to speak of state 'failure', it is important to ask if states were ever 'successful' in the first place. In Afghanistan, for instance, a strong, centralised state has never existed, since governance has always been decentralised — exercised through jirgas, customary laws, and tribal codes of conduct. It might be interesting to ask, therefore, if Afghanistan can ever have a strong centralised state structure, whose writ extends to all the provinces in the country or if a replication of the homogenous nation-state model, which has been established as being inimical to the deeply multi-cultural societies in the region, will lead to greater conflict between the disparate ethnic communities in the state?

Chari points out yet another source of instability in the region which is transnational in character and which the failed states discourse tends to overlook in its zeal to treat state failure as an inherent characteristic of a particular state. The history of the South Asian region has been marked by attempts by states to promote disharmony within their neighbouring states by lending financial, strategic and moral support to their internal conflicts, thereby 'aggravating the security problems of their neighbours'.[47] The Pakistan-sponsored insurgency in the 1990s in the Kashmir Valley is a case in point. In India's volatile northeast, points out Rubinoff, the 'military–strategic dimension' of the insurgencies is 'underscored by the support Bangladesh, China, Myanmar and Pakistan have provided to the separatist movements'.[48]

---

[46] 'World Must Double Food Production by 2050: FAO Chief', *AFP*, 26 January 2009.
[47] Chari, 'Security and Governance in South Asia: Their Linkages', p. 10.
[48] Rubinoff, 'Multilateral Implications of Ethno-Nationalist Violence in South Asia'.

The concept of failed states is also regarded as an ineffective analytical tool since it is vague and imprecise and tends to place a wide range of dissimilar political crises into the same investigative category.[49] Additionally, the concept has been criticised as having a 'catch-all' framework. Practically every problem of governance that faces the Third World today is included in these criteria, including uneven economic development, deterioration of public services, demographic pressures and human flight, among others. Further, the discourse treats states as undifferentiated units. It fails to acknowledge the fact that states can and often do 'fail in parts'. In Pakistan for instance, while the government's writ does not extend to the tribal areas, it continues to remain reasonably strong in provinces such as Punjab and Sindh. Even within India, there are states which have dismal human development indicators (for instance the BIMARU states in the north), while others like Kerala boast of 'relatively equitable educational opportunities, extensive social security arrangements, limited incidence of caste oppression and low rural–urban disparities'.[50]

The idea underpinning the failed states discourse, according to leaders and theorists in the South, is that states in the developing world are incompetent and, therefore, incapable of governing themselves. The conflicts in these countries are not seen as conflicts between legitimate actors in the political realm, but regarded as chaos that 'impartial' third parties, namely Western states, can 'fix' with their policies.[51]

CONCLUSIONS

The starting point for understanding state weakness in South Asia therefore, are the state formation and nation-building processes, and the adoption of a model of a homogeneous and unitary nation-state, which engendered much discontent and conflict in the region, making it 'one of history's most grim blunders, particularly in the traditionally plural societies of South Asia'.[52] The link between the failure of states and armed conflict is not completely straightforward

---

[49] Alex Gourevitch, 'The Myth of the Failed State: Intervention and Third World Sovereignty', paper presented at the annual meeting of the International Studies Association, Honolulu, Hawaii, p. 5, http://www.allacademic.com/meta/p71075_index.html (accessed on 15 June 2008).

[50] Jean Dreze and Amartya Sen, 'Democratic Practice and Social Inequality in India'.

[51] Alex Gourevitch, 'The Myth of the Failed State'.

[52] Neera Chandhoke, 'Exploring the Right to Secession: The South Asian Context', *South Asia Research*, 28(1), 2008, p. 16.

and linear, since their relationship is complicated by other historical, political, and socio-economic factors and state-building exercises within the region.

A fundamental aspect of the predicament facing Third World states, as pointed out by Ayoob, is that 'violence inevitably accompanies the process of state formation and consolidation'.[53] In Pakistan, ethnic nationalism has acquired a violent character owing to the inability of the Pakistani state to allow space to different competing identities and, instead, brutally clamping down on them since regional demands were viewed as anti-state and a threat to the security and cohesion of Pakistan.

Further, states in South Asia have often acted on their own volition to marginalise competing minority ethnic nationalisms. The deliberate attempts by the Sri Lankan state to alter the demographic composition of the eastern province by 'land settlement schemes' in a bid to undermine the Tamil claim for their traditional homeland,[54] led to organised protests against the state which were met with repression, thus fuelling further violent resistance from the Tamils, and setting in motion a cycle of state and separatist violence.

While in some cases states have deliberately acted to marginalise certain sections of their populations, in others, there has been a deliberate attempt to remain conspicuously absent. Suba Chandran draws attention to the FATA, where he argues the state deliberately chose to avoid having any meaningful presence in the region and allowed instead for it to be governed by tribal codes and customs, as the state saw this to be an effective 'strategy to deal with the Pashtun tribes settled along the Durand line'.[55]

Countries in the developing world are relatively new entrants into the international system, and it is only natural that they face challenges in the process of state building. The present discourse on failed states is an attempt by the West to make sense of the challenges that states in the South are grappling with. While state weakness is a reality in the

---

[53] Mohammed Ayoob, 'Inequality and Theorizing in International Relations: The Case for Subaltern Realism', *International Studies Review*, 4(3), 2002, December, p. 43

[54] P. Sahadevan, 'Ethinic Conflicts and Militarism in South Asia', p. 108.

[55] D. Suba Chandran, 'Failure or Functional Anarchy? Understanding Weak/Failing States in South Asia', IPCS Issue Brief No. 100, http://www.ipcs.org/publications_special_details.php?recNo=247&pT=1 (accessed on 21 April 2009).

South, there is need for a debate and a set of criteria being evolved that are more holistic than the existing ones. It needs recognition that ground realities in the 'Third World' are vastly different hence they must be willing to appreciate these disparate histories and socio-economic backgrounds to develop more apposite policy solutions to tackle state weakness.

Notes on Contributors

Sandeep Bhardwaj is currently a graduate student at the University of Chicago, Social Sciences Division. Originally trained as an engineer, prior to this he worked as a Research Officer at the Institute of Peace and Conflict Studies (IPCS), New Delhi, focusing his research on Bangladesh's political and security scenario. He worked as a journalist at *Daily News & Analysis (DNA)* in Ahmedabad for a year. He has also co-authored a report on crime and national security for the National Commission for Centre–State Relations. He has written articles and research papers for several magazines, newspapers and journals, including the *Indian Express, Indian Foreign Affairs Journal, DNA, Design Principles and Practices: An International Journal*, and *Mainstream Weekly,* among others.

D. Suba Chandran is Deputy Director, IPCS. His primary area of research includes Pakistan's internal security, in particular Balochistan, FATA and the Northern Areas. He also works on Kashmir and terrorism, particularly suicide terrorism. Some of his recent publications include *Armed Conflicts in South Asia 2008: Growing Violence* (co-edited, 2008); 'Sectarian Violence in Northern Areas', in P. Stobdan and Suba Chandran (eds) *The Last Colony: Muzaffarabad-Gilgit-Balitistan* (2008); 'Pakistan: Tribal Troubles in Balochistan and Waziristan', in D. Suba Chandran (ed.), *Armed Conflicts and Peace Processes in South Asia 2006* (2006); 'India and Armed Non-state Actors in the Kashmir Conflict', in W.P.S. Sidhu et al. (eds), *Kashmir: New Voices, New Approaches* (2006); 'Intra-State Armed Conflicts in South Asia: Impact on Regional Security', in Dev Raj Dahal and Nishchanl Nath Pandey (eds), *Comprehensive Security in South Asia* (2006).

P.R. Chari is a former member of the Indian Administrative Service (batch of 1960, Madhya Pradesh cadre). He was Director, Institute of Defence Studies and Analyses (IDSA), New Delhi, in 1975–80 and Research Professor at the Centre for Policy Research in 1992–96, and is currently Research Professor at the Institute of Peace and Conflict Studies (IPCS), New Delhi. He has served in several senior positions in the Central and State Governments, including the Ministry of Defence, where he was Additional Secretary. He has also been International

Fellow, Centre for International Affairs, Harvard University (1983–84) and Visiting Fellow, University of Illinois, Urbana-Champaign (1998). He has worked extensively on nuclear disarmament, non-proliferation and Indian defence issues. He has published numerous op-ed articles in newspapers, written over 140 monographs, and contributed articles and chapters to books and journals. His recent books include *Indo-US Nuclear Deal: Seeking Synergy in Bilateralism* (edited, Routledge, 2009); *Four Crises and a Peace Process: American Engagement in South Asia* (co-authored with Pervaiz Iqbal Cheema and Stephen P. Cohen, 2007); *Armed Conflicts in South Asia: Growing Violence* (co-edited, Routledge, 2008) and *Making Borders Irrelevant in Kashmir* (co-authored with Hasan Askari Rizvi, 2008).

Shanthie Mariet D'Souza is Associate Fellow at IDSA and is currently working on the project 'US Counter Terrorism Objectives in South Asia'. Her expertise lie in US policy towards Afghanistan, terrorism, Indo-US relations and Indo-Afghan relations. She received a doctoral degree from the School of International Studies, Jawaharlal Nehru University, New Delhi for her work on 'United States and the Emergence and Decline of the Taliban'. She has conducted field studies in the United States, Canada, Pakistan, Afghanistan, Jammu and Kashmir and India's North East. She has presented papers at International and National conference on Afghanistan and has a number of publications to her credit.

Oliver Housden is presently an Intern with the Asia Programme at the Royal United Services Institute (RUSI), London. Prior to this he was a Research Intern at IPCS, where he worked extensively on Nepal, tracing and analysing the country's transition to democracy. He has also lived and travelled across Nepal to study its peace processes more closely and, in particular, the unresolved issue of the use of child soldiers in Nepal's civil war. His fieldwork has provided the foundation for several reports published by RUSI and IPCS, including 'Nepal: A Failed State or a State in Transition? and 'In a Weak State: the Status and Reintegration of Children Associated with Armed Forces and Armed Groups in Nepal'. In addition he has lectured on his findings from Nepal at universities in the United Kingdom, such as the University of Edinburgh and Birkbeck College, London. He obtained a masters degree in Violence, Conflict and Development

Studies from the School of Oriental and African Studies (SOAS), London in September 2008.

Sonali Huria is Research Officer at IPCS. She is presently engaged in a study on 'Failed States in South Asia' and a project on 'Building Peace and Countering Radicalization in J&K' at the Institute. Her recent publications include, 'Thematic Comparison of Legislations', in P.R. Chari (ed.) *Indo-US Nuclear Deal: Seeking Synergy in Bilateralism*; D. Suba Chandran and Sonali Huria (eds) *Radical Islam and Democracy: Indian and Southeast Asian Experiences* (2008); 'Failed States & Foreign Military Intervention: The Afghanistan Imbroglio', IPCS Special Report No. 67, March 2009 and 'Re-Envisioning Peace', *The Book Review*, 33(3), March 2009. She holds an M.Phil Degree from the University of Delhi awarded for her dissertation titled 'Demystifying the New Military Humanism:' American Military Interventions in the Post-Cold War Era'.

N. Manoharan is Senior Research Fellow at the Centre for Land Warfare Studies, New Delhi. He was a South Asia Visiting Fellow at the East–West Center Washington in 2005 and was given the Mahbub-ul Haq Award in 2006. His areas of interest include Sri Lanka, the Maldives, human rights, ethnic conflicts, multiculturalism, terrorism, and national security. His recent publications include *India's War on Terror* (co-edited, 2009); *SAARC: Towards Greater Connectivity* (o-edited, 2008); *Ethnic Violence and Human Rights in Sri Lanka* (2007); and *Counterterrorism Legislation in Sri Lanka: Evaluating Efficacy* (2006). His forthcoming books include *Counter-terror Laws and Security in Developing Democracies: Lessons from India and Sri Lanka* and *Sri Lanka: A Conflict Dictionary*. He is currently working on 'Comprehensive Internal Security Strategy for India'.

Bibhu Prasad Routray is Research Fellow with the Institute for Conflict Management, New Delhi. He received his doctoral degree from the School of International Studies, Jawaharlal Nehru University, New Delhi, for his thesis on the 'Articulation of Dissent in an Authoritarian Regime: Case Study of Indonesia under the New Order (1947–85)'. He was also Director of the Institute for Conflict Management's Database and Documentation Centre on Conflict and Development (DADC) at Guwahati, Assam between August 2001 and February 2005. His recent publications include 'Tibetan Refugees in India: Religious Identity and the Forces of Modernity', *Refugee Survey Quarterly*, 26(2), 2007 and *Failure of Peace Processes (Armed Conflicts and Peace Processes in South Asia* (2006). His current project is on 'Systematizing Response to Urban Terrorism in India'.

Raghav Sharma has been working as a Research Officer with IPCS since August 2008. Prior to this he worked as a research intern in Pakistan with the South Asia Partnership –Pakistan in 2005, and in Afghanistan, with the Church World Service in 2007. He has also been associated with the Afghan web portal www.afgha.com since 2004. He has authored *Pakistan as a Nation State and Flag Bearer of Islam* (2009), and also project reports 'Drought Response Programme for Hazarajat' (Church World Service, Afghanistan, 2007) and 'Hindu Minorities of Lahore' (South Asia Partnership, Lahore, 2005), among others. He holds a masters degree in International Relations and European Studies from the Central European University, Budapest.

Devyani Srivastava is a Research Officer at IPCS. Her research interests include the study of militancy and extremism in South Asia with special focus on left-wing extremism in India. Her recent publications include 'Naxal Conflict in 2006–07' (co-authored with Mallika Joseph), in D. Suba Chandran and P.R. Chari (eds) *Armed Conflicts in South Asia: growing Violence* (Routledge, 2008); 'Terrorism and Armed Violence in India: An Analysis of Events in 2008', IPCS Special Report No. 71 and 'Terrorism, Religious Radicalism and Violence: Perspectives from India', IPCS Issue Brief No. 120. She also presented a paper on 'Women in Armed conflicts: Case of Naxalism in India' at a conference on terrorism organised by the Qauid-i-Azam University, Islamabad in October 2008 and was part of the team that prepared a report on 'Organized Crime and Terrorism in India' for the Commission for Center–State Relations, New Delhi in December 2008. Her current research is a study of voting patterns in Naxal-affected areas in India. She holds a Master's degree in International Relations from the University of Warwick, UK.

Kavita Suri is Lecturer, University of Jammu. Prior to this, she was an accredited journalist working for *The Statesman* as special correspondent based in Jammu and Kashmir. As a journalist, she has covered the entire State and travelled to the Line of Control, the International border and other conflict areas in the three regions of Jammu, Kashmir and Ladakh. She holds a Ph.D. in Education from the University of Jammu and worked on 'Occupational Stress, Role Conflict and Attitude of Women Teachers, Administrators and Professionals Towards their Profession' for her doctoral thesis. She was a recipient of the prestigious British Chevening Fellowship in 2005–06 and the WISCOMP peace fellowship. She has made many documentaries for Doordarshan's satellite Kashmir channel and Jammu and Srinagar Doordarshan Kendras.

Index

Abdullah, Sheikh 83
'absolute poverty' 223
'Afghan Compact' 40
Afghan National Army (ANA) 22–23
Afghan National Army Air Corps (ANAAC) 24
Afghan National Police (ANP) 23–24
Afghan National Security Forces (ANSF) 22
Afghanistan 11, 21–22, 41, 211–12, 225–26, AF-PAK strategy 17; Al Qaeda 20, 25–26, 30; armed forces, inadequacy of 15; armed groups of 24–25; civilian casualties 32; Congress-led UPA coalitio n 16; counter-terrorism 14; corruption in 222; drugs from 12; as failed state 221; high-profile attacks in 30; insurgency in 20–21; international Coin effort in 39; international intervention 31–32; international networks of armed groups 34; Kabul, attacks in 14–15, 16; Karzai's efforts at reconciliation 37–38; Karzai government in 9; Narco-trafficking 34; NATO in 22, 24; negotiations with Taliban 36–37; and Pakistan 28–29; Obama and 28, 31, 36, 41; problematic neighbours 40; troops from Iraq to 38–39; war in 41; warlords and private militias 26
Afghanistan–Pakistan tribal areas 35
AF-PAK strategy 21, 27–28
Afridi, Manghal Bagh 47
Agency Coordinating Body for Afghan Relief (ACBAR) 32
Al Qaeda 44; as Jaish-e-Muhammad 25; in Pakistan 65–66, *see also* Taliban
All Assam National Liberation Army (AANLA) 130, 136
All Tripura People's Liberation Organisation (ATPLO) 128
All Tripura Tiger Force (ATTF) 129, 131
Anti-Naxal Operation Cell of Maharashtra Police 107
Assam 126–27, 129–30, 133–36, 141–43; Bangladesh-based HuJI in 136; Black Widow (BW) 127, 130, 135, 146; Bodo Liberation Tigers (BLT) 127; Bodo Volunteer Force (BVF) 127; Bodoland region of 134; Islamist militancy in 135–36; Karbi Longri North Cachar Hills Liberation Front (KLNLF) 127, 130, 135, 146; ULFA dominated insurgency 133–36; 'zero tolerance' policy of 142
Awami League (AL) 150

Bahadur, Gul 74
Baloch resentment 220
Bangladesh 154–55, 212; Anti-Terrorism Ordinance 155; armed forces 151–52; elections in 7; bombings in 155; border conflicts and 161–62; civil-military relations 166; counter-terrorism agencies 152; elections in 160; Islamic extremism in 165; *jihadis* in 165; Left-wing 153–54, 159–60; and militancy 162–65; as Muslim nation 150; Right to Information Ordinance, 155; and revolt of Bangladesh Rifles 7; Right-wing groups in 152–53, 156–59; Sheikh Hasina government 167; State-sponsored violence 160–61
Bangladesh Nationalist Party (BNP) government of Khalida Zia 7, 150
Behera 217
Bhutan 8, 212
Bhutto, Benazir 49
bin Laden, Osama 20
'blowback' symptoms 5
borders in South Asia 218, *see also* Indo-Myanmar border
Borok National Council of Tripura (BNCT) 131

Central Intelligence Agency (CIA) 19
Central Paramilitary Forces (CPMF) 110
Chidambaram, P. as Home Minister 107
Communist Party of India-Maoist (CPI-Maoist) 103, 105–6, 138; as Fascist party 112
Communist Party of India-ML as fascist party 112
conflict, Arthur G. Rubinoff on 219; Ted Gurr on 219
corruption, Chabal and Daloz on 221
Cyclone Nargis 1

Daimary, Ranjan 143
Debbarma, Ranjit 129
democracy 224
Dima Halim Daogah (DHD). 127
Disarmament Demobilisation Reintegration (DDR) 36
Disarmament of Illegal Armed Groups (DIAG) 36
Drug Transit or Major Illicit Drug Producing Countries 215
Dusadh, Sanjay 104
Dutta, Jiten 142

Eelam People's Democratic Party (EPDP) 195
Eelam People's Revolutionary Liberation Front (EPRLF) 195
'Eelam War' 191–93. *see also* Sri Lanka

Failed States Index (FSI) 236, 224
'failed' or 'failing' states 222–23; definition of 213–14
Fazlullah, Maulana 82
Federal Limbuwan State Council (FLSC) 172
Federally Administered Tribal Area (FATA) 5, 62–64, 80–81, 220; Afghan guerilla bases in 212; armed conflict in 66–70, 75–77; Jirgas and Tribal Lashkars 77–79; and NWFP and state control 55; Taliban expansion in 71–72
'financial tsunami' 1
forceful poppy crop eradication campaigns 35

gaddi nashin 53
Garlossa, Jewel 130;
Gates, Robert M. 36
Global Peace Index 223
Great Depression 1
guerilla fighters 221, *see also* Naxals

Hasina, Sheikh 7
Hazarika, Mrinal 142
Hizbul Mujahideen 86, 89–90, *see also* Jammu-Kashmir
Hrangkhawal, B K 128
human security 226
Hussein, Mufti Jaffar's Tehreek-e-Nifaz-e-Fiq-e-Jafariya (TNJF) 42
'hybrid warfare' 13

Improvised Explosive Devices (IEDs) 33
India 10–11, 211; elections in 9; Rubinoff on 227; Dreze and Sen on judicial system of 225
Indo-Myanmar border 131, 141, 149
Indo-Sri Lanka Peace Accord 192
Inter Services Intelligence (ISI) 28
International Atomic Energy Agency (IAEA) 215
International Security Assistance Force (ISAF) 3
Iran 29; involvement in Afghanistan 29

Jaish-e-Mohammad, Sipah-e-Sahaba and Lashkar-e-Jhangvi 82
Jalali, Ali 36
Jammu and Kashmir 87–88, 89; conflict in. 83–85; 91–96; 97–99; cross-LoC trade 99; decline of violence 91–93; declining support to armed conflict 94–95; demanding independence 96; elections 93–94, 97–98; fencing of LoC 98–99; *fidayeen* attacks in 86; Hizbul's decline 95–96; and Pakistan 88–89; Pakistan sponsored insurgency in 227
Jammu and Kashmir Liberation Front (JKLF) 86
Janatantrik Tarai Mukti Morcha (JTMM): 171

Jihad 73–75
jirgas 63, 73

Kanglei Yawol Kanna Lup (KYKL) 137, 144
Kangleipak Communist Party (KCP) imposed 'indefinite' ban 137–38
Karzai, Hamid President 22; assassination attempt on 3
Kashmir National Conference (NC) 83, 86
Kashmir, Insurgent violence in 5
Khan, A.Q. 215
Khyber Agency 68, 69
Ki-Moon, Ban 175
Kuki Liberation Army (KLA) 131
Kuki National Army (KNA) 131
Kuki National Front (KNF-Prithvi) 131
Kurram Agency 73

Lashkar-e-Islam (LI) 69, 74
Lashkar-e-Jhangvi (LeJ) 44–45, 49, 51; by Muhammad Ajmal 45
Lashkar-e-Toiba (LeT) 2, 16, 86, 90
Lashkar-i–Islami (LI) 47
Liberation Tigers of Tamil Eelam (LTTE) 4, 191–95; destruction of 8; as 'Foreign Terrorist Organisation' 197, *see also* Sri Lanka
Littoral Combat Ships 15
'Low-Income Countries Under Stress' (LICUS) 214

Maldives 8, 212
Malik, Rehman 48
Manipur 130–31, 136, 143–44, 147; banned *thabal chongba* 137; counter-insurgency operations in 143–44; insurgency in 127–28; Kangleipak Communist Party (KCP) 128; Kuki tribals insurgency 128; media ans militant outfits in 137; Military Council faction of KCP in 137; Okram Ibobi Singh on militant groups in 137; 'Pangals' (Manipuri Muslims) 128; People's Liberation Army (PLA) 4, 128, 131, 137; People's Revolutionary Party of Kangleipak (PREPAK) in 128, 131; People's United Liberation Front (PULF) 128, 131; Suspension of Operations (SoO) agreement 144; United National Liberation Front (UNLF) 127, 143; valley-based UNLF 131
Maoist Communist Centre (MCC) 104
Maoist insurgency 103, 122–23, *see also* Naxals; attacking development projects and infrastructure 114–15; bans by 114; Boat Wing of 113; campaign for conversion to Hinduism 111; Combat Battalion for Resolute Action (COBRA) force and 118; decline in Andhra Pradesh 111–12; and elections 115; groups of 105; trends in 2008 108–17; guerilla warfare 108–9; killing of Laxamanananda Saraswati 106; Salwa Judum campaign 107–8, 109, 116, 123; and Security Forces 112–14; states affected by 112; violence against civilians 115
Mathur, R.N. 142
Mazumdar, Charu 103–4
McKiernan, David General 39
Mehreen Zahra Malik on 'Barelvis' 46
Mehsud, Baitullah 77
militancy, Ahmed Rashid on 56
Mishra, Pramod 104
Mohammad, Sufi 69
Moran, Dibakar 142
Mumbai attacks 12, 14–15
Muqami-Tehrik-e-Taliban 74
Muslim United Liberation Tigers of Assam (MULTA) 127, 135–36; Islamist militancy, led by 130
Myanmar 2, and Nagaland conflict 131–32, 145

Naga National Council (NNC) 125
Naga Reconciliation Forum 146
Nagaland 140–41, 145–46, 147; ceasefire in 141; conflict in 125–26; Democratic Alliance (DAN) 145; managing conflict in 141–46; National Liberation Front of Tripura

and ATTF 143; NSCN-IM 128, 132, 145, 147; NSCN-K 145–46; NSCN-U 140–41; small arms in 141
Namdar, Haji killing of 70
National Democratic Front of Bodoland (NDFB) 127, 130, 147
National Human Rights Commission (NHRC) 107
National Investigative Agency Bill 117
National Liberation Front of Tripura (NLFT) 129, 131, 139
National Socialist Council of Nagaland (NSCN) 126
National Socialist Council of Nagaland (NSCN- IM) 126, 131–32, 138
National Socialist Council of Nagaland (NSCN-K) 126, 132
National Solidarity Programme 32
NATO-Isaf 28
Naxalism 166; task force on 106;
Naxals 17, 103–5; declining activity in Andhra Pradesh 123; conflict in Bihar and Jharkhand 110; counter-guerilla warfare 118–20; counter-Naxal policy 117–18; initiatives for 120–21; murder of Saraswati Lakshmanda 111; Nayagarh attack 111; operational capabilities 116–17; resurgence of 122–23; socio-economic development 120–22; surrendering and rehabilitation 120
Nazir, Maulvi 74
Neog, Prabal 142
Nepal 4, 7–8, 168–69, 170–71; armed political groups in 174; army integration 182; ceasefire in 18; conflict in 176–82; Congress and CPN-UML 174–75; drafting Constitution 182–83; human rights 184; Madhes and ehnic grievances 178–79, 188; Madhesi Janadhikar Forum (MJF) 169, 170–71, 187, 189; Madhes Rastriya Janatantrik Party in 175; and Maoist government 166; and Maoists 181–82; Muslim and Dalit 173, 190; Paramilitary youth structures 183–84; peace process 182, 184; relations with India 185–86; state-sponsored violence 179–80; Tarai_ Madhesi Groups in 171–72, 176–77; Tharu movement in 172; UML's Youth Force and MJF-Youth Forum 187; Unified Communist Party of Nepal-Maoist (UPCN-M) 188; Youth Communist League (YCL) in 4, 174, 180, 187
Nepal Army and People's Liberation Army, tensions between. 8
Nepal Defence Army (NDA), 172
North West Frontier Province (NWFP) 62–64, 75–76, 80–81; as British creation 63; conflict management in 76–77; crmed Conflict in 67–71; negotiations and political deals 77; sectarian violence in 49; Taliban expansion in 71–72
North-east, insurgency in 133–41; Shibashis Chatterjee on 218; demands of insurgents 125; armed conflicts in 125; P. Chidambaram on insurgency in 148

Operation Enduring Freedom (OEF), attack on 3

Pakistan 5–7; 42–44, 53–59, 212; attack on Red Mosque in Islamabad 5; clashes in Saidan Banda 51; control over FATA region 11–12; course of conflict 47-53; Deobandi *Deeni Madrasahs* 42; ethnic nationalism in 228; *gaddi nashin* 47; government of 64–65; Grand Ayatollah Ali al-Sistani 61; Harkat-ul-Ansar 45; Imambargah, attack by LeJ on 49; Islamic identity 42; Jaish-e-Muhammad (JeM) 45; jihadi groups 44–45; Lahore attacks in 15; Lashkar-e-Toiba (LeT) 45; linkages between Taliban and Sunni Deobandi groups 49; Majlis-e-Amal (MMA) 48; Mir Anwar Shah's shrine 51; nuclear assets of 211, 216; political violence in 5; programme of *tafkir* 44; Qari Hussain as Ustad-e-Fidaeen in 53; P. Chidambaram on 211; restoration of civilian authority 48; sectarian violence 59–60; jirga 60; Sipah-i-Mohammed Pakistan (SMP) 45–46; Sri Lankan cricket team attack e in 5; suicide attacks 49, 75–76; Sunni groups 34, 72–73; Swat violence 63–64; Tehreek-e-Nafaz-e-Shariat-e Mohammadi (TNSM) 65; Tehreek-i-Jafariya Pakistan (TJP) 45–46; Tehreek-i-Taliban Pakistan (TTP) 65–66; Swat violence in 70; *zakat* funds 43, 44

Pakistan Muslim League (Nawaz) 6

Pakistan-occupied Kashmir (PoK) 86

Panda, Sabyasachi 111

'Pashtunistan' 218

peace processes 16–18

People's Liberation Organisation of Tamil Eelam (PLOTE) 195

People's Political Party 6

People's War Group (PWG) 104

Pervaiz Musharraf 6

Petraeus, General David 36

Prince Jigme Khesar Namgyel Wangchuck 8

Qayyum, Khalifa Abdul 52

Rao, Muppala Laxman *alias* Ganapati 105

Reang, Dhananjoy 129

Rehman, Matiur 49

Rumsfeld, Donald, 20

SAARC Summit, Islamabad 16

Saifullah, Pir 73

Santhal, Jangal 103

Sanyal, Kanu 103

Sarwat Ejaz Qadri for Pakistani Inqalabi Tehreek 46

security, Mohammed Ayoob on 218

Seetharamaiah, Kondapalli 104

separatist and secessionist movements 217

Shah, Khalid. 69

Shah, Ashraf Hussain 46

Shakir, Mufti Munir 73

Shi'i Islamic revolution in Iran 42

Shia–Sunni conflict 72–73

Shri Amarnath Shrine Board (SASB) 96

Sindhi, 'Abdul Rehman 49

Singh, Maharaja Gulab 84

Singh, Maharaja Hari 85

Sipah-i-Sabah Pakistan (SSP), founded by Maulana Haqq Nawaz Jhangvi 43–45

Sri Lanka 4, 191–93; calls for surrender 209; ceaseless fire 198–205; civilians suffering 209; devolution of powers 209; elections in 8; elimination of LTTE 18; and India 195–96; IPKF to 192; Interim All Party Representative Committee Report (APRC) 206–8; Norwegian mediation for ceasefire agreement (CFA) 192, 196; security forces 193–94; truce offer 208; United National Party (UNP),and SLFP 210; Tamil question in 9; violence in 197, 203–5

state failure 214–16; and armed conflict 216–22

state, Max Weber defining 212

suicide attacks 3; of Marriot Hotel, Islamabad 3; on Serena Hotel in Kabul 3

Sungthagra, B. *alias* Dhiren Boro as NDFB Vice President 142

'Sunni Awakening' in Iraq 35

Sunni organisations. Ansar-ul-Islam (AI) 69, 73

Sunni Tehreek (ST) 46; by Maulana Saleem Qadri 46

Taliban by Mullah Omar 5, 16, 19–20, 25–26, 30, 44, armed conflict by 72–73; 29l; attacks 212; insurgency in Afghanistan 21–26;30, 32–33, 40; in Pakistan 65–66, 166; sources of funding for 34–35; strategic objective of 30

Talibanisation 6, *see also* Afghanistan

Tamil Makkal Viduthali Puligal (TMVP) 195
Tamil National Alliance (TNA) 195
Tamil United Liberation Front (TULF) 195
terrorism, cross-border and domestic 13–16
terrorist attacks 3; at Mumbai 2–3; on Indian Embassy in Kabul 3
Tharuhat Liberation Army (TLA), 172
transnational crime 215
tribal militia 35–36
Tripura 131–2; activities of BNCT 139; Agartala serial blasts 143–44; ATTF and HuJI in Bangladesh 139; Bangladesh Rifles (BDR) 7, 139; insurgent outfits in 131–32; migration from Bangladesh 128; personnel handed over ATTF militants 139; police-led counter-insurgency policy in 138–39; Senkrak 128; serial explosions in Agartala 139; Tripura National Volunteers (TNV) 128

United Liberation Front of Asom (ULFA) 126–27, 129–30, 141–42, 146
United Marxist-Leninists (UML) 174

United Nations Mission in Nepal (UNMIN) 173, 186
United People's Democratic Solidarity (UPDS) 127
United Progressive Alliance (UPA) 9
United States 196; commitment to Afghanistan 40; drone attacks by 80–81; led forces in Afghanistan 66; Global War on Terror (GWOT) of 214; and NATO forces in Afghanistan 38; led Operation Enduring Freedom (OEF) 20, 27–28; in Pakistan 15–16

violence, inspired by religious ideology 61; Mohammed Ayoob on 228

Weapons of Mass Destruction (WMD) 12, 215
Wickremasinghe, Ranil 192

Yuldashev, Tahir 74

Zardari, Asif Ali 48
Zia-ul-Haq 42; and Sunni Afghan refugees in NWFP 43